W0006491

WHITELEY'S
FOLLY

To
Jenni

WHITELEY'S FOLLY

The Life and Death of a SALESMAN

LINDA STRATMANN

SUTTON PUBLISHING

First published in the United Kingdom in 2004 by
Sutton Publishing Limited · Phoenix Mill
Thrupp · Stroud · Gloucestershire · GL5 2BU

British Library Cataloguing in Publication Data
A catalogue record for this book is available from the British
Library.

ISBN 0-7509-3561-8

Typeset in 10.5/14pt Melior.
Typesetting and origination by
Sutton Publishing Limited.
Printed and bound in England by
J.H. Haynes & Co. Ltd, Sparkford.

Contents

William Whiteley's
Guide to Success

Work to live. Everything comes to him who works.
Make your business your hobby.
Think for yourself and rely upon yourself.
Be honest in all your dealings.
Watch the waste.
Remember civility costs nothing.
Avoid extravagance and needless expenditure.
Pay as you go. If you cannot pay, do not go.
Do not despise little things.
Keep cool and never lose your temper.
Be orderly and punctual.
Never, never, never say die.

'If I had my life to live over – William Whiteley',
Weekly Dispatch, 4 February 1906, p. 1

Acknowledgements

My grateful thanks to all the people and organisations who have helped me with this book. The British Library; Colindale Newspaper Library; The Family Record Centre, London; Alison Kenney of the Westminster Archives Centre; Helen Swinnerton and Tina Staples of HSBC Archives; West Yorkshire Archives; Chris Welch of the Wakefield Family History Society; Colonel AC Ward and Wendy Bazill of the Whiteley Homes Trust; Sally Kemp of Whiteleys Bayswater. Especial thanks are due to Jenni, who gave me the idea, and my husband Gary, who understands all about the downside of being married to a writer, and is still unfailingly supportive.

A map of Paddington in the 1870s showing the principal locations referred to in the text.

A Face from the Past

The anonymous stranger who called at the home of William Whiteley at 11.30 on the morning of Thursday 24 January 1907, requesting an interview, cannot have known much about the daily routine of the great man. The self-styled 'Universal Provider', though in his seventy-sixth year, had, punctually as ever, departed his home at nearby 31 Porchester Terrace so as to arrive at the world-famous emporium which bore his name shortly after 10 a.m. Apart from Sundays and his annual holiday, he had attended his business virtually every day for almost forty-four years. A short, square, stocky figure, with flowing white side whiskers, dark grey eyes glancing keenly about him, it was his habit to start the day by walking about the store inspecting each department, and though his smile could be genial and his manner friendly, no one was in any doubt about the storm which would break if he spotted something not arranged to his liking. Eventually, and much to everyone's relief, he headed towards no. 43 Westbourne Grove.

Beside the umbrella counter at no. 43 was a door with a brass plate inscribed with Mr Whiteley's name. Behind it was not an office in the strict sense, but a small windowless space, modestly furnished with a table, chairs and roll-top desk, which was the Universal Provider's own private room. This was not a sign of personal humility, nor did it suggest that the old man was being sidelined by the younger, more active directors who had managed the business since it became a limited company in 1899. William Whiteley would never have sanctioned an office for himself which took up any more space than strictly required. Every square inch not used for the selling of goods was, in his eyes, wasted.

There, he would spend his days perhaps dashing off terse letters to his investment brokers, dealing with litigation, seeing visitors, writing articles, and planning, always planning for the future. Although in the autumn of his career, his iconic status as a figurehead of national and international trade meant that his opinions were still frequently sought, and every word of business advice that fell from his lips was received as a treasure. He had only recently been interviewed for a three-page memoir in the *London Magazine of Commerce*, due to go to press in a few days.

No. 43 was only one of an imposing row of shops, themselves part of an accumulation of properties covering 14 acres, with the Whiteley name everywhere in tall gilded lettering, and a flag waving high above. The retail premises, warehouses, staff dormitories, delivery depots, stables, factories, and laundries employed some 6,000 people. For a man of humble beginnings who had arrived in London with less than £10 to his name, it was a staggering achievement. Recently, his declining vigour had meant that many of the duties he had always attended to personally were now allotted to others, but William Whiteley had not loosened the reins of control. He was still the chairman of the company, and the only director on the board exempt from the regulations which entitled the others to remove one of their number.

Over the years he had been both admired and reviled, acquiring the kind of personal celebrity rarely achieved by tradesmen, but incurring the wrath and jealousy of those unable to keep pace with his all-devouring ambition. By 1907, however, the days of conflict were long gone, and he was now the popular Grand Old Man of Bayswater, symbol of its prosperity. The previous Christmas he had been unwell, and his doctor had told him to take life more slowly, warning that heart disease would probably claim him in another two years. Whiteley had taken the news stoically and determined to spend the time he had left where he felt happiest – at work.

That Thursday, at about 12.30 p.m., the same young man who had called at his house earlier, entered Whiteleys stores asking to see the proprietor. It was not unusual for the Universal Provider to see people without an appointment, and the visitor was told he must first apply to the chief cashier, Mr Goodman. In Goodman's office he repeated his request, saying, 'If you will tell Mr Whiteley I come from Sir George Lewis, he will admit me.'

Lewis was a well-known solicitor, the head of an eminent firm which had once acted for Mr Whiteley in a matter of some delicacy. Goodman cast a searching eye over the stranger. He saw before him a man in his late twenties, tall, well-dressed and gentlemanly, having all the appearance of a managing clerk. There seemed to be nothing remarkable about him, although had Goodman approached any nearer he might have noticed that the visitor had recently fortified himself with several glasses of brandy. The name of George Lewis was enough to gain an interview. Whiteley himself ushered the young man into his room and closed the door.

The business of the store bustled on as usual. It was remnant day, when crowds of ladies would descend upon Whiteleys, and for a time become surprisingly unladylike in their efforts to beat each other to the bargains. The noise was more than sufficient to obscure any sounds of the private interview. Mr Gross, Whiteley's correspondence clerk, looked in briefly, and found the two men still in conversation, his employer testily impatient to bring the meeting to an end.

At about 1 p.m. the door of Whiteley's room opened abruptly and he emerged, looking pale and agitated. His arms were by his sides and his fists were clenched. He strode up to Glyn James, an assistant in the nearby fur department, usually referred to as 'Jules' and said curtly, 'Jules, fetch me a policeman!' The assistant at once did as he was told. Whiteley waited outside his room for the police to arrive. About two minutes passed and he was about to go for lunch when the unknown visitor, who clearly did not, like Whiteley, think their meeting was over, pursued him into the store.

'Are you going to give in?' he demanded.

'No,' said Whiteley, a man for whom not giving in was, as his visitor should have known, a way of life. He made brusque gestures of dismissal.

'Then you are a dead man,' said the stranger. Before any of the horrified staff could make a move to intervene, he took from his pocket a black six-chambered Colt revolver, fired two shots point blank into the head of William Whiteley, then placed the muzzle to his own temple and fired again.

The career of the Universal Provider was over. The mystery of his death was just beginning.

Bankruptcy Avenue

On 29 September 1831 a small parcel of humanity, soon to be labelled William Whiteley, was delivered into the world. It is hard to imagine him as a placid infant. Even a newborn has personality, and he must have been an insistent little bundle, in a hurry to grow up and get bustling.

The scene was Agbrigg in the West Riding of Yorkshire, a hamlet south-east of Wakefield, whose population of less than a hundred consisted mainly of farming folk and artisans. Christmas was of early importance to young William, for he was baptised on 25 December in the parish of Featherstone. His father, Joseph, who was born around 1800 in the Wakefield area, was then a 'mealman' – a dealer in corn. William's mother, Elizabeth, was the eldest daughter of Thomas and Mary Rowlandson, farmers from the village of Purston Jaglin, a rural hamlet on the borders of Featherstone, where Elizabeth was born on 8 October 1810. Her three older brothers, John, James and William, were farmers, and there were two younger sisters.

Joseph Whiteley of Agbrigg married Elizabeth Rowlandson at Featherstone Parish Church on 1 June 1830, but their first-born son was not destined to be brought up by his parents.[1] At the age of just nine months, and presumably freshly weaned, he was handed over to his uncle John in Purston Jaglin.[2] John had married a Mrs Hill of Wakefield. They had no family, but enjoyed an income which suggested they adopt a child – these informal arrangements between siblings were not uncommon for the time. John later moved to Featherstone, where William obtained his first schooling. At the age of 6, he was sent to school at nearby Ackworth, walking there and back each day with Purston-born John Waller, who remained a friend for the rest of his life. The 1841 census shows that the occupants of Featherstone Cottage were John Rowlandson, farmer, his wife Mary, and little William, together with a servant girl. Ages in this census cannot be relied upon as there was a tendency to use round and not accurate figures. William's 34-year-old uncle is shown as 30 and William is recorded as being 5 when he was actually 9. The rest of the Whiteleys – there were now four more children – were living in Thornes, near Wakefield. Mary Whiteley was born in 1833, and Sarah in 1836. Thomas Rowlandson Whiteley, born in 1837, was the first of the family to require a birth certificate, which described Joseph as a 'shopkeeper'. Maria was born in Red Lion Yard, in the Kirkgate area of Wakefield in 1839, where Joseph was a 'manager of a corn warehouse'. By 1841 Joseph's career and, presumably, the family fortunes were in decline. According to Waller, he had been 'rather unfortunate in business'.[3] He is described in the census as a 'corn porter'. In an age when all except the poorest households employed servants, there were none.

At 13, William went to Jefferson's School, Pontefract, completing his education in 1846 at the age of 14. The next two years were spent 'at home on the farm'.[4] He was a vigorous, bouncy outdoor lad, keen on horses and traditional country pursuits. How much contact the young Whiteley had with his Wakefield family is unknown. He later wrote happily about this period of his life, saying nothing at all about his parents, and very little about his uncle, but a great deal about his acquaintance with the local squire, John Gully.

Gully must have been an extraordinary role-model for William. Born in Bristol in 1783, he had found himself, at the age of 21, in debtors' prison following a business failure. Taking up bare-knuckle prize-fighting, he literally fought his way out of debt. He retired from the ring, a champion, in 1807 and, armed with a small amount of capital, an understanding of horses, contacts in the betting world, and a natural facility for figures, began to lay odds for betters. Building up his business and his fortune, he began to acquire horses of his own. In 1832, the year when both the Derby and the St Leger were won by his horses, he bought Ackworth Park, near Pontefract. In the same year he was returned as Liberal Member of Parliament for Pontefract. By 1841 he had retired from politics, but remained on the estate for several more years, living the life of a racehorse trainer and country gentleman. His observations on horse-racing must have made enthralling listening for the farm-boy, who learned early the value of absorbing knowledge from an expert.

I worked well, and sometimes played well [wrote William]. I was very fond of horses and riding, also shooting, and I think I can safely say that by the time I was sixteen there were not many better riders or better shots in the horsey and 'gunny' county of Yorkshire than myself. When I was only ten years old, I used to hunt regularly with the famous Badsworth Hounds, allowed to be the best, strongest and fastest pack ever known.

I used to ride a little snow-white pony, under thirteen hands, but with a wonderfully hard mouth, so that it was quite impossible for me to hold her; all that I could do was stick on, and away she used to go with my small self sticking to her like a limpet. Nothing could stop her; five barred gates, stone dykes, high hedges, wide streams, she either went over or through them, and I never once knew her to refuse.

Besides being well-mounted, I was in very good company, amongst whom I may mention John Gully, the great sportsman, and grandfather of the present Speaker of the House of Commons, Lord Hawke and his brother Stanhope, and Sir Charles Greaves, who rode nearly twenty stone and yet generally contrived to be there or thereabouts. I was the baby of the hunt, and I remember the first time I was out I was fifth in at the kill. They were going to give me the brush, but a lady came up and it was given to her, and I had to be content with the promise of it another time, a promise, I may say, faithfully fulfilled.

The members of the hunt were very proud of me, and very kind, because they thought me a real good sportsman, as whenever the meet was anywhere near my home, I was always there, no matter what the weather might be, and when, after a long run, we called at the nearest gentleman's house, and had the usual crust of bread, piece of cheese and horn of home-brewed ale, they always took care that I was not overlooked and had my full share, Mr Gully in particular paying me special attention.[5]

Gully must have seen something of promise in the boy, for once, when William was working in a field, Gully rode up and asked him if he thought he could catch one of the ponies running loose in the next field. If William could catch the pony, said Gully, then he could ride him home and keep him. This was a challenge impossible to resist and William at once went to get a rope, and after a hard struggle, secured the pony and rode him home in triumph. Whether this was the mount he rode to the hunt, he did not say.

If this is an accurate portrait of the youthful William Whiteley it reveals, apart from a love of the outdoor life, an irrepressible self-confidence, a shrewd understanding of the importance of well-connected acquaintances, a keen sense of what was rightfully due for the effort spent, and a determination to be, and represent himself as being, the best. Whiteley could and would 'stick on' whatever might come, and metaphorically ride out in all weathers, for the rest of his life. Brick walls, fire and flood, every kind of obstruction in his path, once set, would be as nothing. Challenges were simply there to be met and overcome.

Whiteley spent two years on the farm, and during that time, he used to ride around the country with a 'celebrated bone-setter and high-class veterinary surgeon' – the insistence on the elevated status of this gentleman tells us as much about Whiteley as it does about his companion – and had 'many strange cases' to deal with, which unfortunately he did not describe.[6]

William Whiteley must have looked set for the life of a farmer, but the ambitious young man did not relish the prospect of a future tied to his uncle's 12 acres of land. His 1938 biographer, Lambert,[7] states that William thought of becoming a jockey, hoping for patronage from John Gully. If he did, it came to nothing. Despite his perambulations with the bone-setter, he seems not to have been attracted to the career of veterinary surgeon, high-class or otherwise, or perhaps there was no opportunity to continue his education. There was no prospect of advancement through his father. In 1851 the Whiteleys were still in Thornes where Joseph was now supporting two more sons, Benjamin and John, and was employed as a railway porter.

In 1848, William Whiteley at the age of 16½ was bound apprentice to a Wakefield draper for seven years. At first glance, this seems a cruel fate for an all-weather farmer's boy and keen horseman, but he was adaptable, and shrewd enough to see that humble as it was, the position had promise. Taking what fate offered, he could make it his own. The pinnacle of his ambition was probably to be master of his own shop, and if any man could achieve it, it was William Whiteley, armed only with determination, the ability to work hard, and monumental patience.

The firm was Harnew and Glover, and later, Whiteley could not resist the comment that it was 'the largest drapery establishment in Wakefield (now raised to the dignity of a city) . . .'. At the time of the 1851 census, the firm employed nine men and five women. Apprentices were expected to live on the premises and it is here, at 5 Northgate, that we find the 19-year-old William Whiteley, receiving 'a severe drilling into the arts and mysteries of trade'.[8]

Wakefield, a handsome market town on the north bank of the navigable River Calder, was then noted for its fortnightly cattle fairs, and its trade in corn, malt and wool. Once the centre of Yorkshire's woollen trade, it had long been surpassed by Leeds and Bradford. Even if Harnew and Glover's was the largest draper around, it was in a town whose days of glory were over.

The stock of a traditional draper was then divided into two areas, each with its own buyer. There were the heavy goods: rolls of plain and print fabrics, silks and velvets, wool and linen, table cloths, sheeting and towelling. There was little in the way of made-up garments; the exceptions were plain capes of merino wool, and at the luxury end of the market, colourful woven shawls. A woman who wanted new clothes either made her own or had them made for her. The fancy department stocked the smaller items which were kept carefully tucked away in boxes or drawers. There were all kinds of edgings and borders, the most expensive of which were fine lace, as well as sewing thread, handkerchiefs, neckerchiefs, gloves, crisp wide ribbons to trim bonnets, narrow ribbons to tie shoes.

The life of a draper's apprentice was one of unremitting effort. As the lowliest member of the staff, young William would have risen at about 7 a.m., and helped take up the shutters, then cleaned and polished the exterior of the shop. He might also have had to do heavy portering work, carrying and arranging huge rolls of fabric, as well as attending to the wants of customers. The hours were long, and even if the shop shut at 10 p.m. there was tidying and cleaning to do afterwards which could have kept him busy beyond midnight. While the young men assistants would have had a room of their own to sleep in, apprentices were often accommodated on truckle beds underneath the counter.

Hard work was not the least of the trials to be endured, if the master of the place adopted the position described by one contemporary commentator. A draper's shop could be in a condition of

. . . perpetual martial law. Everyone, from the highest rank to the lowest, has to obey blindly the commands which may be given. Soiled goods, inferior goods,

all must be sold in the way which is prescribed. No
scruples of conscience are allowed, the merest
observation receives summary dismissal. One is
painfully impressed by the frightened looks which
announce the sudden appearance of the Caesar of the
establishment. No regiment in parade receives a stern
colonel with greater fear, and whilst the eyes of the
scared servants follow nervously the steps of their
master, this all-important personage, well impressed
with his own dignity, paces majestically up and down
(no doubt, as he thinks), to the intense admiration of
his feminine visitors. If for business reasons you have
to enquire about the character of that man, do not
seek any enlightenment from any of the suffering
beings who live in these places; their mouths are
sealed. . . . Though companions in misery, the
inmates do not even trust one another. . . . But . . . let
the servant leave that master; it is then you will
receive the information you want, for who knows a
master better than his servant?[9]

It is not known if Harnew and Glover operated in this
fashion, and whether Whiteley himself adopted these
traits when he achieved power is a matter which later
aroused considerable debate.

After what he described as 'four years of incessant
toil',[10] William was allowed his first holiday, and he put
it to good use, spending a week in London to see one of
the defining attractions of the Victorian era. The Great
Exhibition of 1851, the largest international collection of
manufactured goods and art ever seen, housed in a
revolutionary glass and iron structure, was opened by
Queen Victoria on 1 May. It was an immediate and
overwhelming success. The building covered an

astounding 19 acres, its soaring artistry combined with a simplicity that did not detract from the glories within. The visitor was struck with a bewildering variety of displays, but the eye was first drawn to the great central fountain, then to the towering trees and colossal sculptures. Here were goods from every part of the world, 17,000 exhibitors, not only European, but from India, Africa, Russia, Persia and the United States; vases, ornaments, jewels, chinaware, lace, embroideries, silverware, clocks, perfumes, and scientific instruments. From Britain there was fine furniture and hardware, cotton and woollen looms in motion, and the best of its silks and shawls. Six million people visited the exhibition, which made a substantial profit. When it closed, the building was disassembled and taken to Sydenham where it was re-erected and opened in 1854. Sadly, it was destroyed by fire in 1936.

One of those swarming visitors was William Whiteley, and it is tempting to suppose, as Lambert does, that seeing such a vast array of goods of every variety, the idea formed in the mind of the 20-year-old draper's apprentice that one day there might be such another magnificent place, called 'Whiteleys', not to exhibit goods, but to sell them. It was a prescience that Whiteley never claimed for himself. Even if he had, the idea of a store selling more than just one restricted class of goods was not a new one, even then. As early as the 1830s Kendal Milne & Faulkner, drapers of Manchester, had diversified into other areas such as upholstery, carpets and furniture, while in 1845 the Newcastle firm of Bainbridges sold furnishing fabrics, furs, mourning and ready-sewn muslin dresses in addition to traditional drapery. Whiteley did, however, at last see his future clearly, and it lay in London. If a man with a good understanding of business and a determination to succeed could not make his fortune in London, then he could scarcely make it anywhere else. 'If the Exhibition impressed me, London impressed me still more, and I was so attracted to it that I there and then made up my mind that as soon as my apprenticeship terminated I would return and make my fortune.'[11]

As early as the eighteenth century, London men of business had begun to find pleasant dwellings away from the heart of the City, and with the later coming of the railways and omnibuses this trend gained pace. With increasing numbers of elegant town-houses in the West End, there arose new centres of luxury shops to serve wealthy customers, establishing the prime shopping areas which flourish today – Oxford Street, Bond Street and Regent Street. The upper storeys of these grand new shops were too valuable to be used as staff lodging and became additional selling space, while windows of the new 'plate glass' encouraged the development of the art of arranging goods in an attractive manner. The introduction of gas lighting enabled goods to be displayed under a flattering glow, and also meant that the hours of shopping could be extended up to midnight, the long hours of the assistants not in those days being a matter of great concern. These developments stimulated a new pastime – window shopping – as if the street itself had become a Great Exhibition, laid on for the entertainment of the passers-by.

Until the middle of the nineteenth century, prices of goods were not fixed, nor even displayed – they were to be haggled over, a point of skill that many a shopper prided herself upon. By the time of William Whiteley's visit, the old custom of haggling was beginning to give way to the fixed price principle, especially in the more fashionable shops. There was to be no abatement, and any attempt to haggle would be met with dignified alarm. The old established shops in the West End took a particular pride in the high standards of honesty in their dealings with aristocratic patrons.

Salesmen were able to supplement their salaries with commissions or premiums known as a 'tinge'. Certain articles would carry this bonus which might amount to anything from a few pence to several shillings. The anonymous author of *Reminiscences of an Old Draper* was able from an early age to earn 12–15 shillings a week from this source. An assistant's remuneration, which could reach £100 per annum including commissions, was, when one included the value of accommodation and food, a modest but liveable salary. Better paid were the trusted buyers on whom the health of the business depended, but the real rewards and of course the risks were for the owner.

The cream of the custom was the 'carriage trade': ladies with money to spend who would be conveyed to the store in their own vehicles, thus advertising to passers-by the high-class nature of the shop and its goods. The carriage would remain impressively outside the shop while the lady was waited upon within, and when she departed a deferential young man was always available to carry her purchases for her. Keen salesmen, anxious for their 'tinge', would vie to display good manners and a smart appearance to cultivate such customers, hoping that they would be asked for personally on the next visit. This valuable connection could also be a stepping stone to setting up an independent business. Such a lady was too grand to pay in cash – or even on time. A discreet bill would be submitted later, often on an annual basis. The more

11

timid, wavering customer of less elevated rank was, by contrast, often the victim of an overbearing salesman, who would reason her into a purchase she did not want, and effect a sale by sheer force of character.

William Whiteley, storing away his observations of the London trade, perforce returned to Wakefield, where his family was now living, to serve out the remaining years of his apprenticeship. The next few years were marked by tragedy. His sister Mary died of tuberculosis in 1852 at the age of 18, and in the following year Elizabeth Whiteley died, aged 43, after suffering from chronic peritonitis for nine months. By 1855, with William's apprenticeship drawing to an end, Joseph was terminally ill. Despite this, William stuck to his resolve and the day after his indentures expired, he went to London. He had just £7 10s and out of that he had to pay 15s for a third-class rail fare. At the last minute his uncle offered him £5, but he refused it, saying, 'I have never received a farthing that I have not worked for, and I mean to stick to it through life.'[12]

The following February, Joseph, aged 56, died of liver cancer, his death certificate describing his occupation as 'railway labourer'. Eighteen-year-old Thomas assumed the position of head of the household. Despite this unfortunate start in life, all the Whiteley siblings did well, which suggests that William was not the only one with a drive to better himself. Thomas joined the prison service as a clerk, and climbed the administrative ladder; Maria later went to London to help William manage his business; Sarah married Henry Mason, a young clerk who was to qualify as a solicitor; John started a successful business as a toy and sporting goods dealer and Benjamin became a reporter with the *Wakefield Express*.

In London, William Whiteley required two things before he could realise the dream of opening his own shop: a thorough knowledge of the drapery trade in London, which he appreciated was of a different order from the solid worthiness of Yorkshire trade – and money. With a single-minded dedication he set out to acquire both. It took him eight years.

He determined always to be his own man, the sole master of himself and his business, never to share either the responsibilities or the profits with another. All was to be by his own effort and at his own risk. He must watch every detail himself, for only his eye would be good enough. He would observe others, learn from them, and as soon as he had mastered what they had to teach him, he would move on.

The East End of London he ignored. The shops of Shoreditch, Whitechapel and Aldgate concentrated on the sale of cheap and gaudy goods to the poor, and there was nothing there that he wished to know. In the West End, the brighter shops with their plate glass windows, exterior lighting and colourful displays must have attracted him, as well as the claim by Shoolbread Cooke and Son, mercers, drapers and carpet warehouse, at 154–156 Tottenham Court Road to be the largest of its kind in London. Nearby was Maples furniture store, founded in 1842, while at no. 203, Mrs Heal and her son were continuing the feather bed and mattress manufacture started by her late husband. Well-established and expanding their businesses were Dickins & Jones of Regent Street and Swan & Edgar of Piccadilly Circus. Peter Robinson in Oxford Street was on his way to managing a block of six shops, which sold, in addition to traditional drapery products, millinery, mourning and flounced silk skirts. Robinson's rivals included Marshall & Snelgrove, founded in 1837, and the rather older business of Debenham & Pooley, whose buyer of silks and woollens was an ambitious young man named John Lewis. He was later to open his own, more modest establishment on the corner of Oxford Street and Holles Street.

It was a promising time for the drapery trade. The middle classes were out to show their new prosperity by the purchase and overt display of consumer goods, which for the ladies included elaborately trimmed and expensive clothing. Large families naturally meant large expenditure; indeed, a professional man, well aware of the financial drain of family life, was often obliged to postpone all idea of marriage until he felt his business was established and secure. London drapers of the 1850s were responding to the new demands by increasing not only the range and quality of their goods, but the size of their premises. This enabled buyers to acquire goods more cheaply in bulk and so attract shoppers with prices considerably lower than those of the smaller retailers.

Meanwhile, a shopping revolution was taking place. A small retail store called the Bon Marché had opened in Paris in 1852, and, like the earlier Newcastle and Manchester shops, diversified its range of goods. American visitors noted the advantages of fixed prices combined with regular sales, high turnover at reduced margins, daily deliveries, and the right for customers to return unsatisfactory goods, and copied the business model when opening their own shops. The modern department store was born.

Whiteley's first employer was R. Willey and Co., an old established retailer at 15 and 16 Ludgate Hill, which was owned by a Yorkshireman. His salary there was £30 a year plus board and lodging. His need to acquire savings imposed a strict economy. Smoking and drinking were pleasures (and expenses) he left to others, and, if his later reminiscences are to be believed, he made work his sole interest and his sole hobby. It may well have been during this time that he began to learn about the wise investment of funds, something that remained a key concern for the rest of his life. He was not a mean man, but he knew the value of money, and every penny spent and every penny forgone had to be for a purpose.

He remained at Willey's for fifteen months, after which he felt he needed to gain experience of the wholesale side of the business, so he left and took an engagement with Morrison Dillon and Co. of Fore Street, which was later known as the Fore Street Warehouse Company. There he remained for two and a half years, when he received a tempting offer. His old masters, Harnew and Glover, had not forgotten the apprentice of obvious ability who had been steadily gaining experience in the metropolis. A partner of the firm was about to retire and they wanted young Mr Whiteley to take his place. He was offered a three-year engagement at a reasonable salary, after which he would become a partner for another three, the whole business to come into his hands at the end of that time.

He hesitated. It was nearly eight years since he had recognised that his future lay in London, but such an offer from the largest draper in Wakefield could not be ignored. Eventually, without committing himself to anything, he agreed to go back to Harnew and Glover's for a trial period of three months. Morrison and Dillon were sorry to see him go, and intimated that should the trial prove unsuccessful they were eager to have him back.

As soon as he returned to Wakefield, William Whiteley knew that it would not do. Many years later, the erstwhile farmer's boy wrote, 'I knew that I could never settle in the country after London . . .'.[13] 'There was that within me which would not let me rest content with the narrow bounds of a provincial town. Here in London, the great centre of the world's commerce, here alone was there a field sufficiently spacious for my energies, sufficiently vast for my ambition . . .'.[14] He returned to Fore Street and stayed there another two and a half years.

The next offer he received was in 1861, from a Mr Graham and a Mr Green who were respectively the foreign and English ribbon buyers for Messrs Leaf, Sons and Co. of Old Change. They were both about to leave their old firm and open their own business, and they were very anxious to have Whiteley join them. As silk buyer he now commanded a salary of £200. Again, it was not exactly the future he had mapped for himself, but again, he allowed himself to be persuaded. The business seems not to have been a success. Before it was a year old, Mr Graham and Mr Green had sold it to another firm, Messrs Borras and Son. Whiteley remained with the new owners until the shop was closed, and at that point began to wonder if the time was at last ripe for him to go into business alone.

His speciality, with the expertise he had absorbed from Mr Graham and Mr Green, was the ribbon trade, yet at that time the market for such items was dear, and he decided to postpone his plans till the following spring. He had an offer from another draper, Messrs Bradbury Greatorex, Beall & Co. At first he declined, for he objected to the travelling that he knew would come with that position. 'The genus bagman does not rank high with me . . . I hate knocking about the country begging for orders, sleeping in damp sheets at night, having to mess in the comercial [*sic*] travellers' room, and drink all round on penalty of being Boycotted.'[15]

The offer of a large salary and the agreement that his travels would be limited to visits once every two months to Manchester, Liverpool and Birmingham, tempted him, and he took the job, but after a year he was determined to wait no longer. He had by then accumulated savings of between £700 and £800, and he deemed it would be enough.

The big question was, where to go? The East End was out of the question and the West End was far too expensive. That left the suburbs. His friends had cautioned him against two places; one was Islington, where the fierceness of the competition made it very difficult to make a profit, and the other was Westbourne Grove, Bayswater. This street was so notorious for failed businesses that it was often referred to as 'Bankruptcy Avenue'.

In the previous two decades Bayswater, which had once been a semi-rural area with scattered dwellings, had been benefiting from the migration of middle-class residents from the city to the suburbs. Substantial houses were constructed for professional men, their growing families and their servants. Wasteland gave way to handsome squares and fine terraces, and a narrow lane had been replaced with a new residential street called Queen's Road (now Queensway). People of fashion – people with money to spend – moved in. The railways had come to the area in 1838 with the opening of Paddington station, and on 10 January 1863 came the London Underground, its Metropolitan Railway linking the City with the new West End. By then, Bayswater was a well-defined urban community, prosperous, and with its own networks of social interaction.

Despite this, shops in Westbourne Grove – the first of which, a chemist, was opened in 1854 – did not do well. The wealthy inhabitants of Bayswater continued to patronise the old established shops such as Shoolbread's which took the trouble to stay in touch with their customers. Bayswater businesses started up and quickly failed, and there were always empty premises to let. One morning, William Whiteley decided to go and have a look for himself. 'Although it had been painted to me in the blackest of colours, I thought it rather bright', he said.[16] He was curious about the apparent anomaly of a flourishing neighbourhood with bankrupt businesses, and there was an empty shop that particularly caught his eye, as having the potential to be made smart and attractive with very little trouble. He determined to come back for a longer look.

On a spring afternoon in 1863, the inhabitants of Westbourne Grove might have wondered to see a stocky young man loitering in the street. There are no pictures of William Whiteley from this era, but from later descriptions we know he had dark hair, curling generously on the temples. He did not wear a moustache or beard, but sported side whiskers, of the 'mutton-chop' variety, which increased in length and bushiness with age. He was round of face with a rather bulbous nose, and clear keen eyes that could deliver an intense frank stare. His mouth was thin-lipped and firm, and close examination of his favourite portrait reveals that what at first might seem to be an incipient smile turns out to be only the set muscles of determination. One can imagine him in 1863 to be neatly though not expensively dressed, gentlemanly although not actually a gentleman.

The loitering stranger seemed respectable enough, and no one sought to enquire after his purpose. He was standing opposite the empty shop on the south side of the Grove, then numbered 63 (now 31) inspecting it with some interest, and gazing intently at each passer-by.

Whiteley had by then discovered that there had been two previous businesses at the shop, both of which had failed, an unpromising omen, but he was undeterred. He noted not only the numbers of people walking past the premises but also their class, and how they were dressed, estimating how much they might have to spend, and whether they were the kind of customers who would support a drapery shop if offered the right goods and prices. He stood there for two hours in all, between 3 and 5 p.m., and at the end of that time he was sure that whatever the reason for the previous failures it was not the fault of the shop. He also saw that businesses in the area were charging inflated prices for their goods, which must inevitably lead to a low turnover. If he were to charge the lowest prices possible consistent with making a profit, customers, he was sure, would compare notes, and transfer their custom to him. From his observations he calculated that he could attract sufficient fashionably dressed people to enter his shop and make a purchase in just two hours to pay the working expenses for one day. Making enquiries he found that a fifteen-year lease of the shop was available at £140 per annum. He took it.

The Making of Westbourne Grove

William Whiteley's first shop was just 12m long. To secure the premises took most of his capital. The lessor required £500 of which half had to be paid in cash. This nervousness was understandable as the businesses of the previous tenants had failed, and there was no reason why the new man should not go the same way. The remainder of the lease was to be paid in three annual instalments, two of £100 and one of £50. Whiteley spent £100 on fittings and £100 on furniture, which left him with just £300 for stock. His previous employers gave him references to enable him to obtain credit and he purchased £600 worth of goods, the usual stock-in-trade of the fancy draper: ladies' hosiery, gloves, ribbons, feathers, flowers and lace. He opened for business on 11 March 1863. There were three employees: two girls and an errand boy. He also brought a sister to London to help him and later said that the business should really have been called 'William Whiteley and Sister'. He did not name her, but it must have been Maria, whom he later installed in a comfortable home in Hampstead. 'At one time [Whiteley wrote in 1884] she superintended the board and lodging of my employees; but now she is fully occupied with the lodging, and no-one can say how much of the efficiency of the "Universal Provider" is due to the business capacity and energy and vitality of my sister.'[1]

It was the day after the wedding of the Prince of Wales and Princess Alexandra, and London was in a festive mood; 10 March 1863 had been a public holiday, and the decorated gas-lit streets, the shops brightly illuminated with special displays had attracted huge crowds. William Whiteley had no time for such entertainments. The careful ticketing and arrangement of his goods ready for the opening of his shop was of paramount importance. He was at last able to put into practice the principles which had become clear in his mind during the fifteen years of preparation for this moment. 'Customers were never pestered to buy things they did not want; everything in the shop was displayed to the best advantage, and everything was marked in plain figures. All goods were sold at a reasonable profit, and there was a conspicuous absence of flaring tickets with "Cheap" and "Great Sacrifice" and similar legends imprinted in huge letters upon them. Purchasers were never given an excuse for complaint, and goods were never represented as other than they are.'[2] He also prided himself on good taste. 'I knew a good article when I saw it. I had the faculty of hitting the public taste, and I had a knowledge of how to display goods when I had bought them in a nice, tasteful way.'[3]

An essential component of his business plan was that terms were to be cash only. A business that sacrificed margins for turnover could not afford to wait for payment. There were to be no exceptions to this rule. In the same way, the price that was ticketed was the price to be paid. No haggling – no discounts.

He also determined not to spend money on advertising in the newspapers. If the *Bayswater Chronicle* was expecting advertising revenue from the fledgling business it was to be disappointed. 'I never advertise [he told the painter William Frith, some years later]. I never spent a shilling in that way in my life. My notions of the advantage of advertising take the form of good things at so small a profit as to make the purchasers recommend their friends to come to my shops; and I have found that method of advertising so satisfactory that I feel no inclination to spend the enormous sums that some of my brethren in trade find, or think they find profitable.'[4]

The shutters had not even come down, and the shop, perhaps because of the demands of that important occasion, was a little late in opening, when a lady (a Mrs Johnson according to Lambert) came in and asked for something out of the window. He apologised for being late and explained that it was his first day. 'Then I suppose I am your first customer?' she said, a notion which must have pleased her. He told her she was and she asked his permission to offer up a short prayer, blessing the future course of the business: '. . . ever afterwards we were the best of friends until her death,' Whiteley later commented. 'She was such a lady as one seldom meets'.[5]

The first few years of the business were ones of long hours and hard work, but the rewards soon became apparent. The little shop thrived, and the pennies he so carefully watched accumulated into pounds, which were used to expand the trade. Whiteley had been correct both in recognising the demand for a drapery shop in the neighbourhood and the effectiveness of low margins in producing a high turnover. Indeed he may have underestimated the explosive effect of giving Bayswater ladies access to reasonably priced fancy trimmings. At first, the shop seemed to the casual observer to be no better than its competitors, but one day a lady who had purchased an item in another shop, mistakenly brought it back to Whiteleys to exchange it, and discovered that what she had purchased for 1s 6d, he was selling for 8¾d. The discovery created 'a profound impression', and when a similar event occurred a few days later, news of the astonishing Whiteley prices spread quickly through the neighbourhood.[6] The number of customers increased rapidly and dramatically, and he was soon obliged to engage more staff – and then still more. After just twelve months of business, he was employing fifteen assistants, a cashier and two errand boys, and had paid off the remainder of the lease. The shop was always full and the young ladies, now crammed shoulder to shoulder along the counter had hardly room to turn.

Many years later a correspondent of the *Paddington Kensington and Bayswater Chronicle* (hereafter referred to as the *Chronicle*)[7] provided a glimpse of the young Whiteley. 'I went to him as a deputation from a Sunday school to ask him to join in the early closing movement . . . I have never forgotten my first impressions of Mr Whiteley. He had only one shop in those days. I found myself in the presence of a keen dark-eyed young man, who seemed to read me at a glance. He had a cup of tea in his hand behind the counter, and was economising the time. A man of very few words, he gave me a brief but courteous dismissal.'[8]

To Whiteley, success in business came not from seeing how much he could make out of his customers, but from providing them with what they wanted. Ladies eager for a bargain soon found that they had only to ask for something not in his usual offerings, and he would obligingly get it for them. Often this meant adding a completely new range of goods. The accounts of the first few years of the business have not survived, but it is possible to piece together an impression of its phenomenal early development. One by one he added more departments – silks, linens, and haberdashery, made-up goods such as mantles, dresses, and hats. All had somehow to be squeezed into the modest premises. Each addition was a roaring success. Ladies outfitting, and mourning wear were important new enterprises, and there were, even in the early years, some notable departures from the sort of goods found in traditional drapers' shops such as furs, sunshades and umbrellas. By 1867 his turnover was nearly £43,000, about £2,000,000 at today's prices, while the original little shop must have been bursting with a seething mass of ever more demanding customers, hard-pressed assistants and a mountainous array of goods. Whiteley started to look around for another shop, but there were other, more personal things on his mind.

Of the two original young lady assistants, one continued to be employed by the business for many years. The other has a more interesting history. Her name was Harriet Sarah Hill, and she was born on 7 February 1845, in Winterslow, Wiltshire. Her father, Thomas, was a linen draper. In William Whiteley's reminiscences about his early life, there is no mention of affairs of the heart. His relationships with women, whether romantic or recreational, are a matter for strict silence and since he always claimed that in the early years work was his only hobby we are presumably intended to assume that he formed no liaisons of any kind during this time, something which, given his later history, is a little hard to believe. It is only in the 1860s that he began to reveal a trait which was to continue for very many years to come – an interest in young shop girls.

It is not known when Harriet Sarah Hill became William Whiteley's mistress, but by the beginning of 1867 it must have been apparent that she was pregnant. They were married on 23 February at St John's Church, Holloway.

Not far from 31 Westbourne Grove there was another little shop to let – no. 41. The idea of keeping his businesses in one area where he could more easily supervise them had its appeal, and so he took the lease.

Many years later, Harriet Whiteley recalled those early days:

I married him just as he had taken his second shop and four years after he started business. What an ordeal it was for a young girl! We lived at the top of the house . . . and how well I can remember times without number sitting on the bottom stair holding a candle while he put up the shutters at night. Sometimes I could hardly keep my eyes open, I was so tired. Then we would go upstairs for a chat in our little sitting room. Occasionally Mr John Barker of Kensington would come to see us. I used to cut thin bread and butter for him. And my husband was always fond of a special custard which I would make for him with my own hands. If anyone else made it he wouldn't eat it.[9]

The total cost of acquiring and refitting this property was £2,000. The extra cost may have been because he was planning to make his family home there, for it was at this address that their first child was born on 30 April 1867. He was christened Walter Herbert. Given that little Walter was born only two months after the wedding it is possible that he was premature. Maybe he was unable to

feed adequately, or absorb his food. He passed away on
9 June, the cause of death given as 'marasmus' or
malnutrition. He was buried at Kensal Green cemetery.

Not long after the move to no. 41, another shop, no.
43a, became available, and Whiteley took that too.
Among the new employees was a young Scotsman,
James Keith, who was to remain with him for over
thirty years and become his trusted general manager. By
the end of 1867 Whiteley owned properties valued at
£2,850 (over £130,000 today). The years of business
failure which had given Westbourne Grove the
sobriquet of Bankruptcy Avenue, played into his hands.
Most of the row of shops belonged to small owners who
could not afford to keep them empty for long, and rents
were low, some as little as £140 per annum. He made
sure to know when a lease expired, or a shop fell
vacant, and then he would add it to his growing
empire, refit it to his requirements and either expand
an existing department into it or start a wholly new
one. When freeholds became available, he bought
those, too. By 1871 he either owned or leased ten shops
in Westbourne Grove.

The family too was expanding. Ada Florence was
born on 11 April 1868, followed by Clara Louise on
24 August 1870. It was soon impracticable for the
Whiteleys to live above the shop, and they moved to
2 Kildare Terrace. The 1871 census return for that
address shows 39-year old William Whiteley, describing
himself as a silk mercer, Harriet, 25, 2-year-old Ada, and
Clara, just 7 months, while lodging with them were
seven drapers' assistants, two females aged 23 and 27
and five males, aged from 14 to 16. A nursemaid helped
Harriet care for the children and there was one general
servant. The household was due to increase again, since

William junior was born on 23 October 1871 and Frank Ernest on 29 October 1872.

The rest of Whiteley's assistants would, as was then the custom, have lodged near to their place of work. It would be easy to view the firm as an extended family, with William Whiteley a demanding but loving father, regarding his employees with a kindly paternal eye. The truth, concealed by his silent, suffering staff, was that Whiteley was a strict, sometimes harsh employer, even when compared to his contemporaries. It would be many years before this would be revealed to his customers, who were often greeted at the door by the smiling owner's expansive and unctuous charm.

By now the firm was moving into a new phase, adding gentlemen's outfitting and tailoring to its departments. These new enterprises were immediately and overwhelmingly successful. The tailoring sales alone were £15,000 in the first year of that department – over £700,000 today.

The public face of Whiteley's care for his staff was the instigation of a number of societies, the first of which was the Kildare Athletic Club, which he founded in 1870. Members paid a small subscription, and Whiteleys supported the club by donation. There was a sports meeting every September, which was open to the public, and for some weeks before the event, the prizes would be prominently displayed in Whiteleys' window – a glittering array of loving cups, goblets, tankards and decanters. The events consisted of flat races of various lengths, pole leaping, hurdles, walking, throwing the cricket ball, and a sack race, the participants being the young gentlemen only. Refreshments were served and a band provided a selection of the popular music of the day. After Mr Whiteley had given away the prizes to great acclaim, there was dancing in a specially erected marquee. These events (tickets 1s each or 2s 6d for carriages) would attract up to 5,000 people. The cost to the business was minimal, the publicity incomparable.

Then there was the Kildare Rowing Club of which the *Paddington Times* commented 'The club, we believe was instituted by the numerous employees in Mr Whiteley's establishment, and has that gentleman's especial patronage and encouragement. In sight of this fact, and seeing what one house may accomplish, we strongly recommend other houses to follow suit. Proprietors get more muscular and sturdy staff to conduct their business by fostering the tastes of their men for the manly pastimes of Old England.'[10]

In the early years of his business, Whiteley probably gave little thought to the activities of the Paddington Vestry, and that organisation may have given no thought at all to him. The Vestry (which later became Paddington Borough Council) was a body of local men, elected by the ratepayers of the parish, whose duty was to set the local rates, and carry out public works, such as street cleaning, and the repair of roads and public buildings. In its early days, the largely rural nature of Paddington meant that the worthies who sat upon its committees were primarily landowners and professional men. The rapid expansion of Paddington into an urban district meant that by 1870 the members were mainly local businessmen and, increasingly, businessmen who regarded William Whiteley as a rival to be reckoned with. They had viewed the march of the Whiteley juggernaut along Westbourne Grove, and many of them did not like what they saw.

The minutes of the fortnightly meetings of the Vestry were published in the Paddington newspapers and, while the members frequently congratulated themselves on the splendid work they were doing, the press occasionally felt obliged to use sarcastic barbs to prick the balloon of their self-confidence. Ratepayers frequently wrote irate letters to the papers complaining about both the level of the rates and the Vestry's expenditure.

In the 1860s it had become increasingly obvious that there was a great need for a public baths and washhouse in Paddington. Many of the poorer inhabitants were engaged in dirty occupations such as coal porter or dustwoman, and the facilities for washing either themselves or their clothing were limited. Some had taken to bathing in the canal during the warmer weather, much to the outrage of those residents whose homes overlooked the indecent display. A washhouse was an expensive item, however. Those of Marylebone and Pancras had cost £24,000 and £25,000 respectively, and the gentlemen of the Vestry, despite two reports by the district medical officer urging upon them the great necessity for such an amenity, were hesitant about adding another burden to the rates.

In July 1870 advertisements began to appear on the front page of the *Paddington Times*, headed 'Baths and Washhouses for Paddington', addressed to the inhabitants of the parish. Their author was a local estate agent and auctioneer, James Flood, who, highlighting the prevarications of the Vestry, proposed to form a company to make good the deficiency. In many ways Flood was not unlike William Whiteley. He was a self-made man, of humble beginnings and basic education, but endowed with a 'native force of character and great power of persistence in pursuit of an object'.[11] He had tremendous energy, an enviable capacity for hard work, and the ability to meet opposition with imperturbable good humour. It was said that he never lost his temper, a quality that anyone who reads the minutes of the Paddington Vestry meetings over the years will recognise as a rarity. In 1870 his persistence showed itself in the doggedness with which he continued to assail the neighbourhood in general and the Vestry in particular with his demands for a washhouse. Eventually the Vestry started taking Flood seriously and a letter from him offering to desist from his own enterprise if they would agree to construct a baths and washhouse was read out at their meeting on 17 January.[12] On approval from the Sanitary Committee the Vestry decided to go ahead with the scheme, recognising the 'indomitable perseverance and ceaseless activity . . .' of Mr Flood.[13] In May, the spring elections for membership of the Vestry were held and Mr Flood put himself forward and was returned unopposed. His powers on the Vestry grew rapidly, and he was soon regarded as one of its leading and most influential figures. On 16 January 1872 the Paddington Vestry took a decision that was to have lasting consequences, agreeing to buy the land and houses at 143 and 145 Queen's Road, for the purpose of constructing the new baths. The site was just around the corner from Mr Whiteley's growing row of shops, where he had recently started a new department of furnishing fabrics which had been as instantly successful as his previous enterprises. Neither Flood nor Whiteley could have foreseen that the Paddington Baths were to be the subject of bitter and angry disputes lasting more than ten years.

In the meantime, despite his increasing affluence, Whiteley, with equal determination, maintained his policy of cash terms without abatement. If anyone doubted that he was serious about this, they were made quite certain of the matter by a case that came before the courts in March 1871.

In September 1870, the store had received in the post an order from a Miss Cleveland, the daughter of the Rector of Romaldskirk near Barnard Castle. Whiteleys had filled orders for the family on two previous occasions, and both had been paid for; however this was altogether of a different magnitude and importance. The lady was to be married on 29 September, and a lengthy letter set out her requirements in detail; a variety of silk and other dresses, petticoats, jackets, mantles, veils, headdresses, embroideries, trimmings and laces. This letter was followed by seven or eight others ordering additional items which included three mantles, and twelve silk dresses which required dress protectors as she was going out to India with her husband.

The goods were duly sent and approved and on 29 September the lady was married to Captain Young of the Royal Artillery. After the traditional month's wedding tour the happy couple departed for India. While they were away a letter arrived at the rectory addressed to Miss Cleveland. The envelope was opened by her father. It contained a bill for £155 5*s* (about £7,750 today). The Rector was 'filled with indignation and astonishment' and at once wrote to William Whiteley.

> Romaldskirk Parsonage
> Oct 6 1870
>
> Sir – I am perfectly astonished at the amount of the bill which you have sent in to my daughter. She chose to forget and you were not aware that she is one of the ten children of a country parson. On her return from

31

her wedding tour she will examine the items of your account.

yours truly
Henry Cleveland[14]

This cut no ice with William Whiteley, who continued to press for payment. Cleveland wrote again, pointing out that the purchases were made without his knowledge or agreement, but suggested that in order to save his daughter's peace with her husband and to avoid further annoyance he would pay a part of the bill if a liberal discount was made and if time was given for the payment of the residue. This suggestion was very firmly refused. Mr Whiteley reminded the Rector that his was a ready-money business. No haggling – no abatement.

If Henry Cleveland thought that Whiteley would not be prepared to take a clergyman to court for debt, he was mistaken. In March 1871 the case of Whiteley *v.* Cleveland was heard before Durham Assizes. Whiteley's counsel told the court that Mr Cleveland was a gentleman of some standing in the county, which was true, and with a private fortune, which was not true. Indeed the unhappy Rector had a living of only £650 per annum to support himself, his wife and their ten offspring. Prior to her marriage, his daughter had been granted an allowance of just £40 per annum (about £1,900 today) for all her clothes and pocket money. The trousseau had been discussed in the family, but the lady had acted alone in placing the order. Neither her mother nor her father had been consulted. The only item Cleveland had seen was the wedding dress itself, and he told her it was a ridiculous one, more fitted for a duke's daughter than the daughter of a country parson. It never seemed to have occurred to him that more than £40

32

might be required in view of the special occasion, and he failed to ask his daughter how she had paid for the ridiculous dress.

Quite where Miss Cleveland imagined the money would come from to pay for her trousseau we shall never know, since her husband was no better off than her father. It was revealed in court that Whiteleys' bill had been only one of many. The Rector had managed to pay the others totalling £300, but the effort had nearly ruined him, and Whiteleys' must have been the last straw. He tackled his daughter about it on her return, and there were some very bitter scenes.

Whiteley was called to give evidence. He said he thought the bill was a very reasonable one and very little for the trousseau of a lady about to be married to an officer. It would not, in his opinion, have been extravagant if it had been three times as much. Cross-examined, it emerged that he did not know the pay of a second captain in the Royal Artillery. He had not written to Cleveland to ask if he sanctioned the order. He thought that such an action would be considered an insult.

His Lordship summed up and left it to the jury to decide whether the family discussions regarding the trousseau amounted to an implied authority by the defendant to his daughter to order the goods. The jury retired and after an absence of four hours gave judgment to Whiteley for the full amount.

This was fabulous advertising for Whiteleys. The case made not only the local newspapers but *The Times*, listing the goods ordered, and their cost. It also demonstrated that no one, not even a man of the cloth under dire threat of bankruptcy, ever received a discount.

Prior to 1872, Whiteleys, like the early department stores, was only providing goods in a number of closely related areas. That was all about to change. On 18 March that year, Whiteley made an application to the magistrates at the Vestry Hall, Paddington, for a wine licence. The solicitor who appeared for him was Charles Mills Roche. Born around 1830, he had by 1872 practised for more than twenty years, with a business at Old Jewry. Roche was a man of enormous energy, clerk to several vestries, and chairman of numerous local committees. He had been a member of the Paddington Vestry since 1860, and represented that body on the Metropolitan Board of Works, precursor of the London County Council. Any apparent conflicts of interest between his professional and parochial life were to the ingenious Mr Roche simply situations which he could turn to his and his clients' advantage. Whiteley recognised that this was a man whose experience, connections and way of doing things were admirably suited to his business. The association was to last nearly thirty more years.

A solicitor called Wright represented the opposition to the granting of the licence. The applicant, he said, carried on the business of a linen draper, a hatter, a bootmaker, an upholsterer and a jeweller. He thought Mr Whiteley had got enough irons in the fire and did not require any addition, but perhaps he had read the article in the *Saturday Review* stating that drinking habits were on the increase among ladies and he wished therefore to offer them a facility for indulging in that propensity. He did not want to say a word against the respectability of Whiteley or his customers, but the bench should bear in mind that many customers might be ladies or females dressed to represent them (a delicate reference to prostitutes), and the place might be made a place of assignation. He added that there were public houses and confectioners nearby where a glass of wine might be obtained. He trusted that the application would be refused in the interests of morality.

Mr Roche said he was not aware that there was anything objectionable in Mr Whiteley carrying on several trades; on the contrary it was a great convenience to his customers, as they could walk from one department to another. On the establishment, 622 hands were employed, and about 1,000 outdoor, and he was very heavily rated, between £2,000 and £3,000. As many as 4,000 customers went into Mr Whiteley's establishment every day, and there could be no doubt that he had been the making of Westbourne Grove. Many of his customers came from the country and were frequently at the establishment for hours; he was constantly being asked for a glass of wine and a biscuit, and it was unlikely that these ladies would go to a public house. He produced a petition in favour of the application which had been signed by six clergymen, a number of medical men and many local inhabitants.

William Whiteley was then called before the bench. He said he now occupied ten houses in Westbourne Grove, and the number of his customers was rapidly increasing. Many were there from ten in the morning till five in the afternoon, and he was, he said, frequently asked for a glass of wine and a biscuit. There was not a shadow of foundation in the suggestion that the establishment would become a place of assignation.

The chairman observed that it was a most unusual application, and pointed out that none of the people who had signed the petition would require refreshment as they all resided within half a mile of the locality.

He did not wish to say anything personal about Mr Whiteley but he thought he had enough to do in looking after his present establishment. The application was put to the vote and refused.

The editor of the *Bayswater Chronicle* commented 'That Mr Whiteley of Westbourne Grove is an enterprising man no-one will doubt, but we must altogether ignore the idea that he has been the making of that locality. . . . We contend that Bayswater has done much to make Mr Whiteley; nor should anyone grudge his success for we maintain that he deserves it. But there is a point where even enterprise should cease being encouraged, and that is when it is likely to form a bad precedent and militate against the law.'[15]

It was probably the lobbying of local publicans rather than morality that prompted the refusal. The *Paddington Times* suspected that there was more to the application than the occasional refreshment of out-of-town customers, believing that Whiteley wanted to sell wine and beer to his numerous employees. 'At the present time, when restrictions of every description are being inflicted upon publicans, it is really a monstrous piece of audacity in a private individual, totally unconnected with the trade, applying for such a license. We trust that the permission sought will be peremptorily refused, and thus inflict a severe blow and discouragement on men who not content with the ordinary profits of their own trade, seek to grasp at everything that their eye sees or their hearts covet.'[16]

One can imagine William Whiteley leaving the hearing with quiet dignity, but a new resolve. If people believed he had enough irons in the fire and as much business as he could cope with, they were in for a considerable surprise. This was just a temporary setback in a vast scheme which would take the business of Whiteleys to a wholly new level. He had looked at the other trades in the area, and believed that the same principles which had led to success in the drapery and clothing trade would hold good everywhere else. He was on the verge of an expansion into areas those magistrates could hardly have dreamed of. He was about to become the Universal Provider.

THREE

Whiteley's Windows

By the 1870s the expansion of Whiteleys had changed the character of Westbourne Grove, which was no longer a commercial backwater but the thriving heart of prosperous Bayswater. In April 1873 a correspondent to the *Paddington Times* wrote, 'Westbourne Grove has become a most fashionable promenade as well as a favourite hunting ground for ladies shopping, and most of the ladies arrive in carriages. . . .' Unfortunately the Grove was not wide enough to accommodate this scale of traffic, especially as the carriages waiting for the ladies to emerge from Whiteleys arranged themselves in Indian file on each side of the roadway, causing a major obstruction.[1]

By January 1874, according to the *Paddington Times*, matters were deteriorating. 'This Grove has evidently become one of the principle [*sic*] highways of Bayswater, and is daily encumbered with an immense vehicular traffic so much so that at certain periods of the day it becomes almost impassable.' Men of business were finding 'an enormous block of carriages, especially opposite Mr Whiteley's . . .'.[2] In May, the same paper was suggesting that the vast amount of traffic meant that the widening of Westbourne Grove 'becomes daily an obvious necessity'.[3] Despite the complaints, there was an evident local pride in the development of a shopping area which had brought Regent Street and Bond Street to Bayswater.

William Whiteley was no longer just a draper. In 1872 he opened a house agency, a move which must have been regarded with some alarm by Mr Flood. Houses must have something to put in them, so other departments followed rapidly – furniture, which he both sold and repaired, carpets, trunks, brushes, stationery, china and glass. Aware of the demand for imported fancy goods, especially from Japan, and perhaps recalling those elegant displays in the Great Exhibition, he created a special department for foreign wares.

In order to house his growing numbers of staff within easy reach of the business he took the lease of houses in nearby Kensington Gardens Square, Hatherley Grove and Westbourne Grove Terrace where they could be lodged, men and women separately. These were not, in a real sense, homes; rather they were dormitories, since the employees did little more than sleep there. Their meals were also provided by their employer, who had converted the basements of his shops in Westbourne Grove into staff dining rooms.

Whiteley now had control over virtually every aspect of the lives of his employees – their working conditions, their homes, their food, and how they occupied their spare time. Gradually he was extending the same compliment to his customers. If customers trusted Whiteleys to provide quality goods at a fair price, why should he not extend that valuable service – to fit them with everything they could want, from the most delicate layette to the sturdiest headstone. Soon there would be no need for a customer to shop anywhere else. Many were already choosing Whiteleys to do the bulk of their shopping, and as each new department started so they gratefully made use of it. Some, after purchasing from several departments, wanted to pay with a single cheque at the end of the day. Why, thought William Whiteley, should they draw on any account but his? He started a bank, offering the attractive terms of 5 per cent interest, and customers flocked to deposit their funds.

Undaunted by the refusal of the wine licence, he opened a refreshment room, which served light lunches, tea, coffee and pastries. Apart from the profits which he made directly, this enabled shoppers to spend more time and therefore more money in his stores. Some newspapers deplored the encouragement of excessive expenditure. The *Graphic* envisaged that once the ladies had refreshed themselves 'in the wild and reckless period that follows things are done in a financial way which would make angels weep . . . the afternoon's excitement has . . . all the attraction of a delightful dream, with a slight dash of an orgie [*sic*] . . .'[4]

The growth of the business – net profits were £26,000 in 1873, rising steadily to £66,000 in 1876 – was achieved without conventional advertising. Whiteley preferred to approach his customers directly, using handbills to advise them of the bargains to be had at the seasonal sales, and distributing copious numbers of circulars and price lists. Whiteleys now claimed to be the Universal Provider, with a logo illustrating the world, in case anyone was in any doubt.

There was, of course, advertising and advertising. Another enterprise of Whiteleys was the creation of the Kildare Dramatic Society, which over the years performed a great number of entertainments that were well attended and received. The *Paddington Times* approved of employers providing suitable activities for those idle spare moments of staff, and stated that the society 'reflects the highest credit on the employer, who not only allows such performances but places his name prominently forward as its encourager and patron'.[5]

Other shops were beginning to copy Whiteleys and in June 1873 there was a race on the Thames between the Kildare Rowing Club and the Great Western of Messrs D.B. Johnson, Edgware Road. Two steamers were chartered to accompany the race, and the crews were afloat and ready to go at 5 p.m. Just as the word 'go' was given, there was an unfortunate incident. Somehow the Kildare steamer was in the way of the Great Western crew, a foul was called, and by the time everyone had returned to their places, the tide was turning. It was decided that the crews would paddle up to Barnes and row the race from there down to Hammersmith Bridge. The crews accordingly paddled to their new starting point, while both steamers chugged up the river with bands merrily playing. As they passed Hammersmith Bridge, the Kildare crew happened to be ahead and were cheered loudly by their supporters who thought this was the race. At Barnes the race was restarted without mishap and the Great Western crew won by three lengths.

Lambert's claim that in this period scarcely an issue of the *Chronicle* came out without a criticism of Whiteley is something of an overstatement. Whiteley was frequently mentioned, often criticised, and may well have deserved it, but the editor had a satirical pen, which he did not reserve for Mr Whiteley alone. The lack of advertising cannot have been an issue. Whiteley did not advertise in the *Paddington Times* either, apart from occasional notices placed by the athletic and dramatic societies about their forthcoming events, and that organ of public information wrote adulatory articles about Whiteleys which nowadays would invite deep suspicion. In December 1874, commenting on the

Christmas Bazaar, the leading article referred to Whiteley as 'that grand caterer and provider of all the wants of our common humanity. With that spirit, energy and business aptitude and tact which have rendered him what he is, he throws open annually one of the prettiest and most recherché bazaars to be seen in London or any of its environs. In concluding our little notice, we can only sincerely hope, that both the bazaar and its founder may enjoy many years of that prosperity they so richly deserve.'[6]

Thus far, the business of William Whiteley had marched on without check or hindrance. By 1875 the full row of shops from 31 to 53 Westbourne Grove was his. He owned most of Westbourne Grove Terrace and two properties in Kensington Gardens Square. He next determined to open a furniture warehouse, but none of his existing properties nor any of those available were suitable for the purpose. He would have to build one. The location was to surprise his friends and enrage his competitors. For the first time, William Whiteley was to encounter fierce opposition to his plans, a conflict he engaged in with ingenuity and relish.

Queen's Road was then a side street off the main thoroughfare of Westbourne Grove, occupied almost entirely by private houses. It was so out of the way that Whiteley was advised that a furniture store there must fail. The building came to be known as Whiteley's Folly.[7] Whiteley was convinced that those customers who had been loyal to his old shops would quickly patronise the new one. He purchased 147 and 149 Queen's Road and submitted plans to the Vestry. There was one factor he had failed to take into account. The new warehouse would be immediately adjacent to the Paddington Baths.

The much-needed baths and washhouses had taken some time to come to Paddington. Some three years after Mr Flood's initial campaign, on 16 June 1873, the foundation stone had finally been laid. The architect, Mr Lewis H. Isaacs, had planned three men's swimming baths, one of the first class, one second-class and one third, as well as a ladies' swimming bath and about seventy-two private baths. There would also be a laundry department, which would include facilities for dry-cleaning and ironing. The building was completed and fitted out in the following year. It was a substantial edifice, with a frontage on Queen's Road 150ft wide, and a total depth of 250ft. The first and second-class customers came through the front door, but the entrance to the third-class baths and washhouses was in Douglas Place (now Redan Place), a narrow L-shaped cul-de-sac leading off the west side of Queen's Road, and turning south to run parallel with it. On 30 May 1874 the Baths were officially opened by the Lord Mayor of London, and the ceremony was followed by a grand luncheon. Mr Flood was accorded the credit he deserved, and that gentleman must have been gratified to see his dream at last made solid reality. From that moment on he protected the building as if it was his own. In 1875, with William Whiteley's furniture warehouse under construction, the Baths were the pride of the Vestry, supervised by a committee known as the Commissioners of the Baths, who frequently published self-congratulatory reports on the number of visitors and the income generated.

When the Baths were built, the Vestry had not utilised all the land at its disposal, and Whiteley's architect saw that he could use this fact to his advantage. If Whiteley used all of his land there would still be a space between the two buildings and this meant that he could fill the high walls of the warehouse with windows. This would provide the necessary light more cheaply than the alternative method of constructing a central courtyard and well-light.

The Vestrymen at once raised an objection to this plan, and William Whiteley met their objection in a manner that was to characterise much of his future dealings with them. He ignored it and commenced building. He felt unusually secure in doing so, for he did not feel himself to be entirely an outsider to the affairs of the Vestry. Acting for him was Charles Mills Roche, who was not only a member of the Vestry but solicitor to the Commissioners of the Baths, and the Vestry's representative on the Metropolitan Board of Works. Another member of that Board was Ebenezer Saunders, who happened to be the architect of Whiteley's new building.

As the building rose, and it became known that it would be a tall edifice with no less than ninety-one windows, the residents of nearby Kensington Gardens Square professed themselves discomfited by the prospect of being overlooked, and a Miss Emily Faithfull threw another and potentially explosive argument into the mix. Miss Faithfull, described by Lambert as 'a prim lady' was actually a prominent social reformer, and lecturer on women's rights, who took a great interest in local affairs. She pointed out that the windows of the new warehouse would directly overlook the Baths. Since the roof of the bathhouse was made of glass, this was a matter of some moment.

Even the *Paddington Times*, which had recently published flowery praise of the Kildare Dramatic Society and its 'enterprising patron Mr Whiteley',[8] now

passed on to its readers the rumour that the baths would
be placed in danger of fire by the display of furniture
and upholstery, 'which by its light and combustible
nature is very dangerous to an adjoining building and
would increase the insurance'. The architect, it said,
'gives instructions to push on the work notwithstanding
the objections raised and a notice of injunction having
been threatened'. Mr Roche's role also attracted some
scrutiny. 'We hear that a very prominent gentleman of
the Vestry and a member of the Board of Works is a
solicitor both for Mr Whiteley and the Commissioners.
This we think is not right.' The building had caused
other problems, too, interfering with the foundations
of the baths and putting the Commissioners to
considerable expense. 'This should never have been
permitted, and we think it never would if "holding with
the hare and running with the hounds" style had not
been followed.' The writer was unequivocal. 'Mr
Whiteley must be told that however pushing he may be,
he must not push himself too far into the bad opinion of
the Paddington public.'[9]

The Commissioners wrote a number of letters to Mr
Roche, saying that Mr Whiteley could not be permitted
to use the window openings. They received a letter from
Mr Whiteley dated 12 February stating sweetly that he
was 'quite under the impression that the matter had
been satisfactorily arranged, and would at once attend to
the matter personally'. Three days later he sent another
letter apologising for any apparent neglect and another
on 25 February regretting that he had not been able to
supply a new plan of the buildings. On the following
day, the Commissioners, who had come to the
conclusion that these letters were designed to create
delay, and moreover delay during which building work

was still being carried on, informed Mr Whiteley that they were not prepared to enter into any compromise, and had instructed their architect to render the openings useless.[10]

Matters proceeded slowly, except for the building which continued to rise exactly as Mr Whiteley wished it. The Vestry, which had been hoping for the support of the district surveyor, now received a setback. At a meeting on 2 March, a report was read from the Board of Works which stated that a side wall was only required to have no openings if it was a party wall to the adjoining building. Since Mr Whiteley's wall was an external wall, he could put openings in it if he wished. This was not at all what the Vestrymen had hoped to hear.

Thomas Fisher, a licensed victualler, and one of the Vestry's more outspoken opponents of William Whiteley, urged support of the Commissioners' proposal to block the windows, pointing out that if they did not act as suggested, the public would think that Mr Whiteley was being shown undue favour. Indeed, local residents who were watching the situation with some interest were drawing their own erroneous conclusions. He revealed that both he and Mr Flood had been asked by members of the public what they were going to get out of it.

Mr Roche tried to calm matters. He said that Mr Whiteley was most anxious to accede to the wishes of the Commissioners. He was prepared to block every window they objected to, and he would pay an annual rent for the windows so that no permanent rights over the Baths' light and air could be obtained. Mr Roche's assurances did not impress the Vestry.[11]

The meeting of the Vestry on 16 March provoked a long and noisy debate. Mr Saunders had sent a letter to the Vestry solicitor, Mr Hortin, and somehow, copies of it had been printed and sent to all the members of the Vestry, no one knew by whom. There was considerable disagreement as to whether or not the letter should be read – in the end Mr Roche's argument won the day and it was not – during which Mr Flood admitted that he had been responsible for it being circulated. Vestryman Young proposed a motion approving the Commissioners' decision to resist Mr Whiteley, while Vestryman Shaw said a man should be heard before he was condemned and proposed adjourning the matter until the Commissioners had reported. The gentlemen of the Vestry were usually very amenable to suggestions that difficult matters should be adjourned. It was a solution they often grasped at with, one suspects, a sense of relief, and the knowledge that there were some things which, if ignored for long enough, really would go away. In this case, however, their blood was up, and Mr Young's motion was carried by a narrow margin.[12]

By April, the *Paddington Times* was reporting that the question 'has not only created great excitement in the Vestry, but appears to be agitating the whole parish. . .'. The Commissioners, affirming their position as custodians of an important public building, asked the Vestry to grant funds to protect their rights by building a wall to block the windows. They believed that the sum of £200 would be amply sufficient. The Vestry expressed its confidence in the Commissioners and left them to take any action they saw fit. Mr Flood, approving the proposal, stated that he recommended it on public grounds, and had no personal feelings in the matter. His colleagues shouted 'Hear, hear!' He added that the position of Mr Roche was a very peculiar one, as he acted for both plaintiff and defendant in the same suit, and this was not to be tolerated.

The Vestry clerk then reported that he had received a letter from Mr Whiteley from which it was apparent that he had seen a copy of the Commissioners' report. No one could understand how Mr Whiteley might have obtained this report, until it was suggested that some member of the Vestry who was a friend of Mr Whiteley might have given him a copy. No names were mentioned.

Whiteley's letter denied that there was any fire risk, and enclosed a copy of a letter from the secretary of the Royal Insurance Society to back up his assertion. Neither did he believe it would be possible for the windows to overlook the baths. He added that in two or three weeks the building would be sufficiently far advanced that it would be possible to arrange a meeting by which the Commissioners and the members of the Vestry would be able to view the premises. If, after seeing it for themselves, they felt their objection to be well founded, he would deal with the matter. Nothing could seem to be more reasonable, and there were a few waverers on the Vestry, but several members including Mr Flood said that no ladies would attend the baths if they thought they could be overlooked. Whiteley's courteous words had not erased the memories of his earlier carefree indifference to both the Vestry and the Commissioners, and Flood said that the letters were nothing but delays. The matter was put to the vote and the Commissioners' actions were approved by twenty-six votes to twenty-two.[13]

The *Chronicle* came down on the side of the Vestry, declaring that the privacy of the baths must be beyond suspicion, although it did not lay the blame for the unfortunate position at the door of the one man who had entire control of the work.

48

Mr Whiteley himself is so accustomed to deal with the public and is so utterly unlikely to challenge unpopularity that he is not likely to have been his own advisor in this unfortunate matter. Anyhow he has lost the opportunity of making a graceful surrender. Public baths are about the last buildings on which to try experiments of the kind just attempted, and Mr Whiteley should have known that unpleasant suggestions of 'Peeping Tom' are inevitably associated with his side-lights in the Queen's Road. But it is now too late. The Commissioners' architect has now commenced the blocking up of the obnoxious windows.[14]

Not everyone supported the Vestry, however. A few individuals had had a look at the glass roof and concluded that the matter was not as serious as had been supposed. In May, the *Paddington Times* made a startling return to supporting Whiteley:

. . . that universal caterer to all our wants, Mr W. Whiteley – the maker of the Grove – through which thousands now daily pass, where but a few years since hundreds were scarcely visible; the man in fact who contributes more to the rates and taxes than any other man in the parish, and gives bread and employment to hundreds of young men and young women, who, without him, might be wanting in both . . . for ourselves, looking on the roof of a bath or washhouse does not appear a very heinous offence, especially when those windows are fixed and glazed with ground glass, thus totally preventing any view of the Bath-house premises. It is only a question of obtaining a little daylight and the opposition to it is as trivial as it is petty. We know what little men, dressed in a little brief authority will do . . . Mr Whiteley for a moment is stayed from carrying out one of those gigantic enterprises by which he has made Bayswater the prince of suburbs.[15]

The Vestry needed to remind itself that it was not a popular body in Paddington, and the revelation that the glass was not, after all, transparent, excited some comment. The following week a letter from someone signing himself 'CANTAB' denounced the Vestrymen as 'jackdaws in borrowed feathers pluming themselves so vaingloriously on their zeal in support of these baths', and accused them of straining at a gnat, 'that gnat being simply a few harmless windows overlooking most harmlessly the roof of a public washhouse'.[16]

Mr Roche had had some time to consider his unusual position. It had caused him no personal embarrassment whatsoever, but Mr Flood's comments had brought matters into the open and forced him to decide where his loyalties really lay. At the meeting of the Vestry on 22 April a letter was read from Mr Roche tendering his resignation as solicitor to the Commissioners. The Vestry approved. Mr Fisher described Roche's double position as 'monstrous', and his conduct as 'extraordinary and unsatisfactory'. Among other things he had interfered personally on behalf of Mr Whiteley, and had actually forbidden the builder of the baths, Mr Elkington, to carry out certain instructions of the Commissioners.'[17]

Whiteley realised that it would be useless to court popularity with the *Chronicle*, which he preferred to ignore, but when the warehouse was opened he invited a representative of the *Paddington Times*, which had already denounced the Vestrymen's wall as 'a useless waste of parochial money',[18] to inspect the new premises. The resulting article was everything he could have desired. The building, gushed the writer, was

> as chaste in its style as it is magnificent in the grandeur of its proportions. . . . On entering the noble vestibule a grand panorama lay before us. Lines upon lines of costly furniture stretched out to our view extending some three hundred feet and more in depth. . . . Riveted to the beauties of the spot we were gently reminded by our most amiable *chaperon* that on the first floor we might discover other objects of attraction equally great. . . . Following his steps we ascended by a palatial staircase and found ourselves amid bedsteads and bedding, drawers and washstands . . . this floor also forms an immense and complete depot of every object necessary to the kitchen and household department.

Ascending, the visitors saw a workshop extending the whole length of the building. In the light of later events it is interesting to note their comments on 'the admirable and perfect organisation against fire . . . we could not help smiling within ourselves at the senseless twaddle we once heard concerning the hazard the baths were exposed to by the proximity of this grand emporium.' They were also impressed by the numerous lavatories and appliances for health and comfort: 'we again perceive the evidence of that great trait in Mr Whiteley's character, that the comfort and well-being of everyone he employs is ever uppermost in his thoughts. This, we believe is the grand secret why all his orders are so promptly, efficiently and ably carried out by a staff of employees second to none. . . . Often have we visited the vast establishments of Mr Whiteley and ever retired impressed with the clock-like movements of every department.'[19]

All was not so harmonious in the Vestry. Mr Roche may have resigned as the Commissioners' solicitor but he was still a Vestryman, and still able to throw barbs and obstructions in the way of Mr Flood and his anti-Whiteley faction. When it emerged that the cost of the wall was not a mere £200 but £760 (about £36,000 today) the two sides argued openly, each accusing the other of lying.

Mr Flood was far from finished with Mr Whiteley. In November he fired the first shot in a war on a different front, casting an eye on the sewage work in the Douglas Place part of the premises, and it was resolved that Mr Whiteley should not be permitted to make his sewers any deeper than 8ft. In December, Flood protested against Mr Whiteley placing a flag across Westbourne Grove, and the Vestry ordered that it should be removed.

Despite it all, William Whiteley ended 1875 on a note of triumph. His Christmas bazaar was as successful as ever. 'There is a prestige in the name of Whiteley', enthused the *Paddington Times*, which cannot have been overstating things too much: '. . . our Universal Provider is ever at his post, foremost in the field to cater for the wants and wishes of the crowds who, bring forth what he may, ever throng to support him.'[20]

William Whiteley was riding high on a sea of popularity, which it seemed that nothing could diminish, and yet the next few years were to be ones of falling turnover, and public ferment.

FOUR

A Sadder and a Wiser Man

The Royal Aquarium and Summer and Winter Gardens were intended to be the great sensation of the London season of 1876, the object being to combine the educational functions of an exhibition with varied yet wholesome entertainment. The public was encouraged to purchase membership tickets, and there was no lack of takers. An imposing 2½-acre presence on Tothill Street, it included art galleries, a skating rink, a theatre, reading rooms, and some very large fish tanks. Unfortunately, at the opening ceremony, presided over by the Duke of Edinburgh on 22 January 1876, there were no fish.

> Never was an institution opened with more *prestige* and promise. [Commented the *Chronicle* that July] Never was there more vulgar haste on the part of the Nobodies of London society to tack themselves onto the Somebodies by purchasing fellowship tickets and so getting the run of a promiscuous company of speculating lords and ladies. . . . Hardly six months ago the Nobodies were paying eight guineas for the five guinea fellowship ticket which would admit them to the circle of the Somebodies and the £5 shares were readily taken up.[1]

William Whiteley was very far from being one of the 'Nobodies' but with his liking for exalted company he must have hoped to add a little gloss to his image by such a noble, even royal, connection. The enterprise would also have reminded him of the Great Exhibition which had so impressed him twenty-five years before, and the opportunity to attach his name to something in the same vein must have been irresistible. And there was the little matter of business, of course. He may have known that as a director and shareholder it was not considered appropriate for him to enter into business dealings with the company, but if he did, it was something he chose to ignore, as he tended to ignore anything that did not suit him. Mr Roche was also involved in the administration of the Society, and should have been aware of the position, and advised his client accordingly. Perhaps he did.

Another influential presence on the Aquarium board was Henry Labouchere, proprietor of the weekly magazine *Truth*, whose columns of reviews and social and political comment were, at that time, mainly written by himself. Labouchere was a personal friend of Whiteley, and must have been fired with a similar zeal since his uncle of the same name had been a member of the Royal Commission for the exhibition of 1851.

Sadly, the Royal Aquarium was not the success that had been anticipated, and at an extraordinary general meeting of the shareholders held on 24 July, matters came under rather closer scrutiny than many people might have wished. Those £5 shares were now worth as many shillings, and their owners wanted to know why. Mr Labouchere chaired the meeting, which became somewhat heated. Just before its commencement a circular had been issued, which included the comments: 'We know that Mr Whiteley has supplied goods to the company, and indirectly, to the refreshment contractors. We have purposely refrained from the suggestion that Mr Whiteley had made any undue profit from such transactions. We think it is a very ill-advised proceeding for any director to adopt; the example set may be followed-up, and we think the shareholders should discountenance such proceedings definitely, and at once.'[2]

Those who were versed in accounts had also spotted something rather worrying. The accounts for the first third of the year which had been presented to the shareholders had shown a profit of £1,798 1*s* 6*d*, which seemed reasonable enough; however, a closer examination revealed that the patient was not as healthy as supposed. The whole of the annual subscriptions had been included in that third, instead of being spread over the year, and some expenditure on prizes had been omitted. The true result, it was believed, should not have been a profit at all, but a loss of nearly £6,000. An angry gathering of gentlemen felt they had been imposed upon by men of no business character on the one hand, and businessmen who had not performed their duties on the other. For those individuals who were not businessmen, and knew nothing of accounts, there was perhaps some excuse, but 'it is different with Mr Whiteley, essentially a man of business, as also with Mr Roche, if we are to believe the flattering encomiums on the financial abilities of that gentleman in the report issued by the Chairman'.[3]

Labouchere admitted that Whiteley had supplied the company with both labour and goods, but said that this had happened in a crisis and at the request of the other directors, to enable the institution to be opened on the appointed day.

I will tell you what has been done [said Labouchere].
Mr Whiteley took a thousand shares in the company,
and I confess I was rather surprised to see Mr
Whiteley taking so very large a number of shares.
Well, Mr Whiteley once or twice enquired to know
how the company was getting on at the commencement. I sent back word and said, 'I really think, as Mr
Whiteley is so very large a shareholder, that it would
be a most advantageous thing to him and the Board if
he would be kind enough to come on the Board, in
order to look after his property and yours.' Well, Mr
Whiteley consented to do so, and it was directly at the
request of the Board that he did so. With respect to
these goods I will now tell you what occurred. At the
opening we had a great difficulty in getting things
done in time, and Mr Robertson the General Managing
Director went to Mr Whiteley with the full
concurrence of the Board, and asked him whether he
would be able, by putting on extra men, to carry out
the arrangements necessary in time for the opening.
. . . Mr Whiteley with the consent of and at the
request of the Board consented to do it; and not only
that, but his charges were less than those which had
been paid before, and he did not charge any more for
it. Therefore I say that you are under a debt of
gratitude to Mr Whiteley for having done so much as
this for you without any recompense whatever.

This provoked cries from the floor of 'No, no' and 'Can't
see it', to which Labouchere replied that the action was
not contrary to the articles of association and if Mr
Whiteley had not stepped in, the work would not have
been completed (applause from Whiteley's supporters).
'Mr Whiteley's business is a ready-money business, but

yet though the amount of Mr Whiteley's claim was £600 we made him wait six months for his money.'

A voice asked how many shares Whiteley now held and when Labouchere said he thought it was 850, the voice said, 'He has made a business of it', to which the retort was 'If you say that a man is not to buy shares and sell them, what next are we come to?' The crowd was far from appeased. It was all very well to claim that Mr Whiteley had helped them out of a crisis, but the shareholders now knew that if he had not intervened, things would have been very much worse.

The *Chronicle*, reporting the later withdrawal of both Labouchere and Whiteley from the company, commented with unusual generosity, 'It is due to the Universal Provider to say that he leaves the Aquarium in good odour with both the rival parties – a sadder and a wiser man. What is the friendship of Labouchere, flattering as it seems to have been, and what the value of his connection, compared with Bayswater to a man in Mr Whiteley's position. Of the two, the ex-chairman had the more to gain, and Mr Whiteley as the result has shown, the more to lose. . . .'[4]

* * *

Having taken a firm stand on not paying for newspaper advertisements, Whiteley was always seeking ways to advertise by other means. He must have approved of the sycophantic outpourings of the *Paddington Times*, and was eager to have similar articles published in more widely distributed newspapers. In May 1876, the readers of the *New York Daily Graphic* were told that, given the necessary funds, a man might be supplied with every necessity of life from a bath to a bank account by Whiteleys. 'At this really remarkable place, one can absolutely and without exaggeration have everything done for him . . . Mr Whiteley will take charge of you from the cradle to the grave, and give you your meals as you go along – if you can pay for it.'[6]

That autumn saw the launch of a highly successful new enterprise, *Whiteley's Diary and Almanac*, which was to become an annual event. In November, *The Essex Weekly News* published what was effectively a grand tour of the premises and all its departments. It recorded that each morning's first postal delivery consisted of a thousand items, with more deliveries pouring in by the hour, and a staff of fifty was employed solely to open this avalanche of mail. In the clothing departments, one could be 'instantly equipped for wedding, garden party, racecourse, funeral or evening party . . .' and the refreshment room, which offered a choice of ten kinds of soup daily, provided 'every requisite for the inner man . . .'. Observing that parcels sent to all the main London districts were labelled W, E, N, S or C, the writer commented, 'Surely these may be interpreted as Whiteley, Energy, Nous, Success and Courtesy, for the last and the second and the third are the keys to the fourth and first.'[7] Whiteley ensured that these flattering articles were reprinted in the *Almanac*.

No trade in Bayswater was safe from the great machine that was William Whiteley. With his formidable resources he set about obtaining foodstuffs in bulk so as to undercut his rivals. Small shopkeepers in the area – butchers, grocers and greengrocers – watched in dismay as, at the start of November 1876, Whiteleys opened a new emporium: a food hall. Naturally there was an invitation to the *Paddington Times* to inspect the result, with the expected paean of praise: 'the most telling genius is the genius of commerce, and this Mr Whiteley possesses in a pre-eminent degree.' The writer described vast pickling vats of beef, pork and ox tongues, sausages being made of 'first rate lumps of solid beef', warehouses crammed with bacon, cheese, potatoes, butter and poultry, and 'the most luscious fruits the eye ever beheld'.[8]

All this was too much for the local traders who suddenly felt their livelihoods being threatened, but like tiny fish about to be swallowed by a whale, there was little they could do. The one thing they did not attempt was legitimate opposition through unified action to undercut their rival. They must have realised it was a war they would be bound to lose.

Threats were made against Whiteley's property, both business and private, according to a correspondent in *Land and Water*. Harriet was receiving regular warnings through the post to be prepared for her husband's sudden death, while he had been advised by the police that he had better not go out after dark.[9]

A disreputable public house in Notting Hill was the focus and headquarters of the anti-Whiteley movement, where, fuelled with copious libations of beer, aggrieved costermongers devised a plan of action. Handbills were circulated 'of a by no means complimentary or savoury character . . .',[10] and by 4 November rumours were flying about the neighbourhood that Guy Fawkes Day would see a full-blown demonstration.

About the middle of the day, when Westbourne Grove was at its fullest, a grotesque and noisy *cortège* entered the thoroughfare. At its head was a vehicle, in which a gigantic Guy was propped up. This figure, evidently meant as an effigy, was vested in the conventional frock coat of a draper; the mask (which represented nobody in particular) being surmounted with an ordinary black cylindrical hat. Conspicuous on the figure was a label with the words 'LIVE AND LET LIVE' while some clumsy epigrams to the same effect were pasted about the wagon. In one hand of the figure a piece of beef bore the label '5½*d*' and in the other was a handkerchief with the ticket '2½*d* – all linen'. A company of butchers in blue frocks followed, making hideous music with marrow bones and cleavers and unearthly cries. A rabble, who soon scared decent people out of the Grove, surrounded the actors in this unwonted scene, whilst the object of the burlesque stood at his own door and surveyed the whole affair with apparent interest and amusement. The company having yelled and hissed to their heart's content, the *cortège* moved on to make the tour of the district, and as far as we can learn, enjoyed a somewhat triumphant progress, the sympathisers being numerous, and the coppers falling very freely into the boxes. The company returned to Westbourne Grove later in the day, and the exhibition was repeated with still greater gusto, and before larger crowds of spectators. Eventually the party moved off, and in the course of the evening, the effigy met with summary punishment in the Portobello Road, in which district as well as Notting Hill, a strong feeling of resentment exists among the numerous trades, which Mr Whiteley's new venture threatens injuriously to affect.[11]

The description of Whiteley's amused reaction is convincing. At no expense he had received advertising which would have cost an enormous amount in the normal way, while the demonstration showed how helpless the opposition were to do any real damage to his business.

A local resident signing himself 'Senex' sent his views to the *Chronicle*.

> I am one of those who have been watching how far the gigantic Westbourne Grove monopoly would go before it would call forth public remonstrance. . . . A new and hitherto untouched class of small and struggling people . . . are now brought into the arena of the Leviathan's victims. . . . Those who have had opportunities during the last week of learning the amount of bitterness which exists among the numerous class whose vocation has been so wantonly interfered with and whose heard-earned living has been so gratuitously jeopardised, are profoundly impressed with this crisis in the social history of the district.[12]

This letter stimulated more correspondence. Many Bayswater shoppers took the view that they would benefit by healthy competition bringing the prices down, although one trader wrote bitterly of customers who entered his shop, found fault with both his goods and prices, and then left, saying they would go to Whiteleys, leaving unpaid bills behind them.

Senex responded to this in the next issue, and if what he wrote was true, it gives an uneasy glimpse into the business methods of the Universal Provider who was so genial to his customers. 'Mr Whiteley does not fight his fellow tradesmen fairly. In the language of the ring, he hits below the belt. Mere underselling is common enough in business, and I am not now complaining of that, but I do say that the kind of underselling which is

characteristic of Mr Whiteley is . . . of the very worst
kind. It is that of selling goods at cost price until you
have worn out your neighbour by sheer brute force of
capital. The war which Mr Whiteley carries on against
his neighbour thus becomes one of extermination.'[13]

This may well have been true. Whiteley often
repeated homilies about the importance of service to the
customer, but it was his customer he spoke of, and he
cared little for anyone else's customers unless it be to
appropriate them for himself, and still less for the fate of
other traders. Whiteley's vision was to be the great
provider of all human wants, and to this end he
continued to expand his business into new areas of
trade, eating into the geographical heart of Bayswater,
never losing an opportunity for self-promotion. 'Our
U.P. [as the newspapers were now calling him] is now
bent on another sensation . . .', observed the *Chronicle*
about Whiteley's plans to build a giant clock above the
Grove. 'A succession of sensations seem a necessity of
Mr. Whiteley's business.'[14] It was left to the *Paddington
Times* to concede that Whiteleys had brought both
prosperity and glamour to Bayswater. 'The Grove has
grown out of its original proportions. Instead of being
the simple grove of a quiet suburb it has become the
grand rendezvous of the metropolis. From all parts of
London we see carriage upon carriage setting down at
Whiteley's emporium, the fair denizens of the West to
whom a few years since the very existence of
Westbourne Grove was as a *terra incognita*.'[15]

The *Chronicle* continued to fire small barbs at Mr
Whiteley. Apart from publishing Senex's attacks, it
declared that placing the vegetable department upstairs
was a miscalculation, and complained of the off-hand
behaviour of the employees to customers who came on

foot. The 'Local Gossip' column contained regular items
described as 'Whiteleyana', which included approval of
the Vestry's asking Whiteley to remove the flag he hung
across the Grove at Christmas. 'Mr Whiteley's way of
placarding becomes the most hideous eyesore that an
English visitor can look upon. We don't want to
Americanize the Grove.'[16]

These articles irritated Whiteley sufficiently that he
decided to fight fire with fire. The instrument of his
defence was the educated pen of Loftus Slade, a 66-year-
old writer and professor of languages, and one of the
correspondents who had defended Whiteley in the
Paddington Times, under the nom de plume 'CANTAB'.
In January, Whiteley wrote to Slade and said he wanted
to see him. Slade duly called upon Whiteley who
explained that he proposed to start a newspaper to
defend himself against the scurrilous attacks of the
Chronicle, and he thought that Slade was the man to
edit it. Slade was most unwilling to take on the task. He
pointed out at some length that the undertaking would
be expensive, and that the same result could be
achieved through the pages of the *Paddington Times*.
Whiteley would have none of this. He was determined
to have a newspaper, and a newspaper he would have.
Slade recommended an acquaintance called John Hope
to manage the paper, and on being offered the sum of £2
per week, agreed, with some misgivings, to be the editor.
The remuneration, equivalent to less than £100 today,
does seem remarkably low; however, it may well have
been a part-time post, since Slade was already engaged
by the Italian embassy.

The new furniture store was by then an undoubted
success, even though it stood in such curious isolation.
Few must have realised that it was just the first footprint

in the march of Whiteleys along the Queen's Road. In January 1877 he took another six houses between Douglas Place and the Baths, to construct a large meat and fish store. The *Chronicle* had little sympathy for the fishmongers, 'as fish has hitherto been too often difficult to get or too dear when got. So Mr W. continues to mete out even handed justice to the tradesmen all around.'[17]

Early in 1877 there was a new flurry of correspondence in the *Chronicle*. A local artist wrote to the newspaper stating that the Universal Provider sometimes offered for sale items that did not exist. He had seen in the window a painting of Harlech Castle, on the frame of which was written the name of the artist, Sir Charles Leslie, R.A. 'As there is not and never was a "Sir Charles Leslie a member of the R.A." this is rather astounding, even for the U.P. I have observed before that Mr W's staff are decidedly shaky in their knowledge of art.'[18]

In the next issue two Whiteley employees flew to the defence of their master. The buyer of the cabinet department said he had bought the pictures himself and the letters R.A. were not on any of them, while the man who had labelled the paintings stated categorically that the letters R.A. had not been used. This stimulated a reply by the original correspondent who insisted he had been correct, and several others who said they had all seen and commented on the offending letters. The matter was becoming a local joke, with some art dealers displaying in their windows paintings labelled 'NOT by Sir Charles Leslie R.A.'.

Once again, CANTAB wrote in Whiteley's support, the only non-employee to do so. In the *Paddington Times* he professed not to be able to see the letters R.A., only 'landscapes of glade-like beauty'. He suggested that the original letter was either a 'humorous skit' or 'intentionally malicious slander'.[19]

The paintings in Whiteleys' windows continued to be unashamedly displayed. The letters 'R.A.' if they had been there, were no longer so, but the labels still gave the artist, who was actually plain Mr Charles Leslie, a minor Scottish landscape painter, an undeserved title.

The meat trade proved to be a successful one for Whiteley, and by March the outcry of rival butchers had died down. The great emporium was proving beneficial to all, since the attraction of bargains at Whiteleys was drawing more and more custom into the Grove. This created a new problem: the fabric of Westbourne Grove, once a quiet semi-rural backwater, was suffering from the increase in traffic. The street was paved with crushed granite which deteriorated into mud and slush in wet weather and threw up blinding dust when it was dry. The constant stream of carriages on the surface also made an incessant and deafening noise. The newspapers and ratepayers of Paddington appealed to the Vestry to do something about it. 'You only have to stand before Mr Whiteley's establishment', wrote the editor of the *Paddington Times*,[20] 'to become perfectly convinced that some change in the whole system of the Grove traffic is more or less an absolute necessity.' The Vestry, in addition to all its other expenses, now found itself under pressure to lay wood paving in Westbourne Grove. One might pity the poor Vestrymen. One moment they were being vilified as 'fussy nonentities whose administrative qualifications are in direct inverse proportion to their personal pretensions',[21] and Mr Flood as 'a constitutional Dictator . . .',[22] while an association of local ratepayers formed in 1875 met weekly with the object of exposing mismanagement and overspending by the Vestry so as to reduce the rates. As soon as action was required, however, the *Paddington Times* declared that one of the chief component parts of the Vestry was common sense, which they were sure would not be wanting in this issue. The question of wood paving for Westbourne Grove caused long and furious debates in the Vestry and the work was eventually carried out in September 1878.

It naturally suited Whiteley to support the actions of the Ratepayers' Association where it threatened the Vestry. The Vestrymen were obliged to retire and offer themselves for re-election every three years, and thus the annual elections each May when a portion of the membership had to try and win back their own seats left openings at which a pro-Whiteley candidate could aim. The Association also had an influential and valuable ally active in their support – none other than Mr C.M. Roche, who was still stinging about his enforced retirement from the post of solicitor to the Commissioners of the Baths. Both he and Whiteley did not regard the matter of the wall blocking the warehouse windows to be final, and sought to reopen matters by having sympathetic candidates elected. In the event they were unable to make any mark on the pro-Flood anti-Whiteley Vestry.

Whiteley had already shown that he could be firm, even vindictive, towards those who owed him money, and over the years he frequently demonstrated the same uncompromising attitude towards shoplifters. In March 1877 a respectably dressed married woman with over £1 in her pocket was caught attempting to leave the shop with two cauliflowers, valued at 6*d*, for which she had not paid. She offered to pay for them, but Whiteley, who had taken a personal interest in the matter, sent for a policeman, who removed her to Paddington police station. Later, at Marylebone police court, an unusually harsh magistrate 'sentenced the prisoner to be imprisoned and kept to hard labour for twenty-one days, remarking that it would teach her not to steal cauliflowers again'.[23]

Perhaps the public was unhappy abut seeing such swingeing punishments and the *Chronicle*'s headlines about 'Kleptomania' may have led to some sympathy for the plight of unhappy shoplifters hauled before the courts by Mr Whiteley. Later that year a Mary Gray was brought before the Middlesex sessions after one of the Universal Provider's sharp-eyed assistants had seen her place a packet of needles in her pocket. Three witnesses gave her a good character and to everyone's surprise the jury returned a verdict of 'not guilty'.[24]

Whiteley, in the meantime, had his own personal court appearance to deal with, for in June he was at the Court of Common Pleas having been accused of libel. Whiteley was an obstinate litigant who liked to use his position, wealth and the machinations of Mr Roche to wear down those with less strong stomachs for the fight, but every so often he took on someone just as pig-headed as he was, and this was such an occasion.

In 1873 Whiteley had decided that he would start supplying his customers with coal, and entered into a verbal agreement with a coal merchant called Tassell, who would both supply and deliver the goods. Initially the delivery notes and invoices had been made out in Tassell's name but later, by mutual agreement, they were made out in the name of Whiteleys. All went well until 1875 when Whiteley decided to obtain his coal from another supplier. Tassell, unwilling to lose such a substantial amount of custom, sent a circular to all those

persons whom he had been supplying through
Whiteleys. 'Having had the pleasure of supplying you
through our agent Mr Whiteley of Westbourne Grove, we
now beg to inform you that in consequence of different
arrangements being made, Mr Whiteley has discon-
tinued receiving orders for us. We shall be most happy
to receive your future favours. . . .' Whiteley was
furious. Not only was Tassell trying to hold on, in his
own name, to the customers Whiteley thought were
rightly his, but he had the monumental cheek to
describe Whiteley as his agent. Mr Roche was directed
to send a firm letter, and he did so, pointing out that
Tassell's circular contained 'two deliberate falsehoods.
. . . It is evident that [the statements] have been made for
the purpose of damaging Mr Whiteley, and obtaining an
unfair advantage to yourselves. Mr Whiteley never was
your agent, and instead of his discontinuing to receive
orders for you, he ceased to deal with you for coals.' The
letter demanded, under threat of legal action, that
Tassell withdraw the circular, retract the falsehoods,
and apologise.

Tassell was going to do no such thing, and so now it
was Mr Whiteley's turn to issue a circular. 'Caution –
Coal department – W. Whiteley having become aware
that a circular containing statements devoid of truth is
being sent to his customers by Messrs Tassell and Co,
begs to warn them against being misled by the assertions
made in it, and to say that he has instructed his solicitor
to take legal proceedings against the authors.'

Whiteley, who had only been accused of being an
agent, had seriously misjudged Tassell, whom he had
accused in print of being a liar. Tassell contended that
the circular, of which 25,000 had been distributed, was
libellous, and moreover that he was the real vendor of

the coals, not Whiteley, who was no more than a 'brass-plate coal merchant'. When the case came to court, therefore, it was not Whiteley who was taking proceedings against Tassell, but the reverse. Tassell claimed that Whiteley simply supplied the names of the customers, and earned a commission on sales. Whiteley claimed that he was in fact the merchant and the 6*d* a ton he received on best coal was not a commission, but a discount.

Mr Justice Denman, who seems to have been mightily unimpressed by both parties, urged them to put an end to the action. 'Is it not really a cruel thing to fight this and bring the jury here again on Monday morning? Why don't you shake hands over it?'

Whiteley was unwise enough to make a flippant remark to his counsel Mr Henry James QC who was even more unwise to repeat it to the Judge. 'My Lord, Mr Whiteley says that he has such an appreciation and admiration of the justice of a British jury that this is recreation to him.' 'Our juries are waiting in 600 or 700 cases', Denman reminded him, coldly. Neither party was willing to reach a compromise so the case was adjourned to the following Monday when Denman observed that it was a deplorable thing to have occupied the courts for three days in such a case. The jury found for Mr Tassell, and expressed their contempt in the traditional way by awarding him damages of one farthing. Each man was ordered to pay his own costs.[25]

In August Whiteley decided for the time being to give up greengrocery, but this was not the defeat that the *Chronicle*, which reported 'joy among the costermongers and water-cress girls', suggested.[26] He may have been unhappy with the quality and reliability of the supply, and had therefore ceased operations until he was able to

engage the one supplier whom he knew he could rely on
– himself. A few months later he bought an estate,
Manor Farm at Finchley, and although this was to serve
him over the years as a pleasant country retreat, he also
set about developing it as a supplier of poultry and
vegetables.

The Kildare Athletic Club having proved to be such a
success both with the members and the public, Whiteley
added several more sporting activities over the years. In
1877 the football club was started, playing in colours of
blue and amber.

In September, after six months' struggle, the
Westbourne Gazette and Belgrave Herald which
Whiteley had set up with such determination collapsed
in failure, with losses of £370. Slade called his
editorship 'one of the most thankless unprofitable
offices I ever undertook'.[27] No copies of the paper
survive, so it is impossible now to judge the reasons for
its demise; Slade cited Hope's mismanagement, while
Hope alleged that Slade was unfit for his editorial post.
Either way it is remarkable that Whiteley, who
habitually gave everything his personal attention, was
not aware of what was happening during the paper's six
months' existence, and took no steps to change the staff.

It had been an eventful and unhappy year, though
Whiteleys' dented reputation did not deter customers.
In December, the *Paddington Times* published its usual
elaborate praise of Whiteleys' Christmas bazaar,
commenting, 'Whatever carpers may say, the energy,
enterprise and public spirit of Mr Whiteley have made
the Grove what it is today – a second Regent Street.'[28]
This was true, but the following years would give
Whiteley's enemies even more reasons to hate him.

FIVE

From a Pin to an Elephant

Part of the mythology of the Universal Provider, which had some foundation in fact, was that from time to time an amateur humorist would attempt to test his mettle by setting him a seemingly impossible task. On these occasions Whiteley would seize the opportunity to turn the joke back on the perpetrator, and acquire some free publicity into the bargain. These were stories he loved telling and re-telling to the end of his life. 'It has, I think almost passed into a proverb that Whiteleys can execute any commission. . . . But on many occasions that boast – if a fact can be called a boast – has been put to a very severe test . . . a gentleman leaving for central Africa commissioned me to find him a suitable wife within six hours.' The match, according to Whiteley, was carried out in minutes. The gentleman having insinuated that Whiteleys could provide him with everything except a wife, Whiteley declared 'Oh, I have brides on the premises, also; pray come with me!' He led the surprised customer to a department, signalled an attractive assistant and presented her to the gentleman. All accounts of this incident naturally report that the resultant marriage was very happy.[1]

One morning, an eminent pillar of the Church called upon me, and said, 'Mr Whiteley, I want an elephant.' 'Certainly, sir, when would you like it?' 'Oh, to-day!'

'And where?' 'I should like it placed in my stable.' 'It shall be done.' In four hours a tuskiana was placed in the reverend gentleman's coach-house. Of course, this was a try-on, designed to test our resources, and it originated in a bet. The vicar confessed himself greatly disconcerted, because, as he frankly avowed, he didn't think we could execute the order. He displayed the utmost anxiety lest I should hold him to the transaction, but I let him down with a small charge for pilotage and food only, at which he confessed himself deeply grateful.[2]

Quite when these events happened is not clear, but in 1877 *Truth* commented that these were old tales. That organ was recounting yet another story, presumably then recent. In Whiteley's words:

On one occasion, some young men, to decide a bet, ordered a secondhand coffin. For the moment, I was nonplussed, as it was hardly practicable to dig one up. But I soon remembered that we had in the cellars a coffin with a curious history. It had originally been made for a man of eccentric habits, who kept it in his room. When he got married, his wife objected to the coffin, and it was given to an old servant of the family, who had it placed on end and fitted with shelves to serve as a cupboard. But her friends disliked it, and she finally sold it to me. Thus, the coffin, though never used for its proper purpose, was undoubtedly a secondhand one, and I duly delivered it in execution of this very original order.[3]

Mr Labouchere supplied even more elaborate details. 'Ascertaining that the would-be wag was giving a grand

dinner party upon a particular evening to some very
choice friends, a cart drove up to the door, and before
the astonished lacqueys [*sic*] in the hall could recover
their senses, two undertakers marched into the dining-
room carrying a coffin on their shoulders, and delivered
themselves, before the assembled company, of the
following message from their master:- "Mr Whiteley's
compliments, and he's very sorry he can't get you a
second-hand one, sir, so he's sent you a *misfit*".'[4]

The *Chronicle* absolutely refused to believe in the
story at all.

Truth of Thursday last contains a silly cock-and-bull
tale, meant to glorify Mr W. The concocter, (who tells
the tale all out of his own head, and evidently has
wood enough to make another) says that Mr W. was
asked to supply a second-hand coffin, and that he
turned the table on the wag (these people are always
'wags') by delivering the coffin to the customer in his
drawing-room, before a party of guests. People who
read this rot are asking what Mr Labouchere's puffery
of Mr Whiteley in *Truth* really means. What new
scheme has he in hand now, in which the Westbourne
Grove U.P. is again to be an instrument? Wasn't the
Westminster Aquarium enough?[5]

Whiteley was often obliged to think on his feet, as when
'another ingenious joker' ordered a pint of live fleas.
The first problem was where to find the fleas. Whiteley
sent urgent messages to the zoo and a dealer in wild
animals, 'begging them to comb the monkeys and any
other animals whose coverts were well stocked with
game, and to send me the captures'. Quite what these
gentlemen thought of the request is unrecorded, but by

evening, the fleas had duly been delivered to Whiteleys when he found that he only had enough to half fill a pint jar. This might have dismayed a lesser man, but Whiteley recalled that the order had specified live fleas. If he had continued filling the jar, he reasoned, the lack of air would have meant that the recipient would have ended up with a jar of dead fleas, which would not have met the requirements of the order. 'So I sent off the collection, with a note explaining that there were as many living fleas as could be got into a pint jar without prejudice to their health!'[6]

On one occasion, some South African chiefs were visiting England, and were to be presented to the Queen at Windsor. She had asked for them to attend wearing their South African cloaks. The chiefs were mystified. They had no idea what such a garment might be, and had nothing with them that might pass muster. No one had the courage to tell the Queen that there was no such thing as a South African cloak, and instead the Foreign Office appealed to William Whiteley. He had the chiefs sent to Westbourne Grove, and fitted them all out in Inverness capes. When they were brought before the Queen, it was necessary to confess what had happened, and Her Majesty, who, contrary to popular belief, did enjoy a joke, was immensely amused.[7] One result of these challenges was the oft-repeated boast that Whiteleys could supply 'everything from a pin to an elephant'.

Whiteley's propensity for believing that he could do anything also extended sometimes to what can only be described as meddling in the personal lives of others, something he felt his position entitled him to do. In 1878 an extraordinary action was brought against him in Brompton County Court by a Miss Emily Montgomery whose property he had appropriated. The young lady had been cohabiting with a Mr John Bear who had lately been a student at Oxford. Whiteley's only connection with this couple was that their house, in Bayswater, had been obtained through his agency. Mr Bear had been living on an allowance granted to him by his father, also called John, a wealthy gentleman who was then residing in Australia, and who knew nothing of Miss Montgomery. The young couple may have hoped that Bear senior would accept their position, but he did not. As soon as he discovered the unusual arrangements, he threatened to stop his son's allowance unless the couple separated. When this did not happen, he carried out his threat. Neither the junior Bear nor Miss Montgomery had the income to support their joint lifestyle, and neither seemed willing to earn it. Instead, they began to place their furniture and valuables in pawn. Amongst the items pledged were some diamond rings, a sealskin mantle, some furs and a bedroom clock. Some of these things had been bought as gifts for Miss Montgomery and were unquestionably her property.

In August 1878 Mr Bear senior arrived from Australia with a view to putting an end to all this nonsense, and William Whiteley, for reasons best known to himself, decided to offer his services to the aggrieved father to settle the matter. A meeting was held between father and son, which took place at Whiteleys on 4 September – presumably in a private room. Here, a document was drawn up which father and son initialled. Under the terms of the document, the son, Mr J.W. Bear, agreed to 'carry out his father's wishes and instructions in every particular . . .'. This included giving up possession of the house and its contents to Mr Whiteley, leaving Miss Montgomery, and departing for Paris, from whence he should in due course leave for either Australia or Fiji as instructed. Mr Whiteley was to release the items from pawn, and hold them till further orders from Mr Bear senior. A sum of £2 2*s* a week was to be paid to Miss Montgomery.

The detailed terms of the document were not revealed to Miss Montgomery, Mr Bear junior informing her only that their relationship was over, and that the house and furniture were to be given up. On the following day, while she was out of the house, Mr Bear junior removed the pawn tickets, and handed them to Mr Whiteley. Bear senior and one of Whiteley's clerks then went to the various pawnbrokers and redeemed the items.

Although the allowance was paid to the lady through Mr Whiteley for a few weeks, it was suddenly stopped on the orders of Mr Bear senior, not through any fault of hers, but because his son had declined to wait meekly in Paris for his father's instructions.

Miss Montgomery, who was made of sterner stuff than anyone imagined, boldly wrote to Mr Whiteley demanding the return of her property. His reply was that he would return the items if she paid him £140, being the cost to him of redeeming all the goods and the interest thereon. Her response was: 'That includes the money for things not mine. Give me back my things.'

Mr Whiteley was not going to be told what to do by Miss Montgomery and must have been somewhat surprised when served with a notice of court action. The trusty Mr Roche was by his side as ever, representing that his client had acted only as an agent for his co-defendant, Mr Bear. Miss Montgomery, it was claimed, by cohabiting with Bear junior, had effectively given him all right and title to the pawn tickets, and the conduct of the young people had given the defendants the right to act as they had done. His Honour was having none of this. Dismissing the first argument, he said that Mr Whiteley's responsibility was equal to that of Mr Bear, and that 'they were both wrongdoers in the transaction, Mr Whiteley appearing to be the active mover in the matter from beginning to end'. Miss Montgomery's pawn tickets had been taken without her knowledge and consent and she was entitled to the judgment. Whiteley could not give in gracefully. He appealed, and in March the following year the case came before the Queen's Bench, where Emily Montgomery was again triumphant.[8]

* * *

By 1878 the ever increasing crush of vehicles in Westbourne Grove was becoming such a serious problem that there was a campaign in the *Paddington Times*, which was ultimately unsuccessful, to open up some of the side streets to traffic to allow carriages freer outlet. 'When this Grove was first laid out, little did its builders imagine the immense traffic that Whiteley's emporium would bring to it from all parts of the metropolis', reported the *Paddington Times* in February.[9] It was not only Whiteleys that enjoyed the carriage trade. As more and more people spent time and money in the Grove, other traders realised that they too could make profits there, despite the presence of the Universal Provider. One of his most prominent competitors, who eventually came to be regarded as second only to Whiteley in the Grove, was William Owen who set up a substantial drapery business offering a wide range of goods which he was happy to advertise in the newspapers. In only a few years Owen expanded his empire from one shop to seventeen. Competition meant that for Whiteley the years from 1876 to 1880 were ones of falling, although still substantial, profits. He was no longer everything to all people in Westbourne Grove, and his constant battles in court and with the Paddington Vestry did not assist his popularity.

In August 1878 there were floods in the Grove, revealing a severe problem with the sewers. Heavy falls of rain had caused an overflow of the drains and many traders including Whiteley suddenly found their premises awash with sewage. His basements measured over 1,000 square feet, every part of which was in use for storage or packing, and the water rose to 3 feet in height. Whiteley was in the thick of it, superintending the work of removing goods to a place of safety.

That Christmas there was a new novelty, the 'steel-blue electric illuminations' of the Jablochkoff candle which lit up the exterior of Whiteleys in the Grove, and attracted crowds of boys until late in the evening. The *Chronicle* gave grudging approval, commenting: 'The gas lights in the Grove suffer much by comparison, being reduced to a dirty yellow glimmer, suggestible of the worst of November fogs.' This cheap, bright and simple lamp was one of the first of its kind to be used for public lighting and in the same year the Metropolitan Board of Works was installing them on the Victoria Embankment, and in the City. Whiteley may well have been one of the first individuals in the United Kingdom to utilise it.[10]

If there were no new Whiteleys departments in 1878 that may have been because a far grander scheme was in preparation. With a magnificent row of shops on the Grove and the start of another row around the corner, one of the chief obstacles to their being united into one seamless empire was the narrow cul-de-sac, Douglas Place, which formed the approach road to the washhouse and third-class baths. But Douglas Place could be so much more: with Whiteley properties to the left, and Whiteley properties to the right, and still more Whiteley properties before, it would not only benefit him to enlarge and widen the way, but, surely to do so would be a service to the whole of Bayswater. So it was reasoned. There, firmly in the heart of the Vestry was that great disinterested public servant, Mr Charles Mills Roche, ideally placed to put to the Vestry a proposal which the ratepayers of Paddington would be delighted to fund. Mr Roche dug deep and found the perfect basis for the scheme, no less than an act of parliament, the Michael Angelo Taylor's Act dating back to the time of George III which he said gave the Vestry the authority to make a compulsory purchase of the non-Whiteley properties in Douglas Place and widen the road. Anything more audacious it would be hard to imagine.

Initially, the Vestry seemed to be in favour of the project, but when the ratepayers of Paddington realised what was happening, they were incensed. 'I hope the members of the Vestry will make themselves acquainted with this Act before they record their votes on the subject', wrote 'A Ratepayer' to the *Chronicle*.[11] 'They will then see what an injustice it is to shape a private interest into a public improvement. . . . If Mr Whiteley required property in order to make his improvements to suit his own convenience, let him buy it in the ordinary way, and not ask the Vestry to put a Public Act in force for his purpose.'

One of the threatened properties was owned by a Mr Gibbon who wrote to the Vestry declaring that the motive of the scheme was 'covetousness, and its object the benefit and aggrandisement of Mr Whiteley . . .

it displays an utter disregard to the rights interests and wishes of the owners of or other persons interested in the property proposed to be taken . . .'.[12]

By the time the 'Douglas Place Improvement Scheme' as it was known, came to be debated there was a strong movement to oppose it. 'Mr Roche', the *Chronicle* pointed out, was present in 'the anomalous capacity of advocate for his client at a tribunal of which he himself is a member.' In the interim, Whiteley had been busy buying up additional properties in Queen's Road, and several householders protested that their neighbours had only been persuaded to sell because their own willingness to do so had been misrepresented by the eager buyer.[13]

Mr Roche argued that Mr Whiteley's only wish was to do what was amiable and agreeable all round, but no one seemed to be in a very amiable or agreeable mood, and the scheme was ultimately rejected. Commenting on Mr Roche's position on both the Vestry and the Highways Committee, the *Chronicle* added, 'If a sense of professional propriety did not prevent Mr Roche from taking such an advantage of his position, there ought at least to be men in the Vestry with some regard for the dignity of their body.'[14]

The *Chronicle*'s opinion may have been coloured by the scandal which was touching Mr Roche at that time. It is said that you may know a man by the company he keeps, and it may also be true that you can best understand a businessman's methods by observing the behaviour and credentials of his solicitor. The events of 1879 and 1880 in the life of Mr Roche caused no flicker of disloyalty in William Whiteley.

On 15 February 1879 the *City Press* published the minutes of a meeting of the creditors of an ironmonger, the late Mr W. Clark, who had been declared bankrupt almost two years previously. Roche was the creditors' solicitor, but matters had been brought to light which had resulted in the creditors instructing another solicitor, Mr Rooks, to make enquiries into the activities of Mr Roche. In August 1878 Mr Clark had been very ill, and much of the time between then and his death in the following November had been spent in the Bethlehem Lunatic Asylum. Despite, or maybe because of the fact that the unfortunate Mr Clark had been in no fit condition to transact business, Roche had purchased from him a number of insurance policies which were worth £1,650. For these he paid the sum of £60. He had already realised £1,000 worth of the policies when the creditors discovered what had happened. Mr Rooks took action against Mr Roche who, asked for an explanation of his actions, wrote a long letter in which he tried unsuccessfully to claim that he was acting for the benefit of Clark's widow who had eight children to support. Quite how his actions were intended to benefit the widow was not apparent, since she received not one penny from his transactions. All Roche would admit to was overlooking the rule that he was not, as solicitor, permitted to purchase part of the estate, a minor error which he felt did not reflect upon his character. Mr Rooks, who must by now have formed his own opinions on Mr Roche's character, obtained an order against him to repay the £1,000 and surrender the other policies, and was granted a warm vote of thanks from the creditors.

Roche was naturally anxious to keep the matter quiet, but the *City Press* had made it public, and at the next meeting of the Metropolitan Board of Works, Roche was openly asked if he was the man mentioned and if so, were the allegations true? 'I will not refer to the taste or feeling which prompted the hon. member in asking me the question,' replied Roche with studied dignity. 'In asking me that question he has done me a far greater service than he thought he would do. My reply is that the statement is untruthful, that it will come before a jury as the subject of libel. Until that time my mouth is closed.'[15] And closed for the time being it remained, apart from a statement at the Vestry's next meeting when he declared the *City Press*'s statement to be libellous. The entire matter was now *sub judice*, although papers relating to the bankruptcy were being freely circulated in Bayswater.

Ever conscious of the advantages of free publicity, Whiteley must have been delighted when, in the summer of 1879, the art critic George Augustus Sala published a series of comments on London localities in the *Daily Telegraph*, one of which was devoted to the delights of Westbourne Grove. He noted that 'the vast majority of the promenaders . . . were exceptionally well-dressed. The reason for this seemed to be clear. Westbourne Grove is less an artery than an organ. It is the centre of the new prosperous and refined district.' He soon found the name 'Whiteley' inscribed in tall gold letters over a large double-fronted shop. '"Wonderful Whiteley," I thought – it was a foregone conclusion in my mind that he was to be wonderful. . . .' Sala found Whiteley 'sumptuous in hares' and 'great in beef', admiring also his sauces, pickles, chocolates, butter and cheese. He then tramped the length of the Grove on the even numbered side 'noting many shops and finding no more Whiteleys', only to be informed that it was chiefly in the odd numbers that Whiteley 'flourishes exceedingly'.[16] The *Chronicle* was scathing about this somewhat ill-planned trip, since the article had occupied two-and-a-half columns in the *Telegraph*, one of which was wholly about 'W.W.', one of 'gossipy recollections' and only half on the 'subject proper'.[17]

Whiteley probably had no input into this article, but he was taking steps to bring himself even more prominently before the public notice in a wholly flattering light. The artist William Powell Frith – who, unlike Charles Leslie, really was a member of the Royal Academy – was a popular and fashionable painter, most noted for his panoramic scenes of contemporary life, although he had since 1863 been honoured with royal commissions. A Yorkshireman residing in Bayswater, who shopped regularly at a certain well-known emporium, he must have had, in Whiteley's estimation. every quality required to immortalise the works of the Universal Provider in paint. Whiteley wrote personally to Frith asking for an interview, and it says much that Frith's first reaction on receiving the missive was to satisfy himself in his own mind that he owed nothing to the writer: 'indeed, the principles on which he conducts his business are such as to prevent the possibility of anybody owing Mr Whiteley anything for an unreasonable time.'

> Punctually at 9.30 . . . the great trader made his appearance, and a shrewd, smart, honest appearance it is. . . .
> 'Sir,' said he, 'I am an admirer of your works.'
> 'I reciprocate the compliment,' said I. 'I sincerely admire yours.'

After some flattering comments on virtually the whole catalogue of Frith's pictures, Whiteley proceeded to the point. He proposed that Frith should paint a new picture, entitled 'Whiteleys at Four o'clock in the Afternoon', leaving it to the artist's discretion as to whether he should paint the inside or the outside.

> If you take the former, you would have the aristocracy making their purchases. You might introduce the young ladies who do me the honour to assist in my establishment, many of whom are very pretty. Then there are what are called shopmen, with fine heads, and every conceivable detail for your back and fore grounds. If, on the other hand you select the outside of the shops, you could introduce the commissionaires, who, as you may have observed, wear a picturesque livery, created by me; you would have the nobility and gentry stepping into their carriages, with – forgive my suggestions, they are subject to your criticism – street beggars, toy-sellers – think of the contrast between them and my customers . . .

Whiteley's only stipulation, if the outside view was chosen, was that '. . . the whole length of the shops should be shown, care being taken that the different windows should display the specialities of the establishment'.

Frith's face must have betrayed his suspicions, as Whiteley immediately denied that the painting was intended to be an advertisement. Frith thought over the proposal which he ultimately declined: 'and I have often thought since, that though I should fear to undertake it, much might have been done with it.'[18]

In the meantime, work was going on at a furious rate on the newly acquired sites in Queen's Road, exciting considerable speculation in the neighbourhood as to the purpose of Mr Whiteley's latest enterprise. He had purchased eight houses, all of which were to be converted into warehouses and shops, and by November 1879 it was known that the development was to include a huge poultry and egg market which was to be stocked from Whiteley's own farm.

The Vestry watched the progress of the Universal Provider's empire with growing unease, especially Mr Flood, who saw his beloved Baths hemmed in on both sides by Whiteley-owned properties. In November, with Roche still firmly entrenched in both the Vestry and the Metropolitan Board of Works, came what was to be the first campaign in a new war. Mr Brass, the builder of the new Queen's Road premises, wanted to take the foundations down to 12ft, but the Vestry surveyor believed it would not be safe to go lower than 7ft, the depth of the adjoining houses, since drainage into London's Middle Level Sewer relied entirely on gravity, and deep drains would not be able to carry off periodic storm waters. The Vestry duly ordered the foundations to be carried no lower than 7ft, but, reported the *Chronicle*, 'Mr Whiteley, acting under the guidance of what Socrates would call his demon, the well-known Mr C.M. Roche, refused to comply, and appealed to the Board of Works. The Vestry must indeed have been sanguine, to think of following Mr Roche into his own lair at Spring Gardens without sustaining an overthrow. Of course they were defeated and Mr Whiteley and Mr Roche are victorious.'[19] The Board had sanctioned a depth of 9ft, which left the Vestry still unhappy and fuming helplessly.

Mr Flood, in the meantime, was not averse to taking a leaf out of Mr Whiteley's book, by trying to establish a foothold in an opposing camp. In July he had been elected a member of the Ratepayers' Association, that very body which had been set up in order to curb the excesses of the Vestry. At the next meeting of the Association, which was conducted very largely in a state of uproar, it was proposed not to approve the minutes of the meeting at which this had taken place, notwithstanding that the minutes were factually correct. The resolution to reject Mr Flood having been carried, a group of his supporters removed themselves to the Red Lion Hotel to set up an alternative ratepayers association which would admit Mr Flood, a division of effort which Whiteley must have found very amusing.

In December, William Whiteley, who did not measure his personal popularity by what the Vestry, the *Chronicle*, or indeed the ratepayers of Paddington thought of him, decided to offer a very special Christmas treat to his customers. In a window in Westbourne Grove wholly devoted to the purpose, he placed on display a portrait of himself, framed and glazed and offered at the introductory price of half a crown, the amount to be increased after a certain date. The *Chronicle* condemned him for 'extraordinary vulgarity . . .', and added, not without some truth, 'How *can* Mr Whiteley so degrade the locality he has so largely helped to create? The public would think much better of him if he would only allow them, but he will not.'[20] After ten days only four copies had been sold, and the picture was quietly withdrawn.

In February 1880 the long-awaited libel action of Roche *v.* City Press was set down for hearing, but counsel for Roche made a formal application to withdraw the case. It was now admitted that the report in the *City Press* was true, although not all the facts had been stated at the meeting. Mr Roche agreed to pay all the costs of the action, but he was far from being out of the woods. At the next Vestry meeting, where questions were due to be asked, Mr Roche was absent, on the grounds that he was feeling unwell. At the next meeting he appeared but was prepared to do no more than read from a verbatim account of the court action, and denied agreeing to pay the costs, even though he had already done so. Thereafter he did not attend meetings of the Vestry or of the Metropolitan Board of Works, thus causing the Vestry no little annoyance.

The Law Society had naturally taken an interest in Mr Roche's activities and in April at the Court of Common Pleas he faced a tribunal, professing on the one hand to be quite unaware of the rule that prohibited him from purchasing his client's property, and on the other asking for special consideration as a man of thirty years' experience. Lord Coleridge pronounced that the circumstances under which the policies had been bought 'could not be considered creditable to him', and moreover 'it strained his powers of belief to the utmost that a practised attorney should be ignorant of such elementary knowledge'. Roche was suspended from the practice of his profession for two years.[21]

SIX

Conflict and Compromise

By 1880, Whiteley's famously bland countenance was concealing a number of concerns. Privately, he and Harriet were on terms of mutual tolerance, she focusing her affections on the children, while he found more congenial female company; an uneasy equilibrium which could not last. Meanwhile, growing trade competition was eating into his profits, and made it all the more urgent that he complete his new warehouses without delay.

With Roche no longer able to represent his interests on the Vestry, Whiteley's building projects along Queen's Road were more than ever open to the hard scrutiny of Mr Flood. Much as Flood protested that he acted only for the good of the parish, there were occasions when his personal dislike of Whiteley became all too apparent. Matters were not helped by Whiteley's tactic of having his work done at high speed before the Vestry could throw obstacles in the way, and local ratepayers complained in vain about the noise of construction going on from early in the morning to midnight. Two residents, including a business rival, milliner John Clarke Record took out restraining orders to prevent the new buildings rising higher than their adjacent properties, obscuring the light. Whiteley had failed to show anyone his plans or indicate just how high his buildings were going to be, but it was soon apparent that they were going to tower over Mr Record's premises, and despite the order, the milliner could only watch helplessly as the walls grew ever higher.

Whiteley's standard strategy was to ignore everything but his own requirements for as long as possible. The law moved slowly, the Vestry met only once a fortnight, and much could be achieved while votes were taken, debates adjourned, and documents drawn up. Events would eventually reach a furious climax with direct confrontation, when Mr Whiteley would suddenly become the most reasonable man in the world, willing to accede to any demand, and pay any expenses. There would always be in the Vestry those men who, while not exactly Whiteley's men, always preferred conciliation, and could be guaranteed to waver under his charm. Before long, the conflict would be not between Mr Whiteley and the Vestry but inside the Vestry itself on the subject of how best to deal with Mr Whiteley – and while the arguments raged, the buildings rose. As ever, Whiteley made sure to have friends in the right places – in this case Mr Saunders, his architect, and Mr Brass, his builder, who could represent his views on the Metropolitan Board of Works.

A typical conflict related to a hoarding around the new buildings in the course of construction in Queen's Road and Douglas Place. In April 1880 Whiteley had been granted a licence which permitted him to erect hoardings 10ft high for a period of 28 days. It suited him better to erect hoardings 30ft high, and leave them there as long as he pleased. Some of them obstructed the footway, compelling women carrying baskets of washing to the washhouse to walk in the road. It was October before the matter came before the Vestry and Mr Flood was incensed. In any other part of London, he said, when a similar hoarding was erected the builders were compelled to remove it, 'But in this case a large capitalist and employer was allowed to go in direct opposition to the Vestry . . . because a man has influence at the Metropolitan Board of Works, there seemed to be an amount of fear on the part of the surveyor . . .'. One difficulty was that the Vestry's representative on the Board was still Mr Roche, who was unable to carry out his duties, yet declined to stand down. The Vestry, powerless to remove him, was effectively unrepresented on the Board until his term of office expired in June.

The way in which Mr Brass had treated the Vestry was 'simply impertinent', fumed Flood. 'The whole of Douglas Place had been taken possession of by Mr Whiteley and his men. To see Mr Whiteley treated different to other people was a disgrace to the parish.'[1] The matter was referred to a solicitor.

An unhappy piece of publicity for Whiteleys in October 1880 was the libel case of a Mr Copping against the *Chronicle*. Not all Whiteleys' young men spent their spare time in healthy pursuits. Some of them had been induced by a cheap subscription known as 'Whiteleys' price' to join a local establishment called the Monmouth Club. The *Chronicle* declared it to be no more than a 'gambling hell' where drinking had gone on late into the night, and Mr Copping, the manager, objected. Some members had run up such serious debts they had robbed their employer. A dismal parade of young men, former employees of Mr Whiteley and now known only by their convict numbers, appeared to give evidence. The *Chronicle* not only won, but was praised for its public spirit.[2]

Throughout 1880 the influence of Mr Saunders and Mr Brass continually smoothed Whiteley's way. Flood repeatedly insisted that there was something radically wrong in the procedures of the Metropolitan Board of

Works. No one, he said, was in any doubt that the
Board's opposition to the Vestry was caused by its
connections with professional men who were working
for Mr Whiteley. Smarting over the Board's agreement to
allow drains to be sunk 2ft below the Vestry's
recommended depth, the Vestry saw that the new
buildings under construction in Queen's Road posed a
similar objection, and once again insisted the depth of
the drains be restricted to 7ft. Unexpectedly, the Board
confirmed the order of the Vestry, but when Mr Brass
continued to construct the drains exactly as Mr
Whiteley wanted, the Board took no steps to prevent
him. Suspecting that a letter of protest to the Board
would simply be put in the wastepaper basket, the
Vestry decided to send a deputation, and in January
1881 the Vestry's case was made in person at a meeting
in the presence of Sir Joseph Bazalgette, the architect of
the London sewer system.

The chief result of the meeting, as Whiteley must
have anticipated, was to refer the matter to another
committee, but the Vestry under the guidance of Mr
Flood was determined not to be thwarted. Mr Hortin
was instructed to issue an order for the partially
constructed buildings to be pulled down so acceptable
drainage could be installed. The potential expense of
having to reconstruct the drains at last produced some
response, and in March 1881 Mr Whiteley employed the
formidable presence of Mr Philbrick QC, who was
accompanied by Mr Saunders, to address the Vestry.
Philbrick pointed out that the drains constructed by Sir
Joseph had never been intended to deal with periodic
storm waters, and could not do so until relief sewers,
currently planned, had been constructed. Mr Whiteley's
sewers had been laid with penstocks – a kind of sluice –

and there could therefore be no danger either to his
building or the neighbourhood. Philbrick and Saunders
were asked to withdraw, while Mr Hortin insisted he
must have a resolution from the Vestry on how to
proceed. One or two members were inclined to be
lenient but the majority led by Mr Flood were not
impressed by Mr Whiteley's penstocks, and saw no
reason to depart from the original order. The *Chronicle*
observed, 'Mr Saunders and Mr Brass had evidently led
Mr Whiteley to believe that by virtue of their position at
the Board of Works he could afford to snub the local
Vestry. . . .' The decision was now final. Either Mr
Whiteley had to reconstruct his drains or the Vestry
could order its officers to 'summarily enter the premises
and destroy the arrangements which those overweening
personages, in defiance of the local authority, took upon
themselves to make'.[3]

Despite all this sabre-rattling, it would be two years
before the drainage question was settled, and another
more serious problem was arising. It had cost the Vestry
some £700–£800 to erect a wall to screen the Baths from
the windows of the warehouse to its north, and now
another tall Whiteley building was advancing rapidly on
the south side. The Baths were beginning to look
hemmed in, and suspicious glances must have been cast
as if by a moment's inattention, the Vestrymen would
one day find the jewel in their crown totally overrun by
Whiteleyana. Mr Flood presented a report showing that
the new construction, a dormitory for employees, was
intended to have a ground floor and four upper storeys
with a total of 120 windows, affording Mr Whiteley both
light and air over the Baths' premises. More importantly
the windows would overlook the ladies' baths, and that
would never do. There were two courses of action: to

ask Mr Whiteley to pay rent for the rights and to glaze the windows with opaque glass, or, at a substantial expense, build yet another wall. It was thought that this would cost about £2,000, and indeed, the deep foundations built so close to the Baths had already forced the Vestry to carry out underpinning work costing over £600.

If Whiteley seemed untroubled by this opposition, it was because he was about to pull off another astounding coup, the opening of his new premises in Queen's Road on 24 March 1881, an enterprise on a truly massive scale, each building occupying several floors, and having a depth of 200ft, with a total run of 8 large plate-glass frontages, all lit from the outside. No. 153 was a showroom for china, stoneware, porcelain and glass, while 155 was devoted to ironmongery. The ground floor of no. 157 was an office for the building, housing and shipping departments, fitted with counters and thirty private desks. Above were to be found paintings, sculptures, pianos and harmoniums. A series of piano and organ recitals were to be held there in June. No. 159 was the new provisions department, with meat, fish, game, poultry, fruit and vegetables, butter and cheese. The basement was a cold-store, where fish cleaning and poultry trussing was carried out, the rooms chilled by many tons of ice, their walls insulated with sawdust. There was also a beer and wine cellar, and apparatus for the manufacture of mineral water. As a result of this expansion, the premises in Kensington Gardens Square which had previously housed the glass, china and ironmongery were to be appropriated for an enlarged refreshment room. The cooking would no longer be done in the basement but in the upper portions of the Westbourne Grove buildings, where a lift would take the provisions up to the kitchens, and convey the cooked dishes down.

Even Whiteley's sternest critics could not fail to be impressed, while trade competitors saw some good in it for themselves. 'They have learnt to accept Whiteley as a fact, and wisely to take a leaf out of his book', reported the *Chronicle*. 'Better for all of us', was the verdict of one local tradesman, 'he makes Bayswater a grand market for us all, except the old-fashioned, who cannot square themselves to the times. He makes the running for us.'⁴

But there was still one major obstacle to his plans, and that was the Paddington Baths, which effectively cut his empire in two. Whiteley must have seen in his mind's eye a continuous row of majestic warehouses along the length of Queen's Road, all with 'Whiteleys' in large gold letters. In April 1881 he approached the Commissioners and offered to buy the Baths, asking them to name their own price. They declined to do so. They were however amenable to his plans to build a bridge across Douglas Place to connect the premises in Queen's Road with those in the Grove. It was an admission that the Douglas Place 'improvements' were not to take place after all.

The storm over the new windows finally exploded in the autumn of 1881. The Ratepayers' Association had succeeded the previous May in getting a number of its members elected to the Vestry, and was prepared to fight any suggestion that a four-figure sum be spent on erecting a wall. Mr Flood on the other hand proposed that the sum of £3,000 be borrowed, not only to save the modesty of the lady bathers, but to protect the future rights of the Vestry over their own building, should they ever wish to make it higher. He pointed out that a lengthy correspondence with Mr Whiteley had failed to reach any compromise, and he believed it was Whiteley's intention to depreciate their property so that he could eventually procure it more cheaply. This comment drew an outraged howl of protest from Whiteley supporters, and a heatedly acrimonious exchange ensued amid yells for 'order'. Vestryman Williams, supporting Flood, revealed that young men had been seen on the roofs of the baths and washhouses looking in at the windows, and that screened or coloured windows would not meet the requirements of ventilation. Accusations of self-interest flew back and forth, and in the midst of an increasingly disorderly debate several other members tried unsuccessfully to have the entire question adjourned until after the summer recess, or at least until they could arrange to view the site of the proposed wall. The Vestry was essentially split between those who wanted to try and agree terms with Whiteley, who they were sure would do anything reasonable, and those who pointed out that they had tried and failed to·agree anything for the last five months which was why they now had to build a wall. No one, said the latter faction, had treated the Vestry with more contempt than Mr Whiteley. Mr Flood finally suggested it was time to vote on his original proposal, and the vote was held and won by a large majority. Naturally, nothing was going to happen overnight. An application to borrow £3,000 was made to the Local Government Board who appointed an inspector, Captain Robert C.T. Hildyard, late of the Royal Engineers, to preside over an enquiry.

At 10.30 a.m. on 3 September at the Board room, Queen's Road Baths, Captain Hildyard, a 'tall spare, military man', took his seat, flanked by the Commissioners, their counsel, solicitor and architect. 'On the opposite side of the table sat Mr Whiteley, looking as bland as ever, but revealing beneath his well-cut face, good brow and powerful features, all the force and persistence of character which had marked his career.'[5]

Captain Hildyard imposed his personality on the proceedings from the start, requiring one of the dissenting Vestrymen to remove himself from a prominent seat at the table, and coolly brushing aside a number of objections to the original motion made on administrative technicalities. Seeing at once that it would be unwise to have too many people clamouring to make their point of view, he also declared that each interest should be dealt with by one spokesman. With that, he arranged a short visit to the site.

On their return, Mr Pollard, a barrister, spoke for the Vestry. There were three objections: the rights of light and air which might accrue to Mr Whiteley over the years, the risk of fire in the huge dormitories occupied as they were by the 'smoking sex', and the privacy of the ladies' baths. He did not wish to impute pruriency to the gentlemen in Mr Whiteley's employ, but in every body of young men there were black sheep. The risk that some might pry would induce in ladies a wholly reasonable dread of attending the Baths.

Mr Isaacs, the Commissioners' architect, presented a plan for a screen wall. He pointed out that Mr Whiteley's dormitories, set up for the accommodation of three men each, consisted simply of wood, sized and varnished. This and the matchbox divisions of the building increased the fire risk. Questioned by Whiteley's counsel, Mr Firth, he provoked a laugh, by commenting that even if the offending windows were glazed with opaque glass and not opened when ladies were there, 'there would still be a possibility of Mr Whiteley's young men getting on the roof of the Baths in order to satisfy their curiosity'. Even if the windows were screwed down, 'a man of prurient imagination could easily take a screwdriver in his hand in order to realise his desires'.[6]

Some excitement was caused by Mr Isaacs revealing that from Mr Whiteley's windows he was able to see the colour of the ladies' bathing gowns as they were swimming and distinguish the red ones from the blue ones. The Reverend J.M. Cox, Vestryman, wanted to know if the bathing dresses were the same as those used at the seaside, an enquiry that Hildyard quite properly stamped on. He did confirm however that the windows he had seen commanded a view of the private baths and the dressing boxes, which were open at the top. Mr Henry Taylor, superintendent of the Baths, said that the attendance of ladies was declining. Men had been seen at Mr Whiteley's open windows, and one lady while in her private bath had seen a man on the roof peeping in through the window.

Mr Firth maintained that his client was agreeable to doing anything that was just. While he had no objections in principle to the Commissioners' wall, as a ratepayer he thought it would involve too heavy an expense. He proposed instead a screen of wood or some other material. There was no difficulty about glazing windows with opaque glass or fastening them up as required. He refused however to pay for the under-pinning of the south wall of the Baths. The costs he said, should be borne by the owners. The enquiry was adjourned, and a few days later Mr Roche wrote on Whiteley's behalf to Mr Hortin outlining a proposition to erect a screen, install opaque glass where necessary and also fit iron bars to prevent anyone getting on to the roof of the Baths from the dormitory.

At the adjourned enquiry on 21 September an alternative plan was put forward: a corrugated metal screen that would cost only £100. Mr Whiteley was willing to pay for this, also a rent of £20 a year to settle everything else. The meeting felt that £20 was on the low side, but closed with the gentlemen entertaining the general impression that matters were heading towards a reasonable conclusion. They were mistaken.

At a special meeting of the Vestry on 25 October, a Mr James Edmeston proposed that the original resolution to apply for the loan of £3,000 to build a wall should be rescinded, but his comment that they could trust Mr Whiteley to do what was right in the matter was met with howls of ironical laughter. Mr Flood now had his say, and a long one it was. The *Chronicle* observed: 'His speech is ragged and halting, and he can relapse into vulgarity at a moments notice, or without any notice at all . . . but he is master of his facts and he is a hard hitter.' Mr Flood professed sympathy in his heart for Mr Edmeston, for 'a gentleman more ignorant of the circumstances than he was never existed'. This provoked loud squawks of amazement from his fellow Vestrymen followed by laughter. He then revealed some of the past history of the Baths. When the building on the north side was being erected there was one plan that the Vestry never seemed to be able to grasp and that was the one with the openings which were described as air-holes. It was quite by chance that they had come to see the plan: 'The air-holes were six or seven feet in length but to Mr Whiteley's gigantic mind no doubt they seemed small.' Representations had been made to Mr Whiteley, correspondence ensued, promises were made by him and not kept, and the commissioners had lost £1,600. When Mr Whiteley proposed to build to the

south of the Baths he was asked not to adopt the same
procedure and had taken no notice. Flood denied that
there was any personal feeling on his part – he and Mr
Whiteley were on the best of terms in business matters,
but his letters were just evasion all through. 'Mr
Whiteley promised and promised but did nothing. . . .
[He] had no right to take that which did not belong to
him, but he thought the Commissioners were men of
low degree and that he could do as he liked. . . . Every
endeavour to come to an amicable arrangement had
been made, but they never could keep him to his word.'
Here a voice interrupted saying 'Never will'. Flood's
speech was greeted with enthusiastic applause, and
Edmeston's proposal was defeated.[7]

By the end of the year, Flood, who must have seen his
day of triumph in sight, was encouraging the Vestry in
another action against Whiteley – for blocking the
footway of Douglas Place with his horses and vans
which were delivering to and collecting from the
furniture department. Mr Whiteley, however, had other
more personal matters on his mind.

It has often been said of Mr Whiteley, usually by
people quoting that gentleman, that his only hobby was
his business. He was said to be a non-smoker, and there is
no reason to doubt that; he was said to be a teetotaller,
and that was very nearly true. At the weekend he would
often enjoy a family outing to the farm at Finchley,
though it is hard to believe that he failed to take care of
any business while he was there. On other weekends,
however, he would go to Brighton, Hastings or similar
places, unaccompanied by his wife.[8] He did not tell her
who his companions were and she seems not to have
asked. If she suspected, she may well have considered
that for the sake of marital harmony, and their four

children, it was better not to know. At the same time, she must have guessed that William Whiteley, true to his claim, was making his business his hobby by having affairs with shop girls very much both his and her junior. Harriet Whiteley seems to have led a quiet, domestic existence and did not have, or seek, a public profile. She is rarely mentioned in the press, except where she and the children accompanied her husband to performances of the Whiteley employees' dramatic society.

It was he who provoked the separation. After years of pretending that all was well, matters were brought out into the open by a simple bunch of violets. He brought them home one day saying that they had been given to him by one of his assistants, 'plucked by her own dear little fingers'. Harriet could not bear to have them in the place and threw them out.[9] She knew what they meant, and he did not deny it. She and the children retired to the farm, and letters passed from Harriet to her husband and from Mr Roche to Harriet. Harriet still believed the marriage should be saved for the sake of the children, but Whiteley was implacable. He did not want a reconciliation, and having Harriet living at the farm was not his idea of a separation.

Mr Roche wrote coldly on 25 June: 'Such a state of things the husband cannot permit to continue, and I am instructed to ask for the address of your solicitor, so that you can be provided with a separate establishment.'

He wrote to her again, more cruelly, on 28 June (unfortunately this letter does not survive), which forced her to reply:

My dear husband
To my surprise and grief, I received another letter from Mr Roche. I am truly sorry you should have

thought fit to proceed to such an extremity, for our dear children's sake. Such an arrangement as you propose would be most indefensible. It would indeed be sad for them to be deprived of a father's care. Mr Roche accuses me of having poisoned their minds against you, which is quite untrue. [There followed a passage which was suppressed when the letter was later read in court] I am gradually getting accustomed to a separate life, but to avoid a public scandal, I am willing to try again to make things go on more pleasantly. With every good wish for your future,

Believe me,
Your faithful wife
Harriet S. Whiteley[10]

What happened in the next few weeks is unknown, but at the end of July matters reached a critical point, and Harriet abruptly departed, taking with her the children and their governess, Clara Harwood Tolputt. The Tolputts were a Folkestone family, and it was here at 115 Sandgate, that Harriet sought sanctuary. There she did the one thing Whiteley did not want her to do – she filed a petition for divorce on the grounds of adultery and cruelty. The charge of cruelty did not excite any comment. As the law stood at the time, a husband could divorce his wife for adultery alone, whereas a wife was obliged to prove cruelty, or some other offence, as well. Whiteley pursued Harriet to Folkestone, but she locked herself in Miss Tolputt's room and refused to see him. Eventually the police were called and he was obliged to retire from the scene.

A petition was drawn up; perhaps rather hurriedly since most of the dates in it, including the children's birthdays, had to be corrected later. These papers were closed to public view until 1984, but they now reveal just why Harriet felt the need to flee the marital home.

Harriet deposed that from her marriage, Whiteley had:

> habitually conducted himself towards your Petitioner with great harshness and cruelty and frequently swore at her and used bad language towards her.
>
> That in the month of December 1873 the said William Whiteley assaulted your Petitioner and pushed her downstairs.
>
> That on or about the end of the year 1873 the said William Whiteley behaved with great violence towards your petitioner, threw her on the bed and put his fist in her face.
>
> That in the month of November 1878 the said William Whiteley seized your Petitioner by the arm and shook her violently and bruised her arms.
>
> That in the month of November 1878 the said William Whiteley behaved with such violence towards your Petitioner that she was obliged to run to the room of her children's governess for protection when he followed her and afterwards assaulted her on the stairs.

Harriet also alleged that Whiteley had frequently committed adultery with one of his employees, Alice Allen, who was also known as Alice Allington, Sarah Ann Lington, or 'Daisy'. In particular he and Alice had visited Tunbridge Wells together on 19 and 20 March 1881 and Hastings on 9 and 10 April, where it was alleged that adultery had taken place. Whiteley and Alice were also frequently alone together in his private room, and, it was alleged, adultery had been committed there, too.[11]

In the ensuing months, rumours flew around Bayswater about the collapse of the Whiteley marriage. One widespread story, which may well have been promulgated by Whiteley and his associates, was that his wife had been induced to leave because of the mischievous interference of Miss Tolputt.

On 27 September Harriet swore an affidavit in which she expressed her confidence that Miss Tolputt was competent to educate the children until they reached the age of 16, and added that she did not feel her husband was competent to judge the governess's ability. While matters remained in dispute, the oldest child, Ada Florence, then approaching 13, was placed in a school in Kensington while William, who was 11, was sent to school in Folkestone. There had been a suggestion that Frank Ernest be sent to a girls' school in Folkestone, to which the lad naturally raised an objection.

On 15 November the case of Whiteley *v.* Whiteley was heard at Westminster Hall before Sir R.J. Phillimore, although the divorce petition was not the issue. Whiteley wanted custody of the children, in order to determine the mode of their education. Some time before the case was due to commence all interested parties were in court. On the back bench, accompanied by friends, was Mrs Whiteley, the *Chronicle* professing to be able to see her refined countenance, blanched features and tearful eyes through her veil. Beside her sat Miss Tolputt, a brown veil drawn tightly across her face. Downstairs, three of the children waited in case they should be required to appear. Behind the benches, pacing the floor in a leisurely way, was Mr Whiteley, 'broad of shoulder, trim of countenance, and apparently quite at his ease'. He was accompanied by 'the inevitable Roche, the Mephistopheles of the play . . .', with whom he occasionally exchanged a few words.

Dr Deane, QC for Mr Whiteley, made a great deal of Harriet's 'clandestine flight' as if it in some way made her unfit to determine her children's education, giving no hint of the circumstances that had forced her to take this action. As regards the two youngest children, he said the governess 'had taken an active part in moving Mrs Whiteley to her present course. To put these two children under her influence would be extremely objectionable to the father.' At this point in the proceedings, Miss Tolputt, labouring under the choice of remaining as an emotional support to Mrs Whiteley or retiring from the scene to save her own embarrassment, took the latter course.

Dr Deane quoted a case on which he said he relied, to show that the law gave the father the right to decide the children's education. Mr Inderwick, for Mrs Whiteley, had done his homework, however, and pointed out that the case quoted related only to religious education. As for Mr Whiteley's supposed animosity to Miss Tolputt, Phillimore read out an extract from a letter written on 25 July in which Whiteley had given her notice, picking out the more flattering lines with 'a dry and merciless emphasis':

> To prevent any mistake, I think it best to tell you that I intend to send the children to school; not that I am at all dissatisfied with the instruction they receive, but on account of private matters. I am very sorry to lose you as a member of my family, and hope I shall often have the pleasure of seeing you.
>
> With best wishes
> I am, yours sincerely
> William Whiteley[12]

Then there was the letter written by Roche to Mrs Whiteley on 28 June, accusing Mrs Whiteley of poisoning her children's minds against their father, a letter, as the judge pointed out, written four weeks before that father had written to Miss Tolputt in such friendly terms. Dr Deane sat down, struck into silence.

Mr Inderwick made an appeal on behalf of 12-year-old Clara Louise and 10-year-old Frank Ernest. Frank, he said, was suffering from a serious bodily infirmity which he did not describe, but added that the boy was expected to be cured. Clara was in delicate health and required a mother's care.[13]

The judge made an order that William and Ada should be sent to schools selected by Mr Whiteley but subject to the reasonable objections of Mrs Whiteley. For medical reasons Frank and Clara were to remain in their mother's care.

'And with regard to the governess?' interjected Dr Deane.

'I make no order in respect of the governess,' said Phillimore.[14]

The matter rested as an uncomfortable compromise, the only winner being the *Chronicle*, which sold 18,000 copies and went out of print.

Clara's delicate condition was never discussed, but in later years when Whiteley was accompanied by his family to public events, he took only his sons and Ada. A photograph of Whiteley and his children taken at around that time shows a fragile-looking Clara with hollow eyes and thin bony wrists comparing oddly with her lumpenly robust older sister.

The divorce was set down for hearing on 24 June 1882. Some dozen witnesses were assembled, counsel for both sides were in attendance, and the 'close and square little court at Westminster . . . was fairly filled by expectant visitors'. The proceedings were adjourned until 29 June; again an interested crowd waited, and 'at lunch time it was impossible to pass down Westminster Hall without seeing the unmistakeable form of Mr Whiteley who stood in the pleasantest of chat and with every sign of complacency, talking with a friend'. The court, however, was taken up by a still more sensational case, and nothing happened until 1 July when all morning there was a bustle of activity between the opposing sides with documents being prepared which Mr Roche took to counsel for signature. Then it was announced that there had been an 'arrangement'. Mr Whiteley, it was reported, no longer objected to the pecuniary settlement, and on Harriet's side, she agreed that there was to be no divorce but a separation.

A young woman who had been in Whiteley's employment for nine years, and who was not named by the press, had been subpoenaed to give evidence for Mrs Whiteley, and had attended the court for that purpose. On returning to work she found a note awaiting her, stating that her services would no longer be required, and she should apply to the cashier for the wages due to her.[15]

True to form, there followed constant obstruction to drawing up the deed of separation, and when protests were lodged on Harriet's behalf, claiming that proceedings were being 'wantonly and vexatiously delayed' to prevent her from receiving the annuity of £2,000 guaranteed by the deed, there were Mr Whiteley and Mr Roche, pleading the natural delays of the law, and most unwilling to hurry matters just to oblige Mrs

Whiteley.[16] Harriet later described the separation as 'a matter of temperament'. There were 'certain things in the background that could, I suppose, have been proved if it had come to the divorce court, but there was a desire to hush it up'.[17]

For a short while, it must have seemed to William Whiteley that life began at 50. The children were to a great extent not his daily concern, and if he wanted to take a mistress, supply her with fine dresses and openly drive around with her in a carriage, that was his own business. After a few years of decline, sales were on the increase, and it looked as if 1882 would mark a new era of prosperity, but while money passed across the counters in ever-increasing amounts, there was to be disturbing evidence of homicidal antagonism, and, unknown to him, the beginnings of his own eventual destruction.

SEVEN

William and Louie and George and Emily

In 1855 Emma Louisa, daughter of Henry Solloway, a publican of Charlton in Kent, married Thomas Turner, a journeyman plasterer. The marriage was to produce five children, two of whom were to have a profound effect on both the life and death of William Whiteley.

Louisa Ellen, who was usually known as 'Louie', was born in 1856, her sister Emily Mary two years later. If there was any family weakness with the potential to mar their future, it was an over-fondness for alcohol. A grandmother had been known to like her tipple and both the Turner parents shared her enthusiasm. Perhaps this was what contributed to the death of Thomas Turner. In 1875 the family was living in the village of Belvedere and one day in February he unwisely decided to cross the railway lines at Erith in the path of an oncoming train, oblivious both to the approaching danger and the shouts of alarmed onlookers. Forty-five-year-old Turner was described as 'paralytic, but not so much so as to render him helpless', which suggests that he may have had a stroke, and could only move slowly. He might have made it to the other side, but one earnest cry finally attracted his attention and, fatefully, he paused. He was struck by the train and flung bodily on to the platform, where he was found to be dead.[1]

As the girls grew to womanhood, both were considered to be very attractive, and neither lacked admirers. Emily was said to be especially beautiful, with wonderful dark eyes. Sketches of Louie in middle age show her as slender with an aquiline nose – striking rather than conventionally pretty. According to her mother, Louie left home between the ages of 13 and 14 although she did not go far, living with a grandmother at Douglas Street in New Cross, and who arranged for her to be apprenticed to a Miss Harper who kept a shop in Belvedere, a toyshop according to the newspaper interviews, a boot shop in the census returns. Louie was there only a year and then decided to take a position as a barmaid at the Dewdrop Inn, Woodpecker Road, New Cross, but it was a bad decision. The work did not suit her and she left. Her next employment was as a cashier at the Ind Coope company brewery in Romford, but somehow, this too, was not the occupation she felt best utilised her talents. The glamour of Whiteleys beckoned.

After the death of William Whiteley, the date on which Louie first went to work for the Universal Provider became a matter of crucial importance. She herself was quite positive that this event had happened late in 1882, and that prior to then, neither she nor Emily had ever met him, and had only ever entered the store as customers. The only contrary evidence is in the interview with Mrs Turner published in the *Star* which suggests that Louie went to work for William Whiteley when she was only 16. The difficulty about Mrs Turner's interview is that when it is possible to check the facts in official records it becomes apparent that either her memory was seriously at fault, or, as is far more likely, the information had become garbled in the transmission from the spoken word to the printed page.[2]

The contents of this interview should therefore be regarded with some caution. Louie's story, on the other hand, was told in court and her statements reviewed by counsel, so there is no ambiguity about what she actually said. If her account is accepted as true, it follows that Louie could not, as suggested by Lambert, have been the cause of the Whiteley separation.

Emily's early history, as told by her mother, is that she went into service, as either nursemaid or companion to the daughter of Sir Samuel Joyce of Endsleigh Street, Tavistock Square. There is no one of that name in Endsleigh Street in the 1871 census, but in 1881 no. 12 is occupied by 65-year-old William Joyce, an unmarried barrister and his 61-year-old sister Mary, together with two servants, a cook and a housemaid. It is quite possible, therefore, that Emily worked as a maidservant at this address in the mid-1870s. It is here, after two years of presumably satisfactory service, that she is said to have made the acquaintance of George Rayner.

Rayner has been variously described as a 'stockbroker', a 'financier' or 'something in the city' which gives, and indeed is meant to give, an impression of a man of some substance and influence. The truth, as revealed by official records, is more mundane, and it should be remembered that at his death his estate was worth less than £8,000 at today's values. George Edwin Henry Rayner was born in Islington in 1849, the second son of William Rayner, a solicitor's clerk. No. 25 Colebrook Row was a bustling household in 1851. Apart from the Rayners, daughter Emma, son William and toddler George, there was a widowed mother-in-law, two servants, a visitor and two lodgers. The family later moved to South Norwood where another son, Bernard, was born in 1859, his father now describing himself as a scrivener. All three sons were destined to go into the mortgage and insurance-broking business.

There are too many versions of the relationship between George and Emily to describe it with any certainty. From Emily, who inherited the family failing for drink, and died in 1898, we have only hearsay; George's story was told many years later when he had his own reasons for wanting to deny what he could; there is the misty-eyed and not a little suspect story from Mrs Turner; and, most convincingly, there are the quiet restrained words of Louie.

The stories all agree that Emily became George Rayner's mistress, and they lived together at 2 Stanley Villas, Teddington. According to Mrs Turner, Rayner had had chambers at Gray's Inn, and initially Emily had 'visited' him there – a popular Victorian euphemism. The house at Teddington was, she said, 'beautifully furnished by Maples'.[3] Emily regarded herself as George's wife, and took his surname. By 1881 the couple had three children, all acknowledged by George; but that comfortable situation was not to continue.

Many doubts might have been clarified by the 1881 census return, except that on census day Louie and Emily were on holiday, staying at a boarding house at 16 Lascelles Terrace, Eastbourne. George – his surname so badly written that he appears on the transcribed return as 'Maynor' was at home, describing himself as married, which suggests that in those days at least, he had no objections to Emily regarding herself as his wife, and he gives his profession as 'late financial agent and broker'. The family move away from Islington during his infancy meant that he recorded his place of birth incorrectly as Dulwich. In Eastbourne, both sisters took two years off their actual ages, and neither declared an occupation.

Louie's surname was so badly scribbled she is on the census as 'Turns' and there were four children with them, whose names were written in varying degrees of illegibility.

One child with the surname Cousins may well have been a neighbour's, along for the trip, or perhaps nothing to do with the little party, but there are two boys and a girl called Rayner, all of whom were born in Teddington. The oldest is just 3, his name transcribed as Ewen, although Edwin seems more likely. Then there is 2-year-old Horace, and 4-month-old 'Evilin' (actually Emily Eveline, who later came to be known as Eva).

Little Ewen or Edwin's fate is a mystery. No child of either name was born or baptised in the area at the time. Not only did George later deny that this boy was his son, he claimed that Emily had admitted to him that she was not even the child's mother, and that the boy was later handed back to his real parents.

It is Horace George Rayner with whom we are most concerned. The future murderer of William Whiteley was born on 10 April 1879, at Stanley Villas, Teddington. Emily registered the birth, gave George's name as the father and declared herself to be 'Emily Rayner, formerly Turner'. George's profession she gave as 'stockbroker'. Some newspaper reports suggest that the couple had rows about Horace's paternity, but in the mad scramble for information after the death of William Whiteley, it is very possible that there may have been confusion between Horace and the older boy. Louie was later adamant that Emily had told her George was Horace's father. The rows led to a separation and Emily went to live with her mother in Thurston Road, Lewisham. She then took a situation as governess with a family at Brockley Park, Forest Hill, but soon afterwards she and George were reconciled.

Trying to piece together these suggestive fragments into a coherent story is not a simple task, but one possible scenario is that before George and Emily began to cohabit, Emily, to ensure George's support, 'adopted' a child and passed it off as hers. After the birth of Horace, she may have felt more secure and confessed what she had done, resulting in the subsequent estrangement. Louie, however, always believed that the older boy was Emily's, and George his father.

The incorrect belief that George Rayner was a man of substantial means has led to the assumption that he was one of Whiteley's wealthy friends. There is actually no hard evidence that Whiteley and Rayner ever met before the 1880s, and from Louie's testimony it appears that it was through the two men's independent involvement with the Turner girls that they first became acquainted. The simple fact that Rayner furnished his Teddington home from Maples is rather suggestive.

Louie first met George Rayner about a year before the birth of Horace, when she visited Emily and George at Teddington, and she also visited the couple when they were staying in Brighton. When Louie went to work in the toy department at Whiteleys in 1882, Emily had been living with Rayner for some three years and Horace was aged 3½.

Whiteley lost little time in making slim, attractive Louie his mistress. She introduced him to Emily and George, and the two couples started to take weekend trips together. Mr Rayner's part in the equation was particularly convenient for William Whiteley. When, in January 1883, Whiteley decided to establish Louie in a house in Greville Road, Kilburn, neither too far from nor too near his own home, a house for which he paid the rent and furnishings, it was all carried out in the name of George Rayner. The fiction was that the house was intended for George, Emily and Louie. The reality was that Louie lived and entertained her lover there, while George and Emily occasionally stayed as visitors. Mrs Turner later claimed that Louie lived at the Finchley farm as a housekeeper. Louie never mentioned this, though of course it is not impossible that this was the case for a time.

The mistress of William Whiteley enjoyed certain advantages. There were new clothes to wear, handsome presents, pleasant drives in a fine carriage, and holidays at the seaside, while of course, the long hours of shop work were a thing of the past. Louie still visited the Whiteleys emporium, but as a customer, ordering any amount of goods she required, the assistants being well aware of what qualified her to do so. Obliging Mr Whiteley even changed the livery of his grooms from gaudy red and gold to a more subdued colour at her suggestion.

* * *

In 1882 an unusual royal visit provided a magnificent opportunity for a massive publicity exercise. Cetewayo, the deposed King of the Zulus, arrived in England in August, with the object not only of sampling everything English, but attending a series of meetings at the Colonial Office, in the hope of being restored to the throne. According to Whiteley, 'The Government was in some doubt as to what to do with its savage guest, when the happy thought struck Lord Kimberley [then the Colonial Secretary] that I, who provide for all men, might provide for Cetewayo.' Of course Whiteley could not resist getting in on the act, and entirely took over the arrangements for the entertainment of the royal visitor. A house at 18 Melbury Road, Holland Park, was provided and furnished for the King and his entourage, which included commanders who had served at Rorke's Drift and Isandhlwana. Every requirement was provided, and during the course of his month's stay Cetewayo developed an astonishing appetite for English beef and a prodigious capacity for champagne, the word 'fizz' becoming an important addition to his vocabulary. He would greet his many visitors wearing a suit of blue cloth with a flannel shirt and brightly coloured necktie.

After Cetewayo's death in 1884 Whiteley provided some amusing reminiscences of the 'grand, kind gentleman'.

When he first arrived, his daily ration of 3½ pounds of beef contented him. Before he left his regular allowance had risen to 7½ pounds *per diem*. He greatly admired English beef. . . . But this huge mass of fresh meat looks larger than it was in reality, because of the way in which it was frizzled in cooking. Cetewayo was very particular about his cooking. The beef had to be cut in steaks two inches thick, and cooked until it was as hard and dry as toast; then it was eaten by itself. . . . In drink he was particularly fond of champagne, although he had no objection to whisky. You know how eloquently he discoursed to a temperance deputation about the curse of intoxicants, and his earnest desire to keep them outside Zululand. If his desire to keep rum outside Zululand was half as keen as his desire to put champagne inside the corporation of one particular

Zulu whom I knew well, Cetewayo must indeed have been one of the most zealous Maine law men on record.

On the day when Cetewayo was told of his restoration, a party was laid on, with 'fizz and beef and beef and fizz all the night through'. As the revellers finally retired to their beds, Whiteley presented Cetewayo with a magnum of champagne, but advised that it should be kept for the next day. The royal visitor, fascinated by the huge bottle, insisted on taking it with him to his room for safe keeping, promising faithfully he would not drink it that night. He hurried back to his room 'hugging the magnum as if it were a precious child. A few minutes afterwards as I went upstairs I saw the big bottle standing outside Cetewayo's door drained to the last drop.' On the following day the King was obliged to call off a visit to Crystal Palace, the newspapers giving out that the royal visitor was suffering from a 'cold'.

Naturally, Whiteley did not lose the opportunity of having the King of the Zulus visit his emporium, and claimed that nothing else in England had impressed Cetewayo as much as 'the great establishment over which I preside'.[4] On 25 August large crowds assembled in Westbourne Grove, and at 11 a.m. the King arrived at Whiteleys accompanied by two chieftains, an interpreter and his suite. There he was received by Mr Whiteley to whom he raised his hat, and proceeded to tour the premises, buying up quantities of curtains, flannels, blankets and rugs, which the newspaper noted with some surprise, 'was by no means in the direction of gaudy patterns'. His Majesty then sat down to lunch in the refreshment room, which was specially decorated for the occasion, finally departing at 3 o'clock.[5]

With all these pleasant things to take up his spare moments, it is possible that Whiteley was in too sunny a mood to allow people like Mr Flood to trouble him very much. Flood, in the meantime, was having his own problems, finding an unexpected resistance to his demands for a loan of £3,000 to thwart Whiteley's plans.

The police prosecution of Whiteleys carriers for the obstruction by the horses and carts in Douglas Place had also come to nothing. Despite the fact that as many as thirty-five Whiteley vans at a time occupied the narrow roadway, the magistrate observed that each was only there for as long as necessary, and dismissed the summons. Licking its wounds, the Vestry retreated to marshal itself for a direct challenge to Mr Whiteley who was now claiming that the footway of Douglas Place outside the furniture warehouse was not public property at all, but his.

Once again, the Vestry was torn with internal strife over Mr Whiteley. When Vestryman Silvester revealed that he had discussed Whiteley's claims with Mr Roche's son, also a solicitor, Mr Flood's comment was 'When Mr Silvester tells you plainly that he is in communication with your enemy, what are you to think?' and a Mr Griffith commented that the Vestry 'knew too well the kind of man to whom Mr Whiteley entrusted his legal affairs'.[6]

Matters were now coming to a major crunch: 'hardly a meeting now takes place in the parish board-room at Paddington Green without dividing the members into Whiteleyites and anti-Whiteleyites, using up some hours of the public time and generating a good deal of latent heat', observed the *Chronicle*. James Sherrard, a local JP, felt impelled to make a contribution. He said, appropriately enough, that he stood for peace, justice and fair play, and thought it was possible even at the eleventh hour to avoid litigation. Flood was not to be swayed. Mr Whiteley's idea of fairness, he said, was to procure all he could, and keep it.[7] The Vestry, curiously unmoved by Whiteley and Roche's argument that Douglas Place was used only by 'washerwomen and third-class bathers',[8] duly set the legal machinery creaking into motion. Sherrard, convinced that he could resolve matters personally, went to see Whiteley's premises, had a good look at Douglas Place and spoke to the man himself, who was all sweet buttery charm. Whiteley assured him that he did not want to go to law and would be willing to place matters before three independent arbitrators, and accede to any reasonable request. This proposal was duly stamped upon by Mr Flood, who threatened to give Sherrard 'a bit of his mind'.[9]

As the sunny days faded into autumn, there was no hint of the events which were to plunge Whiteleys into both physical and financial turmoil over the next five years. Shortly after 11 p.m. on 15 November 1882, a man was standing at the door of his premises in Queen's Road when a passer-by commented, 'Whiteleys is in flames, if you want to see a blaze.'[10] In a few minutes it was clear that this was true, and crowds assembled in Douglas Place where smoke and sparks could be seen at the back of 51 Westbourne Grove, which specialised in fancy trimmings – ribbons, flowers and feathers. Mr Whiteley had just arrived on the spot and, accompanied by policemen and two firemen, he disappeared into the shop. His employees hurried from their dormitories and proceeded to assist both in fighting the fire, and in removing the stock. Before long, however, the fire became too much for the amateur brigade. Flames had broken through the roof and were spreading east to the other shops in the row, no. 53 with its muslins, linings, toys and games, and no. 55 where stocks of stationery and needlework items were easily ignited. Eventually the fire engines arrived, and the police were fully occupied in keeping order among the hundreds of onlookers who had assembled, while the residents of Kensington Gardens Square began packing their belongings for an evacuation. The firemen took enormous risks fighting the blaze, and it was fortunate that there were only a few minor injuries. The following morning it was apparent that although only the top storeys of six buildings had been damaged by fire, water was dripping into the intact shops below, and flooding the basements.

A great deal of work was done in a short time to clear the debris, 'business as usual' being the order of the day, and the next morning those departments that could open were in full swing, crowds thronging the shops as if nothing had happened. The official report of fire chief Captain Shaw told a terrible tale: from nos 43 to 55 the first, second and third floors and their contents were burnt out and roofs gone, while the adjoining and communicating buildings were severely damaged both by fire and water. The only small comfort was that the damage, estimated at £60,000, was fully covered by insurance. The cause of the fire was unknown, but it was generally assumed to be something to do with gas.

With the Christmas season approaching it was an obvious opportunity for Whiteleys to have a sale of salvaged goods, which was widely advertised, presumably by leaflet. Even the great Universal Provider could not have anticipated how successful this would be. Long before the doors were due to open, the Grove was crowded with a great mass of determined women, the early-comers pressed close up to the windows, the tardier spilling over the pavement into the roadway. For several hours they continued to assemble, with new arrivals swelling the numbers by the minute, 'until the street was filled with a struggling mob, presenting a by no means decorous appearance'.[11] From time to time, loud complaints would signal the fact that in the great crush, female thieves were at work. Eventually, the doors of no. 41, which were manned by two apprehensive-looking policemen, were thrown open to the surging mob, which pressed eagerly forward. Ladies of even the more reputable classes pushed, hustled and jostled in frantic efforts to enter the premises, the unfortunate policemen doing their best to prevent injuries. Inside, the seething mass fought to be near the counters, hats drunkenly askew and clothes almost torn from their bodies. Even the announcement that the shop was full did not cause those outside to disperse, and they stuck obstinately to their posts in the hope of entering later. The decision to open only one door had been a huge mistake. Women in bulky winter clothing had to force their way in and out by the same exit, and since it was necessary to remove purchases on the spot, those struggling to leave were encumbered by large parcels. On more than one occasion a fight nearly broke out and it was remarkable that only one lady fainted. 'It is to be hoped,' said the *Chronicle*, deploring what it called 'a sight to make men blush . . .', 'that Mr Whiteley has had his last public fire.'[12]

When, just ten days later, Henry Taylor, superintendent of the Paddington Baths, awoke shortly before 6.30 a.m. on 26 December, his first impression was that there was a bright yellow fog filling Queen's Road. Gradually he realised that the phenomenon was 'something more than atmospheric'. At first he felt sure

that the Baths were on fire, and roused his family and
the engineer. He then saw that the blaze was at the top
of the corner block of Whiteleys overlooking Kensington
Gardens Square. Trying to reach the scene, he was
obstructed by about seventy horses running loose in the
streets – the occupants of Whiteleys' stables which had
been brought out for safety. Once again the local
residents were packing their belongings in preparation
for flight, and a large crowd had assembled. There were
numerous people in the streets whose Christmas
celebrations had lasted all night, and instead of going
home they decided to round things off with a view of
the fire. One of the hotels in the neighbourhood was
obliged to close its doors against the increasing rabble.
Rumours were passing around that six of the horses had
been roasted alive and one or two stablemen burnt, but
this was not the case. When Whiteley appeared, looking
remarkably calm, he took one look at the loose horses
and ordered them all to be collected and returned to
their stables, which was done.

An early concern was for the menagerie which was
housed in a glazed arcade at the end of the provisions
market. This was extremely popular with Bayswater
residents, many of whom enjoyed frequent visits to their
particular favourites. The shrieks of the birds and
monkeys and the panic of animals trapped in their cages
could clearly be heard, and at first it was thought that
some unfortunate resident was in the building.
Fortunately the fire was quickly brought under control,
and the animals were saved.

It later transpired that the fire had broken out on the
fifth floor of the premises where pianos were
manufactured, the fire feeding itself hungrily on
seasoned and varnished wood. At 7 a.m., the roof fell in

and this was followed by the crash of heavy machinery breaking through the upper floor. The hoses continued to play on the smoking debris for several hours after the flames were out. This time, only one building was burnt out, the adjoining ones being only slightly affected. The damage was about £25,000, which included the value of 100 pianos reduced to a blackened powdery heap.

Once again, the cause of the fire could not be determined, and a malicious rumour, for which there was no foundation in fact, passed rapidly through Bayswater that the Universal Provider had been 'run in'. Even the *Chronicle* acknowledged that Mr Whiteley, even after insurance receipts, would be out of pocket by the fire, quite apart from the worry and mortification. But there was a point to the rumour: two fires erupting in such a short space of time, both without an obvious cause, both breaking out while the shops were closed, and in locations where, although there was much easily combustible material, nothing had been left in a condition where fire could arise spontaneously. If Mr Whiteley was not the guilty party, could it be that he was the victim of arson?

EIGHT

Out of the Ashes

The year 1883 did not start well for William Whiteley. He was still coping with the restoration of his premises after two fires, and matters with the Vestry were coming to a head. In January, the Paddington Vestrymen succeeded against all expectations in winning agreement to a loan of almost £3,000 to enable their proposed wall to be built. Whiteley, who had once offered to pay rent of £20 per year for the rights of light and air conferred by his windows, had in the interim withdrawn the offer and refused to pay anything. The two sides were at loggerheads once more. The correspondence on the dispute was printed and laid before the Vestrymen for their perusal. It amounted to 143 pages. Mr Sherrard, even if Mr Flood had, as promised, given him 'a bit of his mind', was unrepentant, and carried the banner of peacemaker into the Vestry. In March he demanded a postponement of four months, to try and reach an agreement. To his surprise he found a bland and amenable Mr Flood, perfectly willing to adjourn for four months, so that 'no more irritating feelings should be provoked than already existed'.

The Vestrymen were just about to agree the four month postponement, when one of them smelt a rat. Why was Mr Flood so calm and agreeable? What was he up to? It was pointed out that in four months, half their number would be out of town, which would suit Mr Flood very well as he would then find it easier to procure a vote in his favour. It was next proposed that the matter should be postponed for seven months instead. Mr Flood surprised them again, by agreeing to that, too. 'He was wonderfully magnanimous and smiled agreement to the mild motions for postponement in the most exasperating manner', observed the *Chronicle*.[1]

The mystery of Mr Flood's behaviour was solved in May when he declined to stand for re-election, revealing to his fellow Vestrymen that for some months he had been under treatment for heart disease and had been advised by his doctors to take things easy. In the meantime, Sherrard had been triumphantly elected Churchwarden, a position which entitled him to take the chair at Vestry meetings. Accepting the new honour with due humility, he said he had agreed to stand as he thought he might be able to bring about peace. He was a great lover of peace. The speech was greeted with loud applause. Under Sherrard's new position of prominence, a committee of three Vestrymen was formed to carry out arbitration with Mr Whiteley, and the wall scheme was dropped.

Whiteley agreed an annual payment of £20 for the windows, which, if anyone remembered, was the figure he had first proposed, and the Vestry also scored a victory over the Douglas Place obstruction, extracting a fine of £300, while Whiteley conceded the parish's rights over the footway. He won his point on the drains, which were not to be altered, 'and the result [observed the *Chronicle*] will be that at times the main sewage for the parish will rise above his own pipes and imprison the house sewage possibly for days together'. In the absence of Mr Flood, the Vestry accepted the committee's recommendations without a murmur.[2]

In the 1883 Vestry elections there were five vacant seats, and Whiteley saw his opportunity to swing the

balance of the membership in his favour. Five pro-
Flood, and therefore anti-Whiteley, candidates were
standing, including Whiteley's chief trade rival, William
Owen, and his old adversary John Clarke Record.
Whiteley duly matched these worthies with five
candidates of his own, and there was a strong and lively
campaign from both sides, creating considerable local
interest. The five Whiteley men had no lack of funds for
their campaign posters, leaflets and newspaper
advertisements, and even enjoyed the services of Mr
Roche who canvassed the ward on their behalf. On the
day before polling, every household in the ward
received, by different deliveries, three letters asking for
support for the Whiteley men.

Polling began promptly at 8 a.m. and in every part of
the ward, cabs could be seen with party broadsides
pasted on them. Mr Whiteley's five candidates appeared
in front of Westbourne Hall 'arrayed in gorgeous rosettes
of orange and purple . . . all day long the scene outside
Westbourne Hall was one of unwonted excitement,
Westbourne Grove very seldom being enlivened with
this particular form of activity'. The polls closed at
8 p.m. and the votes were counted, the results being
greeted with loud cheers. The result was a considerable
blow to Whiteley. Although the voting was close, with
less than 100 votes between the winner and the last man
in the polls, all five of his candidates were defeated and
Owen and Record tied at the top.[3]

With a temporary lull in his battles with the Vestry,
Whiteley could concentrate on one of the sillier court
cases of his long career as a persistent litigant. The case
had been in progress for eighteen months when it came
before the court of Queen's Bench in June 1883, 'and
there was an array of familiar and expectant faces in

court, showing that some important revelations were anticipated'. Mr Whiteley and Mr Roche were in court early, and it was apparent to all concerned that this was a needle match. The case had its roots in an action that took place in 1881 when Edward Rooney, a warehouse-man, had been prosecuted together with Richard Moorhead, one of Whiteley's buyers, for conspiracy to defraud. False invoices had been prepared, Moorhead had approved them, and Whiteley money had been paid out, but no goods had arrived and the cheques had been paid into an account owned by Rooney.[4]

Both defendants were tried at the Old Bailey and convicted. Rooney's brother Robert was a reputable manufacturer of brushes and an agent for purses and bags who had supplied Whiteleys since 1878, doing business worth some £30,000 during that time. He too had been robbed by Edward, who had taken items of stock which were sold to Whiteleys through his own agents. Despite Robert Rooney's impeccable record, Whiteley, having taken delivery of goods valued at £3,400, decided that he was not going to pay for them, claiming that for some years his buyers had been bribed, and the cost of these bribes added to the price he was being asked to pay. Rooney's case was that what Whiteley called bribes were actually commissions; that he, Rooney, paid for them out of his own pocket and ninety-nine traders out of a hundred did the same. He took action for payment.

Whiteley demanded that the whole of Rooney's books be opened and examined for the years 1878 and 1881. In July 1882 the courts, impatient to reach a conclusion, held that this inspection was not necessary and all that was required were details of a few typical cases which could be provided in a week. Somehow, matters ground on for nearly a year, and by the time the case was heard in 1883 it had been before the divisional court sixteen times, and the court of appeal twice, while 140 summonses had been issued. Thousands of pounds had been spent, and it was estimated that the total would probably come to £9,000 – £10,000. Neither man was about to give up, and they certainly were not going to shake hands on it out of court. Rooney said it was 'a matter of public reputation on which any necessary amount of money would be well spent', while Whiteley contended 'that he has been "had" for a series of years and must make an example'.

Meanwhile, Rooney took his own subtle revenge. During the delays he had, unknown to Whiteley, been buying up as an ordinary member of the public some of the goods he had originally sold wholesale to Whiteleys, and calculating the mark-up charged. Matters were being aired in court that William Whiteley would rather not have had publicised. Having said for many years that he sold his goods at the lowest price commensurate with making a fair profit, it now seemed that this did not apply in every department. It is probable that Whiteleys, like so many other stores, promoted loss-leaders – goods on offer at low prices to tempt customers in, while other items on sale were less generously priced. Where Whiteleys differed was that the owner first claimed that all his mark-ups were low, and then attempted to make, and indeed succeeded in making, a personality cult out of it. No one would be able now to examine the many thousands of items in stock and assess what his mark-ups really were, but it is safe to assume that they were exactly as low as they needed to be.

The two opposing counsels crossed swords several times, with claims that Whiteley was making 150–200 per cent profit on Rooney's prices, while laughter rippled through the court and Whiteley sat shaking his head. Counterclaims that Rooney was making excessive profits were denounced as lies, and the judge, with a smile, observed that he would not accept anything as a fact that he did not extract from the witness box. In the end, the tendency of any Whiteley case to create a vast accumulation of paperwork was its own downfall. The judge said that it would be impossible for a jury to master such a huge volume of information, and declared the case 'untriable by a jury'. He dismissed it to an official referee for a report and all 140 witnesses were sent home.[5]

At Whiteleys itself, nothing – not even the prices – had changed. Early in 1884 the *Chronicle* gave a fascinating picture of what it was like in the big store. Without the oleaginous fawning one sees elsewhere and also devoid of any obvious attempts to prick the Whiteley balloon it may well be one of the most accurate accounts we have:

> Crowded as the Grove always is, it is so especially on a fine Saturday morning when all sorts and conditions of men women and children throng the pavement and the string of vehicles on the road makes crossing from one side to the other a dangerous feat. [the Grove's] . . . air of gaiety and absence from dull care is unique in the metropolis. . . . Saturday morning has become a regular institution for shopping . . . Young ladies' schools broken up into small parties, prowl about Whiteleys and buy presents for each of their dearest friends on the principle of selecting a cheap article which looks expensive. The girls are not allowed to remain long in

the dissipated whirlpool of the big shop, but have to meet by appointment under the clock at a much earlier hour than they like. To add to the general crush the larger and more massive is the mamma the larger the number of young hopefuls she drags about with her who seems [*sic*] to go to Whiteleys principally to eat buns, which they munch *sans gêne* as they walk about in the different departments. On Saturdays the shopwalkers at Whiteleys fired with the importance of the day, feel it their duty to be especially exasperating to the customers with their ceaseless 'Which department now, Madam?' In fact in their misdirected energy they often call out the question after a lady who has not replied, although anyone could see by her composed manner that she knew her way perfectly well. In the provision shop, of course, the crowd is dense. Here may be seen anxious ladies selecting fish for the family dinner and husbands and wives eagerly discussing whether some trifle or other should be bought, while the assistant behind the counter patiently awaits their decision; thrifty housekeepers wrangling over their accounts, and arguing that credit should be given for empties; boys eating tartlets with the rapacity peculiar to their age; mothers debating on the respective merits of sugar at 3*d* and 3½*d* a pound; ladies with a good wholesome appetite repairing exhausted nature with the tempting lobster, roll and pat of butter, or oysters with accompaniments for 6*d* or sandwiches; all this refreshment looking very nice, but striking the observer as requiring something to wash it down.

In the street are vendors of flags and clockwork mice and the usual collection of wonderful articles manufactured and sold for a penny each and this gives the Grove the appearance of a fair. No-one seems to mind being jostled about and crushed. Between one and two people start to hurry home. Soon the shutters are up the street hawkers have departed, and by three o'clock the Grove is almost like a deserted village.[6]

At half past three on the morning of 26 April 1884, dense clouds of smoke and an explosion attracted the police to Queen's Road. The blowing of whistles awoke Henry Taylor, and looking out of the back window he saw to his horror an immense volume of flame raging in the shop only two doors away and making its way towards the Baths. Taylor, together with the watchman and engineer, at once fetched the fire hoses and rushed to assist the firemen who were then just arriving. It soon became apparent that this fire was considerably more extensive than the two previous conflagrations, and within minutes all fifty-four stations in London had been telegraphed for assistance. At last help arrived – from Battersea, Clapham, Southwark, Whitehall, the Old Kent Road and many others; 200 fire fighters in all.

At one point Captain Shaw and his men were driven back by the enormous heat and suffocating smoke, as four shops full of furniture, carpets, drapery, oilcloths and linen disintegrated in the roaring flames, and onlookers feared that the men had lost control of the fire, 'which roared and burnt within the immense pile of buildings with appalling strength'.[7]

The smoke had already penetrated to the stables, and the stamping straining horses were set free. For a time they galloped about the streets in great confusion, before some of Whiteleys' employees collected them and took them to a cul-de-sac. Douglas Place was already filled with women and children, the families of carriers who had been driven out of their homes. Within minutes the fire had spread to the shop next door to the Baths, and in a yard at the rear several furniture vans full of goods were in full blaze. As Taylor struggled with his puny hose, the fire spread to the walls of the Baths, and suddenly strands of red-hot telegraph wires fell on the Baths' woodshed setting it alight and threatening the main building. The much-ridiculed wall did its work, however, and though it became so hot as to bulge 5 inches out of perpendicular, it held, and the Baths were saved.

As the hours passed, 'ascending lofty clouds of flame and lurid smoke began to attract crowds to the scene. The glow on the clouds was seen by countrymen coming with their hay carts from Sudbury and Harrow, and market gardeners coming with their carts up the Uxbridge Road caused a serious block of traffic on the Queen's Road.'[8]

An official was sent for from the gas company to cut off the supply. This should have been accessible from an iron box sunk into the pavement, but he was unable to open it. A pickaxe was sent for, and then a crowbar, and much effort was expended in getting the box open, the man having to remain dangerously near the burning premises, becoming steadily drenched through and through by the firemen's hoses. When the box was revealed, the key would not fit and another had to be sent for. In all it took over an hour to turn off the gas.

The 'most serious and alarming fire in the annals of Bayswater'[9] naturally attracted sightseers. The traffic in the Grove was almost completely blocked, police were everywhere trying to get the goggling crowds to move on, 'wooden barriers were erected across Queen's Road and a great unwashed and evil-looking crowd from the East End of London thronged the streets apparently enjoying the sight of the firemen and the smoke and the

131

sound of the unceasing working of the engines'.[10] The motley crowd which included 'street singers, performing Zulus and other itinerant followers of London's sights took up positions in Kensington Gardens Square, the residents of which probably saw more of the masses of London in one half hour than during the whole of their previous existence, and probably devoutly wished they might never gaze upon again'.[11] Some of the omnibus companies saw the chance of a quick profit. They came up from the city to Westbourne Grove laden with passengers inside and out, with large placards bearing the words 'TO WHITELEYS FIRE!' as if it was a popular entertainment.

Whiteley had naturally been early on the scene, and when the *Chronicle* reporter caught up with him, he was offering an appearance of 'unruffled equanimity . . . speaking with his wonted urbanity and without the least sign of a disturbed mind'. He had obviously been at the centre of the action, with 'his coat collar up to his eyes, his face smoke-blacked, his hands thick with dirt, and the spray from the fire-hose standing like dew-drops on his ample whiskers'.[12] Whiteley was about to look in on the provisions department, to take care of numerous matters including ensuring that the men received their dinner, and the reporter had to conduct his interview on the hoof with his subject 'directing here and ordering there . . .'[13] as they spoke. While dazed by the destruction, Whiteley was already estimating his losses and planning for the future. 'Why the place is the apple of my eye, built on my own freehold of the best materials – no expense spared, I can tell you! No jerry materials. All my experience was brought to bear in the planning and devising, too. It was to be a monument for myself, for my sons, and my sons' sons after them. It is

really cruel.'[14] The value of property and goods
destroyed he estimated at £250,000, not counting the
contents of the pantechnicon where his clients were
allowed to store goods. 'We shall begin to build as soon
as possible again, of course. I am no sooner down than
up again.'[15] 'All former catastrophes . . . have been
eclipsed by the magnitude of this last conflagration', said
the *Chronicle*'s reporter.[16] Arriving at 9 a.m., he found
the eastern end of Westbourne Grove and the entrance to
Queen's Road closed to traffic, and an army of police and
firemen guarding the highway. Able to pass the cordon,
he saw that 'the lofty mansard roof, usually surmounted
by the well-known Whiteley flag, was missing, and a
broken frontage of smoking blackened and roofless walls
was all that remained of the once imposing façade of
shops.'[17] Four out of the row of Whiteley's seven great
shops had been completely destroyed.

The fire had broken out in the carpet fitting and
planning department which had been left perfectly safe
at 7.30 p.m. the previous evening. Nothing there could
have provoked such a massive fire. The other mystery
was how the fire had managed to take such a
determined hold in so short a time, gutting the massive
premises in just four hours. Captain Shaw later reported
that one building of four floors, 300ft by 500ft, had its
contents burned out and roof destroyed, while the other
buildings of five floors with covered yards and stabling
were very severely damaged by fire, heat and water.

But it was business as usual wherever possible. The
provisions market had not been damaged, and 'at half
past eleven the dainty young ladies in their white caps
and black dresses were displaying their goods with
remarkable impetuous ability notwithstanding the
clatter around them; but that is Mr Whiteley's way'.[18]

Those who had suggested in 1882 that Mr Whiteley was setting his own premises on fire were silent now. His rate of insurance had been raised considerably, as had that of some of his neighbours including Mr Record, and his losses far exceeded the amount of cover. Whiteley's accounts at the year end eventually showed he had lost £123,000, of which only £62,000 was recoverable in insurance. The turnover was naturally affected and he suffered a trading loss of £105,000.[19]

Two days after the fire, firemen were still playing jets of water on the piles of blackened debris, and thousands of visitors continued to throng in from all parts of London. Mr Isaacs, the architect of the Baths, came to inspect the premises and found to his concern that the Vestry's wall separating the Baths from the smoking ruin of Whiteleys shops had been so badly warped by the fire as to be a danger, recommending that it be pulled down. The workmen took considerable risks to do this, scaling the wall and sitting astride the top, taking it apart brick by brick. Later, they tried fastening ropes to projecting angles and pulling from below, the numerous narrow escapes from the crashing rubble eliciting gasps of horror from the crowds of sightseers, who sometimes had to scatter for safety. Four days after the fire, a huge part of the wall was brought down causing a general stampede, and filling the street with blinding dust which took some time to clear.

On the following day it was felt that there was no more danger of the wall coming down on the side of the Baths, and the workmen were erecting scaffolding to take off the upper part, when a strong gust of wind caused it to topple. The upper part of the 70ft wall did fall on to Whiteleys' already ruined site, but the bulging caused by the fire brought the rest down into the woodyard of the

Baths, burying seven men. No one was killed, but all the men were badly hurt and, on being offered compensation of 12s per week for three weeks, were obliged to go through the courts for a better settlement which was not reached until the following year. The Baths also suffered – bricks had fallen through the roof and the building was closed for repairs for five months.

One remarkable effect of the fire was to create a mood of sympathy in the neighbourhood for Mr Whiteley. The Universal Provider was human after all; he could be hurt; he could be a victim; it was possible to pity him. Early in May, the Revd Spencer, chairman of the Paddington Vestry, moved a vote of sympathy for Mr Whiteley. He felt it would be a gracious act. Now that the legal actions were concluded, they were in a position to 'melt him down by kindness and sympathy, thus proving that in all the Vestry had done they were actuated only by considerations of the public interest'. He asked for the vote to be passed unanimously, and a letter presented to Mr Whiteley, and this was done.[20]

The *Pall Mall Gazette*, which loved both heroes and villains, decided to cast Mr Whiteley in the former role and interviewed him at length, revealing that there was one thing the Universal Provider did not sell. 'I deal in everything that the world produces except fresh milk', said Whiteley. 'Fresh milk . . . is against my principles. Condensed milk you shall have in any quantity, but fresh milk – not one gill.' The reporter asked the obvious question – why? Whiteley 'with an air of conscious rectitude', declared, 'Because it is against the Sabbath.' The *Gazette*, with uncharacteristic restraint, declined to comment on the contrast between Mr Whiteley's virtuous upholding of the fourth commandment and flagrant breach of the seventh.[21]

Having mourned the death of Cetewayo in February, Whiteley was on the lookout for another exotic foreign monarch to grace his establishment, and in June there was considerable excitement at the sight of the Maori King Tawhiao lunching in the refreshment rooms. On leaving by Kensington Gardens Square the King was naturally escorted by the Universal Provider himself. The crowds may have been a little disappointed by the amiable looking King and his entourage arriving in ordinary English dress, and appearing very civilised.[22]

Meanwhile the building work was proceeding as fast as it could go. In November the *Chronicle* observed 'the work has been rushed on with marvellous celerity. The builder is to complete his task by 31 December or pay £50 penalty for every day he may require after that date to complete the contract . . . fortunately for other tradesmen during the short season when Mr Whiteley *does* take his £15,000 daily over the counter, they, too, are filling their coffers. In Bayswater money by no means flows only in one channel.'[23]

The causes of the fires remained a mystery, the possibility of recurrence a constant worry. Whiteley took the unusual step of employing trained firemen both inside and outside the premises, to keep watch overnight. Although he still maintained his home near the business, he no longer felt the need to be on the spot at all times, and liked to spend the months from June to August living on the farm at Finchley. At 7.15 a.m. on 17 June 1885, a hansom cab drove up to the farm with the news that yet another fire had broken out in Westbourne Grove between 5 and 6 o'clock, in the same shops that had been burned down in 1882. In less than an hour Whiteley was in Bayswater, to find that the conflagration, which had begun in no. 41, was raging

through all the shops from no. 39 to no. 43, destroying
the valuable silks and lace stocked for the summer
trade. The young men who slept in the nearby
dormitories had been rousted out of bed to help remove
goods from the premises. In the counting house at no.
39, books and ledgers were quickly taken from the
strong-rooms and pitched out of the windows on to the
ground below where they were gathered up and carried
to a place of safety. When the flames eventually died
down, only bare walls were standing, and several
adjoining shops had been damaged by smoke and water.
Whiteley viewed the devastation with his usual cool
demeanour, and as twenty engines continued to pump
water on to the smoking debris throughout the morning,
in other portions of Westbourne Grove customers were
being served as if nothing had happened. One item of
value for which Whiteley asked for a particular search
to be made was a diamond ring, which was in his
private room. The article was discovered undamaged.

Once again, a fire had torn through Whiteley's
premises with astonishing speed, leaving no clue as to
how it had begun. Once again, the hoardings went up
and the work of rebuilding was put in hand.[24]

It was rumoured that the fire was the work of rival
tradesmen in the area, but, as the *Chronicle* pointed out,
the feeling between Whiteley and other retailers was
more akin to solidarity: 'it is a strong contrast to the
feeling of former years, when Mr Whiteley was looked
upon as a sort of Aaron's rod, destined to swallow all
the little rods of the locality.' As an anonymous
correspondent pointed out, Mr Whiteley's success had
'made the neighbourhood what it is for trade'. This
opinion was borne out when the local tradesmen jointly
sent Whiteley a letter of sympathy. In an effort to

discover the identity of the arsonist, Whiteley offered a reward of £1,000 for the apprehension of the guilty person or persons, but nothing was ever discovered.[25]

The increased fire precautions made the staff understandably jumpy. In July an employee, noticing some smoke, rushed out into Queen's Road, and smashed the glass on a fire alarm post. Fire engines raced up from Notting Hill at full speed only to find a small chimney fire at the Baths. In the meantime, rebuilding was in full swing and by August 1885, to the astonishment and admiration of the neighbourhood, the burnt-out buildings were fully refitted and restocked ready for opening.

Public opinion had certainly softened towards the Universal Provider, but his draconian prosecutions of shoplifters and thieving employees was to continue and even, on the evidence of newspaper reports, to escalate. Every so often he came unstuck, as in the case of Mrs Georgina Ryan, a middle-aged lady of impeccable honesty and a Whiteleys customer for many years, who was brought before the Central Criminal Court in September 1885 for stealing a piece of ribbon. Mrs Ryan had initially purchased a piece of ribbon then, realising she did not have enough, returned for more, examining the original piece for comparison before replacing it in her bag. Challenged by an assistant, the lady, who was a little deaf, did not give a satisfactory reply, and ended up being held in police custody where, despite her desperate entreaties, she was unable to contact her family for several hours, and was not released for two days. When her plight became known, her son, who lived in India, was obliged to return to London to be with her. The case collapsed in court, since the department's records were found to be deficient. The *Chronicle* was scathing. 'It is a tradesman's business to make quite sure his system and his assistants are reliable before he sets down "leakage" to some other source. Failing this, he is too likely to fly at the throat of one of his customers . . . to run the ship on a rock is scarcely the way to reform the evil. In this case it may prove that the rock and not the ship has naturally received the most damage.' In the following year, Whiteley recognised the situation by reimbursing the lady with the £300 cost of her defence.[26]

Shortly afterwards Whiteley the great prosecutor found himself the defendant instead. He had opened a new photographic studio, issuing the specification that it had to be 'the best studio in the world'. This did not include employing an assistant with the requisite knowledge of the Pharmacy Act of 1868, and the courts were most disapproving when it was shown that cyanide of potassium was being sold across the counter 'just in the same way as would be a yard of ribbon'. With such a cut and dried case, a simple admission of guilt and an apology would have been the best reaction. Typically, Whiteley found it necessary to employ Mr Roche to protest that the prosecution was 'prompted by a spirit of vindictiveness' and that one of Mr Whiteley's 'kind friends' had informed on him. This made no impression and the result was a fine of 20s with costs of 25s 6d.[27]

Mr Flood, who had been re-elected to the Vestry in 1884, necessarily remained a prominent and influential figure and it must have seemed that he was simply biding his time until the next conflict would again project him into a position of power. On 29 October, however, he died suddenly at his home, aged 58, and with his passing it could be said that the years of serious warfare between Mr Whiteley and the Paddington Vestry were over.

NINE

The Burning Fiery Furnace

By the 1880s it was well-known that Whiteleys was regularly patronised by royalty, and although Queen Victoria did not make personal visits, other members of the family did. Princess Beatrice was an almost weekly visitor, and the Princess of Wales was often seen there, as was the Duchess of Teck and her children, who included the future Queen Mary. These royal personages were the superstars of the day, enjoying an adulation, deference and respect of which today we see only the faded remains. Their presence in Whiteleys accorded it enormous prestige, especially as they took a personal interest in its fortunes. The Princess of Wales, 'one of the most courteous and kindly of the Universal Provider's visitors . . .', had, according to the *Chronicle*, penned with her own hand a sympathetic letter to William Whiteley after the fire of 1885. These ladies often arrived incognito – Princess Louise was known as 'Mrs Thomson'. Also to be seen were 'notabilities in society and art . . .', including Mrs Langtry who arrived under the name of 'Mrs Levi'.[1]

The Queen's many grandchildren were often granted the pleasure of 'wandering at large in the various departments'. In December 1885 the *Chronicle* described the annual visit of the Duke of Edinburgh to Bayswater to buy Christmas presents. Arriving at 149 Westbourne Grove, he 'greeted the Universal Provider with his wonted frankness and was then conducted as usual to the toyrooms'. One of his tasks was to choose the ornaments for the royal children's Christmas tree at Clarence House. Being familiar with the premises, the Duke noted and commented on changes made since his last visit. He then went to Westbourne Hall, where Whiteley, finding even his monumental premises too small for the festive season, held an annual supplementary bazaar.[2]

* * *

Whiteley's public respectability was in marked contrast to his private life, and the merry outings of William, Louie, George and Emily. Whatever rifts there were between George and Emily regarding the parenthood of the oldest child had healed, and their son Gordon was born in February 1885. By then, Louie had an announcement of her own. She was pregnant by William Whiteley. On 15 September at 4 Park Crescent, Brighton, Herbert Cecil Whiteley Turner was born. Louie gave her full name on the birth certificate, 'Louisa Ellen Turner' and, since she was posing as a married woman and was obliged to supply a maiden name, put 'Turner' for that, too. She declared the child's father to be a tea-dealer named Herbert Whiteley Turner. Louie brought up the child herself, maintained by an allowance of £150 a year from his father. There was also that useful account at Whiteleys, which she visited with her little boy in tow.

If Whiteley's staff disapproved, they remained silent on the subject. In any case, they had more onerous matters to worry about. The first inkling of this in the newspapers came in 1886 with the prosecution of Horace Bailey, an employee accused of theft. His defence was that Whiteleys operated such a stringent system of fines that he had felt entitled to try and recoup his losses. Many establishments had a system of fining employees amounts ranging from sixpence to half-a-crown for misdemeanours such as lateness, or staying out of dormitories after hours, but Whiteleys, it seemed, had a more punitive system than most. Having been fined every month since he had taken up the employment, Bailey had stolen three silk handkerchiefs worth 3*s* 7*d* and tried to pawn them, the value, in his opinion, being equivalent to the fines of the last month. Bailey was only 19 and it was a first offence so the court was lenient, giving him the option of a £10 fine or twenty-one days in gaol. The *Chronicle* commented: 'But is there not something defective in the system of this establishment that so many cases of the kind crop up from it? It is said that the fines are heavy and inflicted for so many things that an employee cannot possibly escape a good many. If this be so it is scarcely an equitable state of things.'[3]

Such a minor concern did nothing to ruffle Whiteley's general air of success and popularity, in which public events only served to add lustre to his image. June 1887 was a time of uncommon bustle in Bayswater, the forthcoming Golden Jubilee creating an outpouring of energy. The streets echoed with constant hammering and sawing as Venetian masts and triumphal arches were erected while, in every inch of spare space, stands were constructed for the sightseers. A large block of premises in Trafalgar Square had been hired at a cost of £350 (the name 'William Whiteley contractor' figuring prominently on the door), to provide seating for onlookers. All the main streets in the locality, and premises both private and commercial, had plans for decorations and illuminations, whether or not the royal procession would pass by. There was a scheme, to which Whiteley was one of the many contributors, to provide an entertainment for the 'aged deserving poor' and children of the parish.

It was generally anticipated that William Whiteley's display would be the principal attraction of the district. The massive frontages comprising the Queen's Road premises and the twenty-seven shops along Westbourne Grove, gave ample opportunity for a showy display. Local residents eagerly watched the preparations which revealed that the entire length of the property would be decorated from roof to ground level, a particularly exciting prospect in view of the height of the Queen's Road shops. The dominant feature of the street was a central tower with a mansard roof, topped with a flagpole and housing a large clock, which was already becoming a local landmark and favourite meeting place.

In the event, Whiteleys did not disappoint, and the decorations when completed drew large crowds. On the summit of the mansard tower was a ship's mast bearing the royal standard, from which pennons stretched either side along the whole of the block of seven shops. In the second storey of the tower the windows were concealed by drapery on which patriotic mottoes were inscribed, and on the balcony around the clock was a rich bank of tall leafy subtropical plants. A strong feature of the display was the names of British colonies and dependencies emblazoned in bold characters on a red ground with shields and trophies between, with space also devoted to England, Wales, Scotland and Ireland, assigned mottoes such as 'South Britain loves you!', 'The Emerald Isle greets you!' and 'We're a' prood o' ye!' in white on scarlet. The most admired part of the

PLAN OF WESTBOURNE GROVE AND KENSINGTON GARDENS SQUARE PREMISES

FIRST FLOOR PLAN

TO QUEEN'S ROAD

SHIRTS	BOYS' CLOTHING	YOUTHS' CLOTHING	CORSETS	YOUNG LADIES' OUTFITTING	BABY LINEN	LADIES' OUTFITTING	MILLINERY	LADIES AND CHILDREN	BOOTS AND SHOES	FANCY GOODS	TOYS	LADIES' EVENING SHOES
31	33	35	37	39	41	43	45	47	49	51	53	55

WESTBOURNE GROVE

GROUND FLOOR PLAN

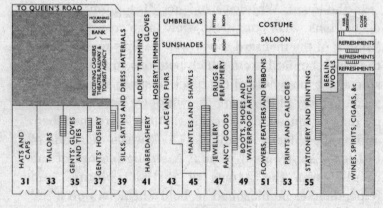

TO QUEEN'S ROAD — MOURNING GOODS — BANK — RECEIVING CASHIERS THEATRE RAILWAY & TOURIST AGENCY — SILKS, SATINS AND DRESS MATERIALS — LADIES' TRIMMING — GLOVES — HOSIERY TRIMMING — UMBRELLAS — SUNSHADES — FITTING ROOM — COSTUME SALOON — HAIR DRESSING — CLOAK ROOM — REFRESHMENTS — REFRESHMENTS — REFRESHMENTS

HATS AND CAPS — TAILORS — GENTS' GLOVES AND TIES — GENTS' HOSIERY — HABERDASHERY — LACE AND FURS — MANTLES AND SHAWLS — JEWELLERY FANCY GOODS — DRUGS & PERFUMERY — BOOTS, SHOES AND WATERPROOF ARTICLES — FLOWERS, FEATHERS AND RIBBONS — PRINTS AND CALICOES — STATIONERY AND PRINTING — BERLIN WOOLS — WINES, SPIRITS, CIGARS, &c

| 31 | 33 | 35 | 37 | 39 | 41 | 43 | 45 | 47 | 49 | 51 | 53 | 55 |

WESTBOURNE GROVE

144

PLAN OF QUEEN'S ROAD
AND DOUGLAS PLACE PREMISES

FIRST FLOOR PLAN

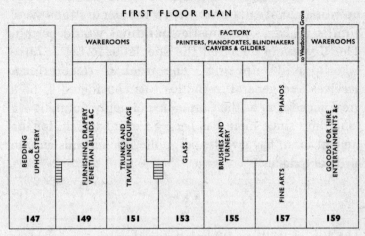

WAREROOMS

FACTORY
PRINTERS, PIANOFORTES, BLINDMAKERS
CARVERS & GILDERS

to Westbourne Grove

WAREROOMS

BEDDING & UPHOLSTERY

FURNISHING DRAPERY VENETIAN BLINDS &C

TRUNKS AND TRAVELLING EQUIPAGE

GLASS

BRUSHES AND TURNERY

PIANOS

FINE ARTS

GOODS FOR HIRE ENTERTAINMENTS &c

147   149   151   153   155   157   159

QUEEN'S ROAD

GROUND FLOOR PLAN

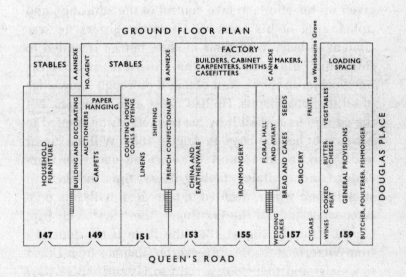

STABLES

A ANNEXE
HO. AGENT

STABLES

B ANNEXE

FACTORY
BUILDERS, CABINET
CARPENTERS, SMITHS
CASEFITTERS

C ANNEXE MAKERS, &

to Westbourne Grove

LOADING SPACE

HOUSEHOLD FURNITURE

BUILDING AND DECORATING
AUCTIONEERS

PAPER HANGING
CARPETS

COUNTING HOUSE COALS & DYEING
LINENS
SHIPPING

FRENCH CONFECTIONARY

CHINA AND EARTHENWARE

IRONMONGERY

FLORAL HALL AND AVIARY

WEDDING CAKES

BREAD AND CAKES

SEEDS

FRUIT

GROCERY

CIGARS

WINES

COOKED MEAT

BUTTER CHEESE

VEGETABLES

GENERAL PROVISIONS

BUTCHER, POULTERER, FISHMONGER

DOUGLAS PLACE

147   149   151   153   155   157   159

QUEEN'S ROAD

145

decorations was a double festoon in red, white and blue with white stars running the whole length of the building. In Westbourne Grove the decorations were similar as far as the smaller buildings would permit. The *Chronicle* declared the spectacle to be 'at once tasteful and imposing'. The week of decorations, services and general festivities was considered to be a great success, or as the *Chronicle* pointedly put it, 'It is a long time since there has been an event which, for the time at least, has sweetened public life and hushed the strife of tongues.'[4]

* * *

The life of William Whiteley was, however, rarely free of strife. Since the separation from Harriet, he had not given up his efforts to take control of the education and upbringing of his sons. His two daughters he was content to leave with their mother, but he intended to introduce his sons into the business as soon as practicable, so they could obtain a thorough knowledge of all its departments. He had many able managers, but the empire he had built by his own efforts he wanted to hand on to his two boys. In August 1887, William junior and Frank, aged 15 and 14, were on vacation from college and Whiteley, feeling it was time for them to stretch their wings, decided to take them with him on a three-week tour of the Continent, their first such trip. On Saturday 6 August 1887 the little party departed from Victoria at 8 a.m., crossed the Channel from Dover to Calais, and then took a train to Ostend where they spent the night at the Hotel Fontaine. On the following morning they were sitting down to enjoy a cup of coffee when the British Consul arrived with an urgent telegram. The news brought an immediate end to the holiday. The Queen's Road premises were in flames again, and the fire was so extensive that it was believed they could not be saved. Whiteley was 'astounded though not overpowered'. He asked the quickest route back to London and was told that if he hurried he could catch the 10 o'clock boat. He at once paid the bill, and gathered his luggage, and an obliging hotel porter drove them to the waterside. They reached Dover at 3.30 p.m., and Victoria two hours later. At 6 p.m. William Whiteley was at the scene of the fire. The telegram had not exaggerated.[5]

At 7 p.m. the previous evening most of Whiteleys was closed for the night, apart from the provisions stores, and the night watchman had started his rounds, noting nothing out of the ordinary. At about seven minutes past, the foreman horsekeeper was relaxing with a quiet pipe when he noticed smoke and flames coming from the third floor of the furniture factory in Douglas Place. He at once summoned the watchman, and the alarm was sounded. While waiting for the fire engines the men tried to fight the fire themselves, but the smoke was so thick they were obliged to retreat into the street. The caretaker and inside firemen employed by Whiteleys activated the hydrants which were kept constantly at the ready with hoses attached, but soon found that the water pressure was insufficient to reach the conflagration on the upper floor, and were obliged to give up. Meanwhile, the employees inside the provisions stores had been alerted and quickly made their escape, which was just as well for it was soon consumed by the flames.

The cries of 'Fire!' had naturally drawn a huge mob to the area, crowding the thoroughfares which soon became almost impassable. Police constables also hurried to the scene, trying against enormous odds to control the suddenly collected seething mass of people, and some unpleasant scuffles took place. 'The quiet street was changed in a moment [wrote an observer]; doors and windows were thrown open; men and women began to run down the road; they scrambled off the 'buses and rushed out of the houses. . . . Every shop disgorged its customers; every house its inhabitants. . . . We could feel the heat now, and the smoke was rolling down into the street. I found myself in the midst of a fighting struggling mass of humanity; women and men pushing different ways, some fighting to get forward, and some struggling to get back.'[6]

By 7.25 a manually operated engine had arrived. Volunteers ran up to man the pumps, but the streams of flame bursting from the building showed that the fire had taken hold and was spreading without restraint. Two firemen, Ambrose Lester and James Brown, at once dashed into the building with a hose, and managed to reach the second-floor landing outside a room in which the fire was blazing fiercely, where, without any protection other than their uniforms and helmets, they endured the heat, directing the water through the doorway on to the flames.

Outside, men were working hard at the pumps when there was a noise which some witnesses described as a rumbling and others as like a cannon-shot or thunderclap, and the walls, weakened by the heat, fell outwards. There was a single shout of warning, and everyone ran, but for many, there was no time to get away. The falling rubble cascaded on to the engine, smashing it beyond recovery, and burying the men, debris injuring several of the spectators. For a moment,

William Whiteley, the Universal
Provider.

Whiteley with his children, *c.* 1882
– from left to right: Clara Louise,
Frank Ernest, Whiteley, Ada
Florence, William junior.

Whiteley's Westbourne Grove premises, *c.* 1900. *(Living London)*

The interior of Whiteleys, Bayswater, *c.* 1999. *(Courtesy of Whiteleys)*

Whiteleys Ltd motorised delivery van, *c.* 1915. *(Courtesy of Eddie Adams)*

RULES OF W. WHITELEY'S ESTABLISHMENT.

Every Employe is liable to be discharged without previous Notice, and has the same privilege of leaving.

Every Employe shall, on admission, sign the Engagement Book, and thereby admit the terms of the Engagement, and that previous Notice to Leave is neither given nor required.

These Rules to be returned to the Counting-House on leaving.

I.—HOURS OF MEALS, WINDOW DRESSING, &c.

	Fine for Non-observance
1. Assistants must be in their places at 8 a.m. ...	6d.
2. First Party, Breakfast, Apprentices 7.30 to 7.45.	
Second „ „ Young Men 7.45 to 8.0.	
Third „ „ „ 8.5 to 8.20.	
First „ „ Young Ladies 8.0 to 8.15.	
Second „ „ „ 8.15 to 8.30.	
3. Half an hour is allowed for Dinner, and a quarter of an hour for Tea	6d.
4. Assistants must not go to any other than their right parties	1/-
5. On Saturdays, the 2.30 Dinner Party must remain at their Counters until the bell rings.	6d.
6. Ten minutes allowed for washing hands before 10.45 after which time Assistants must be at their Counters ready to serve	6d.
7. Window Dressing must be finished by 11.30. No one to commence undressing them until the bell rings for closing.	
8. Young ... and Young Ladies to Dust as per List from 8.0 to 8.8	6d.

II.—DRESS

	Fine for Non-observance
9. Each Young Lady in the shop to be dressed in a Plain Black Stuff Dress, made to clear the ground, Plain Linen Sailor Collar and Cuffs. No Colours, and only Black Jewellery	6d.
10. Young Ladies in the Show Rooms to be dressed in Black Silk Dresses, Plain White Collars and Cuffs. No Colours, and only Black Jewellery	6d.
11. No Rings to be worn in business by any one.	
12. Young Men must wear Black Coats and Waistcoats, Light Boots, and Dark Ties	6d.

III.—ATTENTION TO CUSTOMERS.

	Fine for Non-observance
13. Up to 11 o'clock a portion of each Counter must be kept clear for Customers	6d.
14. Assistants must do their very best to please Customers, and use the utmost civility to all.	
15. No Assistant to allow a Customer to leave the Shop unserved, without speaking to the Shopwalker, under pain of dismissal.	
16. Serve well and quickly, but do not hurry Customers on any account.	
17. Never have much Stock before a Customer at once. When practicable, put away one article before bringing another.	
18. Anyone disengaged is expected to render assistance to anyone serving	6d.
19. Each one to serve in their own place, unless it is the Shopwalker's or Customer's wish to the contrary	6d.
20. No one to refuse to bring Goods from any part of the Shop, but to refer to the Shopwalker ...	6d.
21. No Assistant to give over a Customer to another without permission of the Shopwalker	6d.
22. A Shopwalker must always be called to conduct a Customer from one part of the Shop to another	6d.
23. The price of Goods must be told to Customers distinctly. Never quote the price of an Article over 1/- in pence. Instance—14½d. should be told 1/2½	6d.
24. Customers wishing to exchange one Article for another must be referred to the Shopwalker ...	6d.

IV.—READY MONEY, CHANGE, &c.

	Fine for Non-observance
25. Always bear in mind that this is a Ready Money Business, and endeavour to get paid for Goods sold at time of purchase. Never ask Customers if they will pay on Delivery, or have Goods entered, but present the Bill for payment ...	6d.
26. On receiving Money from Customers always tell them the Amount before removing from Counter; and place same in left-hand corner at foot of Bill. Do not anticipate the Coin about to be tendered, wait until you see it before putting it on the Bill	6d.
27. Examine Change carefully before leaving the Desk and handing it to the Customer	6d.
28. Any Assistant taking Bad Money must pay the full amount.	
29. In case of any dispute as to the amount of Money received from or given to a Customer, the Assistant must pay half the amount disputed.	
30. In handing Customers Coppers place them in a Pence Envelope	6d.
31. All Bankers' Cheques, Provincial Notes, &c., must be shown to the Chief Cashier before accepting them as Payment.	
32. Assistants are strictly enjoined to pay in all Monies to the Desk immediately they receive them from Customers; any infraction of this Rule will render the Assistant liable to instant dismissal.	
33. ... ... before the Goods are packed up	...
34. Any Assistant selling an Article and neglecting to charge for it will be liable for the amount.	
35. Assistants are requested to pay particular attention to their position on the Weekly Takings List.	

V.—BILLS, DUPLICATES, CHECK SHEETS, &c.

	Fine for Non-observance
36. In making out Bills write perfectly legible, define each Article by name and department, and place the figures in the proper columns. This is very important, as from inattention large sums may be dissected to the Wrong Department, while the Right Department loses all, and after a lapse of time Customers cannot recollect having purchased an article not particularized, for instance —in the Dress Department articles must be specified as under:—	
12 Dress Merino ⎫ In the Print Department.	
12 Dress Lustre ⎬ 12 Dpy. Muslin.	
12 Dress Barege ⎭ 12 „ Lawn	6d
37. All Bills must have Assistant's number and date. The Goods must be called back and the Bill examined by next Assistant	6d.
38. In the event of an Under-Charge the serving Assistant and Examiner will be liable for the amount.	
39. Directly a Bill is made out the amount must be entered in the proper column on Check Sheet ...	6d.
40. Assistants must be careful not to put names and addresses of Customers at foot of Paid Bills ...	6d.
41. Assistants must not make out Bills in books other than their own	6d.
42. Care must be taken that Duplicates and Parcel Dockets are not lost or mislaid	2/6
43. Particulars of Duplicates passed through any channel other than the Cash Desk must be furnished to the Cashier on a form provided for the purpose	6d.
44. No Assistant to touch a Duplicate after it has been filed nor question the Cashier respecting it	6d.
45. Check Slips must be added correctly and alterations must be avoided	6d.
46. All Check Sheets must be filed between 6 and 6.30, and on Saturdays between 1 and 1.30	6d.
47. After the words "Check Forward" are shown at the Desk a New Check Slip must be obtained and no further amounts put on the old one ...	6d.

Page 1 of The Rules of W. Whiteley's Establishment, c.1887.
(Courtesy National Archives)

The fire of 1887, according to a contemporary engraving.
(Illustrated London News)

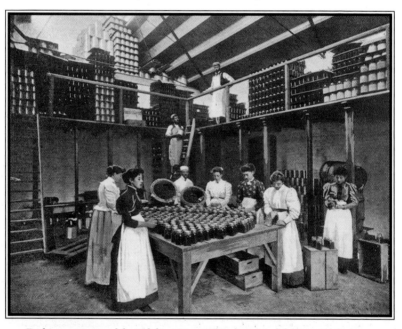

Packing syrups and fruit delicacies at Whiteley's model farm and factory,
Hanworth, 1895 – his only major business failure.
(Orchards and Gardens, courtesy British Library 7028.de.28)

The inquest on William Whiteley at Paddington. *(Daily Graphic)*

Harriet Whiteley and son Frank leaving the inquest.

An artist's impression of the murder of William Whiteley. *(Illustrated Police News, 1907)*

Horace George Rayner.

Rayner in the dock at the Police Court.
(Daily Graphic, 1907)

HORACE GEORGE RAYNER
IN THE WITNESS BOX

RAYNER IN THE DOCK

MR MUIR
THE PROSECUTING
COUNSEL FOR THE
PROSECUTION

THE RAYNER TRIAL
AT THE NEW
OLD BAILEY

LOUISA TURNER

ALICE MAY RAYNER
PRISONER'S WIFE

ANNIE KNOWLES   SARAH KNOWLES

From *The Penny Illustrated Paper*, March 30, 1907

Personalities at the trial of Horace Rayner. *(The Penny Illustrated Paper, 1907)*

An artist's impression of the funeral
of William Whiteley.
(Daily Graphic, 1907)

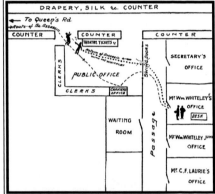

A sketch plan of where the
murder took place. *(Daily Mirror)*

An aerial view of Whiteley's model village, founded with his legacy.
(Courtesy of The Whiteley Homes Trust)

there was panic in the scattering crowds, then they turned and ran back to the scene of devastation, police, firemen and civilians alike, some of them bleeding from scalp wounds, to extricate men from the ruins, and give first aid to the injured. Mr Wrayson, the new manager of the Baths, although severely injured, led the rescue work. Four men were pulled from the rubble. One was taken to hospital, the other three, their skulls smashed by the falling masonry, were obviously dead.

Inside the stricken building, firemen Lester and Brown had suddenly found themselves enveloped in a mass of flame. The roof above them crashed in, and, struck by the burning debris, both men were hurled bodily down the stairs. Bruised, half blinded, his face and hands scorched, Lester realised that he had been carried down to the landing below. Somehow he managed to grope his way down the stairs and eventually emerged into the street. There, getting his breath back, he looked around him and realised that Brown was not with him. The staircase was by now ablaze, but undeterred, he ran back into the building, climbed back up to the landing and there found Brown buried by debris, and semi-conscious. Somehow he managed to get him to his feet and both men made it to safety. (They recovered in hospital, and it is pleasing to note that by 1901 Lester had been promoted to Superintendent.)

The steamers started to arrive, racing to the scene from all over London, and soon, every street and court from which the fire could be reached was filled with engines and miles of hose. The fire was both fierce and rapid. Much of the stock was highly inflammable, and matters were made worse by a lengthy summer drought which had dried the outside timbers. Deep in the heart of the vast building, lead gas pipes were melting in the heat, creating fresh bursts of flame, and the iron doors between the blocks of buildings were red hot.

News of this latest and greatest Whiteley fire soon spread to all parts of the city, and the sightseers flooded in. 'Never did Bayswater see such an invasion of cabs as that Saturday night [wrote the *Chronicle*]. All the hansoms of the West End seem to have driven hither. All the highways and byways around Queen's Road were blocked with them. They stood in long files in Bishop's Road, Inverness Terrace, Porchester Gardens, Porchester Road, Westbourne Grove, and the cry was "Still they come!" People drove in from Acton, Ealing, Willesden, and even from Uxbridge, but the cab traffic from the West End from 9 to 3 o'clock was quite unparalleled in the annals of Whiteley's' fires. At Oxford Circus the hansoms were actually touting with "Whiteleys' fire, sir? Whiteleys' fire!"'[7]

Crowds also made their way on foot, women with perambulators, and with children in their arms, pressing forward for a better look. 'A "Whiteley's' fire" crowd always know where to go for the different points of view of the fire', observed the *Chronicle*,[8] and Kensington Gardens Square was particularly patronised. One determined onlooker took up a position on the roof of 166 Queen's Road opposite and stayed there all night. As the evening wore on, and the fire-fighters toiled, the fire made its way inexorably along the handsome stone-fronted block of shops. Afterwards, it was said that it was like seeing a volcano – perhaps in more ways than one, since onlookers who approached too close felt the fierce heat and were peppered with showers of sparks and burning debris, the children cheering when fragments landed on a gentleman's top hat. Some of the

customers of the Paddington Baths, having just made
themselves comfortable, were bawled out by an
attendant and were obliged to cluster into a waiting-
room semi-clothed and grumbling. This time, however,
the building was not affected.

As in previous fires great efforts were made to save the
animals in the menagerie. The birds were rescued and
safely housed, but when the dogs and puppies were
being carried out in a box, the bottom dropped out, and
the terrified animals ran back into the building to their
deaths. The monkeys and marmosets were so bewildered
that they cowered behind screens and could not be
reached. It was necessary to leave them to their fate.

At 9 o'clock a ladder was raised so the firemen could
reach the mansard tower, and to some observers it
looked as though they now had mastery of the fire, and
the excitement was all over. Enormous amounts of water
were poured on to the flames in an effort to save the
tower, but finally the flag fell into the road, and was
hailed with loud cheers from the crowd. Slowly but
surely the fire was winning. The third and fourth floors
over the clock caught fire and eventually the men were
driven back, while burning zinc flowed from the roof in
a blue flame.

An extensible ladder was brought and placed against
a high building, six men climbing to the top so they
could observe the fire better and direct the efforts of
their colleagues. It was while they were doing this that a
sudden burst of flame set fire to the lower part of the
ladder. It was only the support lashing that prevented
catastrophe and the men were able to make their rapid
but charred escape.

By late evening, the fire was at its height, the columns
of flame and dense clouds of smoke reaching up into the

sky. The tower was a mass of flame, presenting, according to the *Chronicle*, 'a magnificent appearance'⁹ but at 10.55 p.m. the whole structure fell bodily into the abyss below, and flames shot up for 30ft from the roof and continued to do so for another 20 minutes.

Another danger was the massive stone cornices on three of the shops, and Captain Shaw was only just in time to warn his men to move out of the way before the blocks, some of them weighing more than a ton, fell into the road. At 11.35 the ornamental arches below the mansard roof fell, and an hour later the much-loved clock, which had continued ticking throughout, was knocked down by a falling block of stone and rolled into the road. The greatest and most brilliant sight of all was saved till last – the burning of the linoleum warehouse, which must have been seen 30 miles away.

By 1 o'clock in the morning much of the row of seven shops had been destroyed, as had a number of houses in Kensington Gardens Square. Seven families in York Mews had lost their homes, and in Douglas Place the houses of Whiteley's old adversary Mr Record had also suffered. Two days later fire engines were still pouring water on the smouldering ruins, and it was anticipated that it would be several more days before the last embers were extinguished.

Interviewed by the *Chronicle*, Whiteley followed his usual extraordinary policy of putting a cheerful and unruffled face on the disaster, which, in view of the deaths, might not have been in the best of taste. He met the reporters with a broad smile on his face, seeming not in the least depressed by events. 'I came back fully prepared for the worst, but I scarcely thought matters would prove so bad as they have done. It is the most disastrous loss I have as yet sustained, and would paralyse most men. But I am not disheartened. I have inexhaustible energy and indomitable business pluck, and with the aid of these I do not doubt as to my ability to face this reverse, great though it may be.'[10] 'Business as usual' was, as ever, the motto, and Whiteley informed the newspapers: 'May I beg the favour of your making the announcement that, notwithstanding that the fire which took place at my Queen's Road premises on Saturday last is the most calamitous that has yet occurred, I have been enabled to complete arrangements for carrying on the business of every department without delay or inconvenience to my customers.'[11]

Desolate as the scene was, with the smouldering ruins, buckled girders, the roadway filled with piles of debris and blocks of fallen stone, and the dangerously teetering walls of the burnt-out buildings, the Westbourne Grove shops opened as usual, and no. 147 Queen's Road, which escaped unscathed, was also opened, despite the difficulty of the public reaching it through a police cordon.

Whiteley convened an enquiry at his premises, assisted by Mr Roche and several of his most prominent managers, James Keith, Richard Burbidge (later Sir Richard and managing director of Harrods) and John Arthur. All were convinced that the fire was the work of an arsonist and also that some explosive device such as dynamite had been used.

There had never previously been a full enquiry into a Whiteleys fire, since coroners had for some years been prohibited from enquiring into fires unless a death had occurred. This time, an inquest was convened in the schoolroom under Westbourne Park Chapel on the morning of Wednesday 10 August. The eldest victims were Robert Hyde, a 63-year-old picture restorer who had distinguished himself in fire-fighting on many previous occasions, and had once been awarded a testimonial, and John Hampden Gill, a painter, aged 41, both of whom had left a widow and child unprovided for, while the youngest, 22-year-old Henry Mugridge, an assistant foreman in the packing department, had been the sole support of his widowed mother.

William Penfold, the engineer of the local fire station at Hermitage Street, Westbourne Grove, had some awkward questions put to him by Mr Roche, who wanted to know why there was a delay in sending out the steamers. Penfold explained that due to the time required in getting up steam, the manuals were always sent out first. But why, Mr Roche pressed on, were the steamers not sent out soon afterwards? Embarrassingly, it emerged that the steamers did not follow at once because, due to lack of finances, the station had only two horses, which took the manuals out first then had to return to take the steamers. The jury was suitably appalled by this state of affairs. In view of the suggestion that an explosion had taken place before the wall fell down the foreman of the jury said that they would like to hear from an explosives expert. He expressed the jury's condolences to the families of the victims, and Mr Roche took the opportunity to thank the hundreds of people who had sent letters of sympathy to Mr Whiteley. Even as the hearing proceeded, a fourth body was found in the debris. It was that of 29-year-old James Johns, a carman, who left a widow and three small children.

On the following day the funeral of the four victims took place. The procession consisted of four cars and nine coaches, and the streets were crowded with onlookers who watched in respectful silence, while at

Brompton Cemetery thousands more awaited the ceremony. The cortège had hardly begun when it was noticed with some dismay, that although three of the coffins were covered with floral tributes, that of Johns stood out starkly from the rest, having no decoration at all. As the cars passed by the Café Royal the flower girl who stood there ran impulsively into the roadway and threw her entire stock of flowers on to the bare coffin.

On 17 August, the inquest – now into the deaths of four men – was resumed at the Westbourne Institute. Colonel Majendie, chief inspector under the Explosives Act, who had made a detailed examination of the premises, read a very long report. He believed that the fire had been alight but 'bottled up' for some considerable time before the wall fell, but saw no sign at all of any explosive devices. Any sound like an explosion as reported by witnesses he attributed to the noise of the falling building or some minor secondary explosion of gas or inflammable substances. Other scientific evidence agreed with his conclusions.

In evidence, Whiteley said that he was convinced that every one of the fires at his premises had been deliberately started, although he had no idea by whom. He thought it very likely that the culprit or culprits were familiar with the layout of the premises, and that it was less likely to be a past employee than someone currently employed, who, since the doors were guarded, would have had easier access to the building. The jury agreed, but in view of the complexity of the case, proposed to adjourn until 24 October. In the meantime, appeals had been launched through the local newspapers for the families of the fire victims, and a sympathetic public ensured that money soon poured in to assist the destitute.

Whiteley offered a reward of £2,000 for information about the arsonist, and his buyers put up another £1,000 out of their own salaries, but without result. The police, one of whom was Inspector Abberline who was to achieve fame in the following year when investigating the Whitechapel murders, were busy interviewing the numerous Whiteleys staff, but also drew a blank.

The shopkeepers of Bayswater were extremely anxious to show their support for and sympathy with Mr Whiteley, mainly in order to defuse any suspicion that the fires had their roots in business rivalry. On 16 August a meeting of local tradesmen was held at the premises of Mr William Owen, who chaired the event. Present were all the most prominent of those men who might at one time have been considered Mr Whiteley's enemies, including Mr Record. Mr Owen made a splendid speech. A disaster to Mr Whiteley, he said, was a disaster to the neighbourhood. He thought they should be proud to have such a wonderful man among them. Mr Whiteley's establishment was the most wonderful place he had ever been into. 'There was not a square yard in the vast and extensive premises but was utilised, for even small and out-of-the-way corners were occupied, even if it was only with one woman at work.' Mr Whiteley, he said 'must be a genius'. All of them must sympathise with him for he had suffered a great financial loss, not being insured.

Mr Bell, the Hon. Secretary, added that 'Mr Whiteley had contributed more than any man to make Bayswater a splendid centre for business, therefore he was deserving of their sympathy. . . . It was utterly untrue that the trading classes were opposed to him, as had been suggested in some quarters.' There were cries of 'hear, hear'. The meeting decided to send Mr Whiteley a

signed document, expressing their sympathy, and, on a
more practical note, a subscription was opened for the
families of the victims.[12]

The newspapers too had nothing but sympathy. 'He is
an enterprising man who has raised himself to his
present eminence as a tradesman by keen foresight,
quick perception of his chances, untiring perseverance,
and indomitable pluck, qualities which, while trade
holds the important place it does as a factor in the
fortunes of Englishmen, will always be highly prized',
commented the editor of the *Paddington Times*.[13] The
American newspapers were less sympathetic. The
Chronicle reprinted the report in the *Boston Evening
Record* of 10 August: 'Merchant Whiteley's sixth fire in
five years almost obscures politics as a topic of
conversation. Everybody has his own theory of how the
fire originated. Whiteley . . . who is a self-made man,
vulgar, pushing, egotistic, has built up an immense
business from a very humble beginning.' The *Chronicle*,
deploring the sensational mode of reporting with
'a profusion of headlines in large capital letters . . .',
commented: 'The chief feature in the narrative is
"Whiteley's enormous wealth" – a notion evidently dear
to the American retail mind.'[14]

Meanwhile, the *Pall Mall Gazette*, a newspaper noted
for its highly colourful reporting and love of the
sensational, was asking the question which had to be
uppermost in the public mind: 'Why is Whiteley's so often
burned down?' For the *Gazette* it went without saying that
the fires were due to arson, and for the purposes of
revenge against Mr Whiteley. But for what motive?
Dismissing the theory of a business rival, some small
tradesman who had been 'crushed under the Juggernaut
car of low prices and unlimited competition . . .', also the

romantic revenge of some injured lady, the third theory emerged. An informant who said he had a relative employed at Whiteleys had approached the *Gazette* and painted a picture of the store at once shocking and yet perhaps hardly surprising. 'The place . . . seethes with discontent. So far as I know, whether male or female, those who are employed by Whiteley regard their master with feelings of intense dislike. I was surprised at the extent and vehemence of this sentiment; but my surprise died away when I saw the rules of the establishment.' He then produced the list of rules which numbered 176 in all, imposing fines for a wide range of offences: 'in no place that I know of in London or the provinces is there anything approaching to the wholesale system of fine for this, for that, and for everything else, that exists at Whiteleys. But in every other place that I know of the fines go to a fund for the benefit of the employees themselves. In Whiteleys the fines go to the employer.' Whiteleys, he revealed, even had a fines department with its own team of clerks.

And this was not all: 'his whole system is one of slave driving from top to bottom. Whiteley himself patrols the establishment like a roaring lion. Like master like man, and all Jacks in office in Whiteleys pattern themselves upon their chiefs.'[15]

These fines seem extraordinarily petty nowadays. The standard fine, 6*d*, equivalent to about £1.70 today, was imposed for flouting such rules as taking meal breaks at the incorrect time, standing on a chair, failing to put copper coins into a pence envelope when giving change, failing to call a shopwalker to conduct a customer to another part of the premises, or not amending a ticket when a length was sold off a piece. An assistant taking bad money was liable to pay the shop the full amount. An assistant who allowed a customer to leave a shop unserved without speaking to the shopwalker would be immediately dismissed. Rule number 176 was that any offence not covered by the previous 175 was subject to a fine of 6*d*.

An old established rule which Whiteley always believed was utterly fair to all parties, was that every employee could be discharged without notice, while no notice of leaving was required from the employee. On admission every employee was obliged to sign an engagement book, effectively agreeing to the rules, so that any attempt at later redress was doomed to failure.[16]

This article produced a torrent of correspondence, both for and against the Whiteley regime. It was revealed that after being fined, the name and department of each miscreant was posted on a green baize board in the dining hall for everyone to see. Many of the employees who contacted the newspapers nevertheless expressed the view that the fines were necessary and if anyone was fined they deserved it. Some correspondents complained about the food and the accommodation though others said they had never been better fed or housed. Another declared that the fines were spent on subscriptions to hospitals, and grants to the house library. The contradictory nature of the letters makes it hard to arrive at any picture of what life at Whiteleys was like, or, importantly, whether it was substantially different from that in other large establishments. The matter having been aired, however, the question of whether Whiteleys' fines were illegal was examined by the Home Office in the following year, but ultimately no prosecution was brought. This scrutiny may well have signalled the beginning of the end of the fines system in general.

* * *

On 20 October 1887 an unusual deputation arrived at 31 Porchester Terrace, the handsome villa which had been the home of William Whiteley since the mid-1880s. Led by William Owen, the object was to present Whiteley with an address expressing the sympathy of local tradesmen. 'Our presence here this evening,' said Mr Owen, 'will I trust be a sufficient answer to any ill-founded opinion that may be entertained that you have not the goodwill of your fellow tradesmen and neighbours.'

Whiteley was appreciative in response. 'Well, gentlemen, I am not quite ruined either in pluck or purse. I have still left me a clear conscience, a light heart, a good constitution, and some true friends, so that after all I am bound to consider myself rich.' When the speeches were over the gentlemen retired to the dining-room for 'an agreeable hour'.[17]

The adjourned inquest was reopened on 24 October. The police had seen every employee and conducted over a hundred interviews. Every clue offered by anonymous correspondents had been followed up, but nothing had been discovered. Inspector Abberline pronounced himself baffled. In summing up, the coroner commented that it had been pretty well proven that there had been no explosive device, and there was no direct evidence of incendiarism. Despite this, the jury returned the opinion that the fire had been started deliberately.

Against all expectations, Whiteleys arose from the ashes in time for Christmas. On 6 December, the provisions department was reopened, while the annual bazaar was in full swing. The person who had set the blaze was never identified, but perhaps the loss of life had had a sobering effect on his hatred. Whiteleys was never again to be the victim of an arsonist's attack.

TEN

Old Farmer William

Although the last nineteen years of William Whiteley's life lacked those scenes of public conflict and high drama which characterised the period from 1871 to 1887, nevertheless they were packed with incident and activity. The approach of old age did nothing to quell his endless desire to expand the business; striving, and indeed invariably claiming always to be the world's best in every new venture he undertook. The trumpeting of these claims made it more noticeable when, as sometimes happened, he came unstuck, and attempted with varying degrees of success to wriggle out of the consequences, his way oiled as ever by the ingenious Mr Roche. It was a time when he could bask sunnily in the regard and admiration of his business associates, customers and, to a great extent, his employees, while at functions such as concerts, dinners and sports days, he was hailed as a jolly good fellow with satisfying regularity. To the world he displayed a permanent, and well-nigh indelible geniality, and was generous with his homilies to younger men, advising them that business success came with hard work, ingenuity, attention to detail and scrupulous honesty. The private man could be tyrannical and insensitive, all cordiality when he had his own way, but cold and implacable when he did not.

In 1888, owing to a quarrel about which the four participants were understandably cagey, there was a

major and final falling out between William, Louie,
George and Emily, originating when Whiteley accused
George of paying his attentions to Louie. While these
matters were simmering, Louie went to Whiteleys to
have it out with her lover and a very stormy scene was
enacted in his private room. Screams of 'Murder!'
brought assistants running into the room where they
found their employer struggling with his erstwhile
mistress, trying to cover her mouth with his hand, while
she threatened to make her grievances known to the
world. Louie stormed out, and as a parting shot,
declared, 'You know you are the father of this child! Are
you going to let him starve?' Whiteley gave orders that
from then on her account was to be closed.[1]

George took action for slander but it never came to
court. Sir George Lewis acted for Whiteley, and
negotiated a private financial arrangement of which no
records remain. The incident naturally left some
residual bitterness, especially with George Rayner. It is
possible that he was unaware, or maybe over the
ensuing years forgot, that Emily's acquaintanceship
with Whiteley did not commence until after Horace's
birth. The row over the oldest boy's parentage still
rankled, and years later it suited Rayner to wonder
about Horace, too.

In February 1888 the scaffolding was finally taken
down in Queen's Road, the clock, 'the most favoured
trysting place in Bayswater',[2] was restored, and no sign
remained of the great fire. It had cost Whiteley dear – he
had been obliged to pursue through the courts one of the
few small insurances he had been able to take out,
finally winning a verdict for the insignificant sum of
£1,461 7s 9d. The installation of an automatic sprinkler
system enabled him to obtain a moderate amount of

insurance for the new buildings. There remained a
natural anxiety at the merest hint of fire, and in July
when a dropped match burnt two holes in a carpet in
the trunks department, rumours at once flew around the
neighbourhood of a serious conflagration avoided.

That month, enquiries into corruption at the
Metropolitan Board of Works threw an interesting light
on the reasons behind the rapid spread of fire through
Whiteley's premises. Horace Gundry, the district
surveyor of Paddington, said that in 1875 he had called
the attention of the Board to the building of Mr
Whiteley's warehouse in the Queen's Road. He believed
it to be in contravention of the Building Act because its
substantial cubic measurement should have been
subdivided by party walls.

Lord Herschell, who was conducting the enquiry,
asked, 'Who was the architect of that building?' 'Mr
Ebenezer Saunders', the witness replied, creating a
sensation, since Saunders was a member of the Board.
Gundry added that following his report on the
contravention of the Act, the Board was a long time in
coming to any decision, while in the meantime, the
building work was proceeding rapidly. Eventually the
Building Act Committee of the Board decided that as the
building was a warehouse, it would not be used for
retail purposes, so it was not necessary to instruct the
district surveyor to proceed against the builder.

'This place was burnt down?' said Lord Herschell.
'Yes.'
'It is partly as a protection against fire that these
subdivisions are required by the law?'
'Yes, in order to enable the firemen to check the
progress of the fire.'

Gundry also confirmed that Mr Roche was a member of the Board of Works at that time.[3] The enquiry must have thought Mr Whiteley had been sufficiently punished for his contravention of the Act, as it seems no action was taken against him.

From time to time, rumours good and bad would circulate about Whiteleys, causing a storm of excitement over the tea tables of Bayswater. A small flurry was created by the opening in Westbourne Grove of a new butter-market, proving that Whiteley did not always offer the lowest prices, although his side of the road scored in the matter of elegance. 'I do not wish to imply any disparagement,' wrote a correspondent to the *Chronicle*, 'when I remark that [the new butter-market] appeals to a very different class of buyers than those who are accustomed to shop in the Grove, and that the hurry of the customers, the pushing of the spectators, and above all the loafing of the loafers, which still continues on the field of action, would not for a moment be tolerated on the opposite side of the street – the Whiteley promenade.'[4]

When the budget of 1888 introduced a tax on carts and vans, it was natural that the newspapers should turn to Whiteley for an opinion. 'I must confess that this will make a rather heavy item in my expenses, since I employ over 200 carts and vans,' he observed; 'Then I see there is a horse tax. That is a good measure altogether, I consider. If a man has the money to keep a pleasure horse, he can afford to pay £1 per annum for a license; and the £5 on racehorses is a tax in the right place. No, I do not deal in horses; I will have nothing whatever to do with the turf.'[5]

In 1889 it was widely believed that he would be starting a branch in Holloway, a suggestion he was quick to dismiss. 'I would sooner think of establishing a branch at Bombay or Calcutta than at Holloway. If the Holloway people want to buy my goods they can come to Westbourne Grove. . . . The truth is,' he added, 'I am against branches, for I believe in the master's eye being everywhere, and I have hardly enough eyes to keep this place always straight. This very day I have discovered that for the last three years I have been cheated at the rate of £15 per week. . . .'[6]

He was referring to a scheme devised by Wallace Colbourne who had obtained a place as a ledger clerk to Whiteleys using false references, while his wife Amy impersonated a customer with a deposit account. They had obtained £300 worth of goods a year which they had then sold on to a licensed victualler.

Whiteleys suffered from numerous such schemes in this period, of varying ingenuity. Embezzlement and shoplifting prosecutions were common, and in 1895 a couple attempted a complex fraud, one they had carried out before. They would rent a house and furniture and, when the rent was unpaid and the bailiffs arrived, one of the couple – they took turns – claimed to be the lodger of the other, and owner of the furniture. Having worked this scheme on Whiteley, they then, with some effrontery, accused him of levying an illegal distress on his own goods. This proved to be a trick too many, as the entire fraudulent structure was revealed in court.[7]

Interviewed in 1894, Whiteley stated that shoplifting was on the increase. The offenders were almost all women, and of the middle and upper classes. Large pockets and loose cloaks made it especially easy to conceal small items of finery. He had once discovered that the three daughters of an eminent barrister were frequent offenders, and, perhaps anticipating a difficult day in court, did not have them arrested, but called on their father. The parent, refusing to believe that his daughters were thieves, became livid with rage and threatened Whiteley with ruin. An appointment was made for 10 o'clock the following morning, on which occasion, said the irate father, Whiteley should be prepared to be given into custody. Whiteley retreated, and promptly at 10 the next day, the barrister appeared, a changed man. 'When I saw the poor man's face I almost wished I had been able to keep his daughters' misdoings from him. He was a self-confident, bouncing kind of man, but in those few hours he had grown old and haggard and depressed.' A grovelling apology was naturally forthcoming, with gratitude at having been spared a public scandal. According to Whiteley – adding a touch of melodrama to the story – the man shortly afterwards sold his house, gave up his position at the Bar and left England.[8]

Another feature of the closing decades of the nineteenth century was the increasing number of substantial parties, festivals and carnivals which were catered for by Whiteleys. In March 1889 a successful ice carnival at the Albert Hall raised £2,000 for the West End Hospital, while in August that year Whiteley organised a trip to see a naval review, a special train taking passengers to Southampton where the paddle steamer *Juno* waited in readiness to convey them to Spithead to enjoy the best possible view of the manoeuvres, with all meals being provided on board. In October 600 guests lunched in a marquee at the opening of Mansfield College, Oxford, and an Assyriologist present wondered if in old cuneiform records would be found accounts of Whiteley's old-world prototypes.

Royal events were always a favourite, and at a visit of the Princess of Wales to Westbourne Hall in May 1890,

Whiteley was at the centre of things as usual. 'Stout, stalwart, good-looking Mr Whiteley was well in evidence, trying to regulate matters in the crowded lobby of the Hall', reported the *Chronicle*. He later presented two bouquets of white flowers to the Princesses Victoria and Maud.[9]

That month it was reported that Whiteley had purchased several acres of land near Ealing where he proposed to establish a flower farm. There may have been some element of competitiveness in this move. William Owen was a grower of chrysanthemums and a regular prize-winner at shows. Each October his shop would put on a show of his award-winning plants and, excellent as Whiteley's own show was, he was unable to equal that of Mr Owen. Whiteley could only stand so much of being second best. Unable to beat Owen at chrysanthemums, he decided to grow orchids. By May 1891 the *Chronicle* was reporting: 'The "Universal Provider" has taken to flower-farming on a large scale, and his acres of grounds and glasshouses at Hillingdon near West Drayton, and other parts of Middlesex are a sight to see. During the present week he is exhibiting, at the pretty conservatory in Queen's Road a beautiful collection of grand prize orchids, for which he has just been awarded silver and bronze medals by the Royal Horticultural Society.'[10]

In July, a reporter from the *Chronicle* accepted an invitation to visit the farm and was given the full tour, with Whiteley acting as his personal guide. The resulting article was everything Whiteley must have hoped for.

Few people are aware that Mr William Whiteley has become a country flower and fruit grower on a grand scale. . . . This is a fresh revelation to those who do

not know the versatile genius of the man, and his
power of taking up with entirely new branches of
industry which at first sight appear to be outside the
ordinary commercial *rôle*. . . . I had already heard of
the great strawberry farm at Finchley . . . but the
Hillingdon enterprise is one of far greater pith and
moment; it is an experiment in commercial gardening
on a grand scale . . . the Middlesex town of Hillingdon
is a mile and a half from Uxbridge. A wall 15ft high
encloses 11 acres. A square water tower overlooks the
entire farm. The frontage is the stables, van-entrances,
and five or six gardeners' cottages. Inside the area is
divided by another wall of the same height as the
boundary. One half is conservatories, forcing houses,
gardeners' sheds; the other is open and is for the
growing of hardy root and fruit crops. . . . Mr
Whiteley is an excellent talker, and a man of perfect
manners and unfailing courtesy. After acting as
attentive guide and interpreter for four or five hours,
he leaves you with all the freshness, politeness and
suavity with which he began. Fortunately he is
blessed with a splendid physique – with a giant's
strength in a square-set, well-knit frame.[11]

There were seventy-one glasshouses for growing grapes,
peaches, nectarines, tomatoes and mushrooms, while
the forcing houses provided luxury flowers, palms and
foliage plants. Careful planning and forethought ensured
the distribution of water all over the farm. Whiteley,
admitting that he was not an expert in these matters,
explained, 'It is for me to buy the best advice I can get;
to select my men, and then to give them a free hand.'[12]

As in the stores there was an impressive economy of
space. No area went unused – even the boundary wall was

occupied by the cultivation of wall fruits such as apricots and nectarines. 'The Universal Provider though by no means a nervous man, would absolutely shudder at the sight of a single superficial foot of unoccupied space.'[13]

One of the more unusual items of merchandise Whiteleys dealt in was the provision of young single men for parties, where, it seems, a man who could 'talk and dance and make himself agreeable . . .' was a scarce item in the Christmas season. The *Pall Mall Gazette* heard that there was a selection to be had at a guinea a head and sent a lady investigator. The tale was told in full by the *Chronicle*. The lady struggled through the Christmas crowds to be shown, among others, 'a dapper little man, nice looking and on the right side of thirty . . .' who danced well and undertook to rescue any wallflowers, and a bronzed, military looking fellow with battle scars and a luxuriant moustache, who promised to wear his uniform and amuse the ladies with anecdotes. After departing she found it 'positively painful' to dash their hopes by writing to say that the gentlemen would not, after all, be required.[14]

Thomas Anstey Guthrie, author of humorous works under the name F. Anstey, was inspired by this article to write a comic sketch entitled *The Man From Blankley's*, which was published in *Punch* in 1893. In this piece, a snobbish Bayswater couple hire a man from Blankley's for their dinner party, then realise he is not needed. Unsure if they have successfully cancelled, they assume that the stranger who arrives claiming to be a member of the nobility is actually a jumped-up shop assistant. The amusing but fairly predictable consequences do not need to be described. The sketch was later extended into a full-length play and performed in London's West End in 1901 and 1906, and it was filmed in 1930.

William junior and Frank were now working with their father, having followed the course he had designed for them. After school, they had gone to college at Eastbourne, and on leaving went to live at Porchester Terrace and were introduced into the business, Mr. Keith acting as mentor. The 1891 census finds Whiteley and his sons there, each boy's occupation described as 'assistant to his father', the only other members of the household being a housekeeper, a butler, a groom, a cook and two housemaids. Whiteley held a grand celebratory dinner for each of his sons when they reached the age of 21. Whether he marked the majority of his daughters is not known.

Not content with the farms at Finchley and Hillingdon, Whiteley determined on a bigger and better project – the establishment of a model farm and factory where he could not only produce fruit and raise animals, but convert them on site into products which would then be delivered to his shops. In 1891 after a year of searching for the right property, he purchased the freeholds of Butts Farm and Glebe Farm at Hanworth, 3 miles west of Isleworth, which he combined into an estate comprising 200 acres of land. He at once started extensive conversion work. In April 1892 he acquired the freehold of another block of houses on the Queen's Road, and a large plot of land in Kensington for a furniture warehouse, which was to be lit solely by daylight and electricity.

All this activity stimulated another rumour; that the leases of the shops in Westbourne Grove were about to cease and Whiteley was therefore giving up his business there, leaving twenty empty shops. The only thing that was empty was the rumour. The acquisitions he had made were for the purposes not of retreating from the

Grove but of consolidating the whole of his business in Bayswater. The public heaved a sigh of relief; 'there has scarcely been an afternoon tea during the last month at which this absurd "Whiteley scare" has not been brought up,' a lady wrote to the *Chronicle*. 'Mr Whiteley must not think I am flattering his vanity when I add that in every case the rumour was discussed with something like panic.'[15]

The work at Hanworth was carried out with a strict eye to the practicalities and none to beauty. Whiteley's first act was to cut down the trees and sell the timber. All the hedges were removed and replaced by oak posts and rails with a galvanised iron wall 6ft high. A hawthorn and privet hedge was planted next to the wall, and on the inside of all boundary walls stretched six strands of galvanised iron wire. The land was then laid out into plots of approximately 5 acres each with a 7ft roadway between them. A network of pipes was installed for drainage, and the land planted with over a million fruit trees. No space was wasted. Between the trees were fruit bushes, and at ground level there were strawberry plants. The walls around the property were used for growing fruits such as peaches and nectarines, the differing temperatures of the north and south walls ingeniously used to extend the season.

The farm homestead, and a 27-room house that had been built only four and a half years previously were not needed, so Whiteley had them pulled down. He built villas for the chief vegetable grower, cow-man, horse keeper and pig-man, and numerous workmen's cottages. For the armies of fruit pickers there were dormitories, mess rooms, lavatories and washrooms. The farm steward and general manager each had a double-fronted villa, and between these was a bungalow built especially for Whiteley's personal use when he visited the farm.

The vegetable gardens covered 40 acres, and there were also hothouses, an apiary, piggeries, cowhouses, a poultry farm, pigeon aviary, rabbit warren, and kennels for breeding dogs. There were several blocks of factory buildings, for jams and preserves, potted meats, soups, pickles, sauces, jellies and syrups.

One and a half miles away was the Rookeries Farm estate which Whiteley bought in 1894, comprising a manor house, with gardens, lawns and greenhouses. There was 'thickly planted woodland between the house and the church with many shady walks and quiet retreats'.[16] Not for long, since he had the trees cut down and sold, and the area planted with root vegetables. This understandably aroused the dismay of the Selborne Society, founded in 1885 to continue the pioneering environmental work of naturalist Gilbert White. Mr Whiteley, said the secretary, 'has desolated and disfigured a whole district. No words can express a sense of the enormity inflicted upon the public thus robbed of the beauties of trees, hedges and fields, and the singing and movement of birds. The work of destruction still goes on. A belt of splendid trees bordering the roadside in Hanworth Park, adjoining the church, has just been felled. A beautiful wood nearby is also falling to the axe.'[17] It is probable, however, that there were others in the area who were in favour of the farm, which employed a considerable amount of local labour, and provided pleasant accommodation with such amenities as a lecture hall and club room.

In the following year, Whiteley commissioned as a Christmas book, a handsome volume of what would now be called the 'coffee-table' type, with over 140 photographs of every aspect of the model farm and factory's activity, and a text eulogising both the achievement and its instigator. The book is now a collector's item, but in 1895, when Whiteley took 50,000 copies to sell at 5*s* apiece, there were few takers and he made a loss on the project.[18] The text, which one assumes was approved by Mr Whiteley, is nauseatingly sycophantic. 'As we gazed with admiration at the forest of fruit trees that have sprung up under Mr Whiteley's magic wand, and saw them under their most advantageous dress, pendant with their beauteous burdens, and cast our eyes along the acres of vegetables of every variety in their cheerful verdure, all so productive and flourishing, it seemed almost impossible to believe that one man alone had been instrumental in contributing to this happy sight.'[19]

The 'pretty model cottages' had 'every modern improvement'. In the factories, no expense was spared, everything was of the 'newest design and construction', clean, bright, modern and scientific. The workmen were 'pictures of propriety', the women 'equally admirable' and all 'appeared to be of quite a superior class'. Here were 'expensive fruit dainties' and 'trembling jelly', while lemon squash was an 'ambrosial drink'. Beef tea lozenges were made from the finest quality beef boiled in beef tea, and set with gelatine. 'We are informed that a box of these nutritious tablets would keep a man alive for a week.'[20] Most luxurious was the real turtle soup, for which live turtles were imported from the West Indies and killed on the premises.

Not everything on Whiteley's farm was as perfect as claimed. In April 1894 he found himself summoned to court by the County Veterinary Inspector for Middlesex. Swine fever had broken out at Butts Farm, yet contrary to Acts of Parliament, and the Swine Fever order of 1878, no notification had been made to the police. The Inspector had only come to hear of the matter by being told privately that there was a serious outbreak. He at once inspected the farm, and found some pigs separated from the rest, and carcasses in the slaughterhouse dressed and ready for market. Mr Roche, conveniently forgetting that Whiteley had claimed to have bought the best advice he could, urged before the bench that while the symptoms would be apparent to an expert, an ordinary person such as his client might fail to understand them. The magistrates imposed the maximum fine.[21]

Part of the reason for such laxity at the farms may have been the pressure that they were under to supply the food halls with top quality produce which was then expected to be sold at Whiteleys' famed low prices. The equation did not add up, and the farms ultimately ran at a loss, something the proud owner was later at some pains to conceal.

There were also problems back at Bayswater. In 1893, in an echo of the butchers' opposition of 1876, the journeyman tailors employed by Whiteleys protested against a reduction in their hourly rate, and a procession with bands and banners marched along Westbourne Grove for several hours, accompanied by an effigy of their employer on horseback.

In 1894 there was concern in the upper echelons of the wool trade that the term 'flannelette' as applied to a fabric made of cotton was calculated to mislead the public, since it was believed the public understood flannel to be made wholly of wool. The term had been in use for thirteen years, and the suggestion caused some consternation among drapers. A test case was needed, and who better to be the object of this case than William Whiteley. Accordingly a private detective was sent to Whiteleys. He observed a number of items for sale labelled 'flannelette', purchased some samples and sent them to a public analyst, who, after a series of tests reported that they were made of cotton, which was not surprising as the shop made no secret of it. Whiteley was duly summoned before the Marylebone magistrates for an infringement of the Merchant Marks Act. The action ended with a decision in favour of Whiteley, and later that year some representatives of leading Lancashire manufacturers and merchants presented him with an illuminated address, a silver cup and a cheque for his expenses.[22]

In the same year he started a new enterprise as an omnibus proprietor, starting a service between Camden and Bayswater which previously had no direct transport link. Early reports of a rivalry with the London General Omnibus Company ceased when it was revealed that they were co-partners. The chocolate-coloured buses with yellow wheels were said to be lighter than ordinary ones and so less of a strain on the horses, a feature which, it was believed, would appeal to the ladies.[23]

One annual social event which was growing in magnitude with each year was the Whiteleys house dinner, where hundreds of employees and invited giants of the commercial world took their seats at a plentifully loaded table, were entertained with musical interludes, listened to speeches about William Whiteley and drank enthusiastic toasts. Senior manager James Keith made a speech in 1895 revealing his personal admiration for his employer seasoned with knowledge of the hard master that lay beneath the smiling geniality. 'Honesty of purpose, directness of aim and an indomitable pursuit

of his object, had marked him through life.' [Cheers]
Speaking of those who had sought a 'berth' and been
refused, he said that:

> Some had gone so far as to say it was a positive
> pleasure to have a refusal in such gracious words. . . .
> Some of them might occasionally get a lick with the
> rough side of his [Mr Whiteley's] tongue, but he bore
> them no animosity, and the best advice he [Mr Keith]
> could give them was to treasure it up as a token of his
> interest in their welfare. [Laughter] As the years went
> on and the business increased so their chief's energy
> seemed to increase in proportion. High-minded,
> despising meanness and deception, he had
> commanded the homage of men of business in all
> parts of the world. . . . In the midst of his prosperity
> he was ever humble and unassuming, so that even the
> smallest of his employees had easy access to his
> sanctum . . . the outer world looked at such a man in
> wonderment, but they inside the circle saw not only
> the immense energy and enterprise of a great captain
> of industry, but a simplicity and modesty in daily
> living which were an admirable lesson to young men
> in these luxurious days.[24]

In the following year Keith described Whiteley as:
'erect, alert and resourceful as ever, carrying the secret,
if not of perpetual youth, yet of abounding elasticity, his
order being "Full steam ahead!" [Great laughter and
cheers]; '. . . the success they celebrated was mainly
achieved by the direction of one mind, sagacious in
apprehension, decided in opinion and tenacious in
execution – in fact a committee of one.' There was also a
toast to William junior and Frank. 'They came in quietly

eight years ago, and had taken root in every direction.'[25] Trusted managers like James Keith meant that it was possible for the founder to take longer holidays if he wished. That year he spent the whole of August in Switzerland. Whiteley was now 65, but showed few signs of slowing down, and there were still some glittering honours to be won. In 1896, for the wedding of Princess Maud, Whiteleys carried out the whole of the decorative and furnishing arrangements at Buckingham Palace, both for the Royal Chapel and the adjoining rooms, and provided tents, alcoves and seating for the garden party. Queen Victoria was so delighted that she granted a Royal Warrant as General Furnisher to Her Majesty, the first time that such a warrant had been given unsolicited. The framed and glazed warrant was at once placed on display at the picture gallery in Queen's Road. As a result, Whiteleys was in even more demand than before for gala functions, the greatest challenge probably being Trafalgar Day 1896, when Nelson's Column was decorated by a band of laurel 4ft wide and weighing 7 tons, spiralling from base to top.

The year 1897 brought the excitement of the Queen's diamond jubilee, when, despite a petition from the local tradesmen, the route of her visit on 21 June did not include Westbourne Grove. Much was expected in the way of decorations from Whiteleys, and the spectators were not disappointed. A double series of festoons in light green foliage ran the whole length of the third tier of windows, with added flags, and the night was illumined with large fiery stars with monograms and the Royal Arms, while the clock was framed with lights. The sight drew applause from the passengers of the passing omnibuses. Inside, a special edition of jubilee chinaware sold in huge numbers. Many members of the royal family and of Lord Salisbury's government patronised the display.

In the following year, as full of energy as ever, Whiteley arranged to erect substantial new warehouses to store the items used in his hire department, such as decorations, tents, garden fête furniture, and temporary theatres. He had recently had charge of the arrangements for a Grand Ball held in Edinburgh, with two others under contract, a cycle show in Birmingham, and an electrical exhibition. At the opening of the Blackwall Tunnel he had lent 2 miles of chairs. 'I thought I was going to have a bit of a rest', was his observation, 'but it looks as though I am going to have a busy summer.'[26]

As the century drew to its close, William Whiteley's position as the great genial lion of trade was unassailable. While not especially noted for large charitable works, he did nevertheless contribute sums to worthy causes, and continued to support the numerous clubs and societies formed for his employees. It was considered to be a prestigious feather in the cap of the Association of Grocers' Assistants when they received his endorsement for their campaign to reform working hours.

In 1898, however, there was a new personal attack, launched by the writer of a series of articles called 'Life in the Shop' commissioned by the *Daily Chronicle*. The main object of the series was to expose the unseen side of the working conditions of shop assistants, and for the most part, specific shops and individuals were not named. In the first article, however, the portrait of William Whiteley is unmistakable.

Everyone who goes shopping will recall the gentleman with the particularly charming manners and the deferential smile. His personality has in the course of years become quite a feature of the street as well as of the great emporium of which he is an ornament. You can see him from the outside of the 'bus, as it slows up for the shopping ladies to alight, diffusing an atmosphere of subdued and grateful welcome among the arrivals, patting the heads of the children, and bowing to right and left quite in the grand, forgotten, style. No verger showing the dean's lady to her stall has a more adequate manner, a finer blend of reverence, blandness, and gentle authority. His black frock-coat, his expressive hands, always indicating, even in repose, welcome, expectation, gratitude, or farewell, his air of respectful friendliness, constitute a pleasing personality, and lend a tone of distinction and downright benevolence to the whole establishment.

When the rumors [*sic*] concerning the other side of this attractive gentleman's character first reached me I could hardly credit them. The young ladies and gentlemen of the house – the term 'shop' is not used by those 'in business' – declared that he has an abominable temper, and that he could lay aside his purring ways and become a regular drill sergeant in a flash. 'You should see him early in the morning' they tell you, 'when we are unwrapping the goods and getting our stock in order for the day. He just stands there and explodes – goes off in a crackle of temper by the hour.' 'Now then Miss C—. Take care what you are doing. You shall be instantly dismissed, Miss, if I see any more of those remnants lying about. And Mr D— what do *you* mean by putting that stuff in the window?' And so he would go on, storming, browbeating, threatening fines, reports, dismissals, until the customers begin to come in, and then it was time to take up the post by the door, with the obsequious smile, and the chilly-looking hands, softly polishing one another. But, without suggesting for an instant that my friend is a universal type, I am afraid there is something in the charge.[27]

One particularly dreaded item was the 'private letter', 'an instrument of oppression which assistants view with terror and detestation. It was invented, I believe, by Mr Whiteley. He is a particularly shrewd man, and his simple but effective method of enlisting customers on the side of discipline, of bringing them in as a sort of supernumerary body of shopwalkers as it were, has a touch of genius in it. Other houses in the West-end are adopting it, and the assistants view the progress of this new terror with positive dismay.'

The instigator of this terror was an innocuous-looking framed notice hanging in every department, which read: 'Customers will oblige if receiving incivility or inattention from assistants by reporting at once, or sending a letter marked "Private" to William Whiteley, Westbourne Grove.' A complaint of that nature usually led to summary dismissal. The writer had observed 'a note of panic among the assistants when the private letter is mentioned, which is new to me and very painful'. It transpired that the 'private' letter was not so private after all. In one probably not isolated incident, Whiteley had had a letter of complaint printed, and copies distributed throughout the store.[28]

If Whiteley knew of these criticisms he chose to ignore them. There were no more obstacles in his life, just occasional minor annoyances which he could bat away as if they were flies. Nothing could harm the personal regard in which he was held by those who experienced his suave and accommodating charm. As a correspondent in the *Chronicle* said, 'Those who have lived here for some time, and watched the growth and expansion of his splendid business, and have been brought into contact with the man himself, have had their misapprehensions corrected, and found him the frank, hearty, straightforward and scrupulously honest man that he is.'[29]

The letter had been prompted by a rumour that had been 'the talk of Bayswater'. Whiteleys was going to become a limited company. For many years it had been the heart, the spirit and the pride of Bayswater. Now, it seemed, everyone was going to be able to own a part of it.

How to Succeed in Business

The new company was being discussed at every dinner table in the Grove, and Whiteleys was deluged with enquiries from both brokers and investors. In July 1898 it was necessary to halt the flood by issuing a circular to announce that the conversion of the business to a company would not take place until the late spring of 1899. The statement emphasised that the company would be a profit-sharing concern, in which the employees would be considered first, then the banking customers, and finally the general customers.

Whiteley was fortunate to see the company launched, since in October that year he was driving a phaeton along Bayswater Road, accompanied by a lady (who was not named) and a footman, when the driver of a cart, who later admitted he had had a few drops of beer, lost control of his horse, and the two vehicles collided. The occupants of the phaeton escaped with a shaking.

Whiteleys' house dinner that year was both a happy and in some ways a sad occasion. It took place at the Hotel Cecil, and 550 sat down to dinner. According to the *Chronicle*, Whiteley 'as he stood in the reception hall to greet his guests, looked every inch the "chief o' the clan" and the author of his own fortunes – his fine and powerful physique, standing "four square to all the winds that blow", his frank, open face, hearty manner and ready courteous speech, all as noticeable as the enormous strength which lies beneath the invariably gracious manner'.

'I wish Mr Whiteley could be more often heard in public [commented an observer]. He has some notable gifts of the public speaker – a pleasant voice, always easily audible in a large room; and a placable and courteous manner. He is fluent and choice in his language, and although a typical Yorkshireman, has nothing provincial in pronunciation, except the admirable roll of the letter *r* at the beginning of a word, in which northerners excel and southerners are sadly deficient.'[1]

James Keith in his toast to the chairman gave some insight into the reasons behind the proposed incorporation which suggested that Whiteley's stout appearance might bear a less favourable interpretation than the *Chronicle*'s. It was 'a very special occasion because it was the last on which they would meet as a body owing allegiance to an individual. . . . The time had arrived when, for the health of his mind and body, as also for the welfare of the business, their chief had deemed it advisable to take the momentous step of converting the grand concern into a company.'

Underneath the gracious smiles, Whiteley was far from pleased with the prospect. 'The business was never intended to be made into a Joint Stock Company', he wrote later, 'but at my age I am compelled to take life easier . . . and although most remunerative it is more than my two sons care to take upon themselves – preferring less anxiety and less income.'[2] The *Irish Financial Times* provided more background. 'From observations made to a brother journalist, we learn that it is owing to the pressure of his two sons and his three best friends that he has agreed to turn the business into a public company.'[3]

If anyone was under the impression that the founder was about to take a back seat they were in for a surprise

– he still had the reins grasped firmly in his hands, and had no intention of letting go. A notebook in the HSBC archives contains what is probably Whiteley's proposal for the company prospectus, 47 pages, all in his own handwriting. He naturally appoints himself chairman, and selects the directors, banker, broker, solicitor and accountant. Disdaining precise figures, he launches into a detailed description of the business, its strengths, its policies and its many departments. Importantly, he is 'To retain full power as at present and to have the power to discharge any person in any way connected with the Company from the Directors downwards', a suggestion totally in keeping with the man, but not, as had to be pointed out to him, to be countenanced by the Stock Exchange.[4]

The correspondence retained by Greenwell and Co., Whiteley's stockbrokers, show that the pre-eminent salesman was surprisingly ignorant of the requirements of a limited company. On 5 December 1898 this was his reaction to the idea that the assets of the firm needed to be valued for the benefit of prospective investors. 'I am told that Mr Young [of Turquand and Young, accountants] is going to send up two men to go though the books – that everything will have to be valued – I have been served by Mr Roche with two notices to that effect – well if that is so it will take months to do, and will be a very expensive matter that will have to be paid for by somebody – but who is that to be? I do not want it done – my customers do not require it – and I do not know of anybody that does except Mr Roche. If I do not want it why should I pay for it?'[5]

In the same letter he complains that he is being kept in the dark about the proposals, and some consternation must have been caused by his suggestion that he was thinking of continuing as he was for another three years. Somehow that ripple of disquiet must have been smoothed over and the valuation done, mostly by the firm of Cluttons, but stocks, buildings, fixtures and plant amounting to £469,000 were valued by Whiteley himself. By May 1899 the prospectus was eagerly awaited, the general consensus of the financial press being that the shares were well worth applying for, and likely to yield a handsome return.

A letter from Cluttons dated 1 May 1899 set out the full extent of the Whiteley empire.[6] The central business establishment consisted of fourteen shops in Westbourne Grove, seven shops in Queen's Road, and four houses in Kensington Gardens Square. Dormitories were provided by 141 Queen's Road, twenty-one houses in Westbourne Grove Terrace, and two in Hatherley Grove. There were also nearby properties used as auction rooms, building yards and offices, and stabling in eight of the surrounding streets. There were eight freehold houses, while another twenty in the immediate area had recently been purchased with a view to development, as had two freehold plots of land. There were eight suburban distributing depots, and massive depositories in Avonmore Road, Kensington, with four staff houses. In addition there was the Hillingdon nursery of 9 acres and the Hanworth Farm of almost 200.

When the prospectus was finally issued in June 1899 there was, for all but those few in the know, a substantial shock. The share capital consisted of 900,100 £1 shares. Of these, 100 were management shares, allocated to directors and heads of department, and the remaining 900,000 were all taken by William Whiteley, in part payment of the purchase price of £1,818,100, the rest being paid to him in cash. The public was only permitted to subscribe for debentures, essentially a loan stock which entitled the holders to interest. The dream of the ordinary customer being able to own a piece of Whiteleys was shattered. The *Financial Times* commented,

> The long looked-for Whiteley prospectus is out at last, and we are afraid it will be a great disappointment to the general public, and especially to the numerous customers of the 'Universal Provider'. Indeed, except as an example of how a business should not be floated, it is of very little interest to the public at large. . . . Mr Whiteley is simply borrowing close upon a million of money at a little under 4 per cent., without giving the public any chance of participating in the profits of his business. . . . Thousands upon thousands of Whiteleys customers have been looking forward to the forthcoming conversion of the business into a limited liability company in the hope that they might obtain an allotment of shares, and we have little doubt also that a large number of people have been induced to deal with the firm for the same reason. All these persons will be bitterly disappointed. . . . There is a tendency nowadays among promoters of Industrial Companies to keep the plums of the financial pudding to themselves, and to offer the dough to the public, and if there be any plums in this new Company, Mr Whiteley has retained them religiously for himself.[7]

The *FT* was not alone in that opinion. *The Economist* dismissed the flotation as 'only a device for borrowing money at something under 4 per cent'[8] and the *Investors Review* commented, 'neither speculators nor investors

get much for their patience', and while admitting that
the debenture stock was 'run after like hot rolls . . .'
added, 'William Whiteley has certainly not dealt
generously with investors.'[9]

The *FT* was gloomy about the prospects of the new
company. It pointed out that Whiteleys' profits had
decreased in the last few years, those for the period
1895–7 averaging £103,400, but for 1897–9 (both
periods including the exceptional Jubilee year), the
average was £99,600. It was felt that they might decline
further as disappointed customers took their business
elsewhere. An unusual feature of the profit figures
submitted which was not commented on until later was
that the accounts of the Kensington properties and the
farms were excluded. It was generally known that the
Kensington properties made £12,000 a year, but the
trading results of the farms were undisclosed.

Money, also predicting a falling off of business due to
the bitter disgust of customers, added pointedly: 'Mr
Whiteley, in addition to being a Universal Provider,
appears to possess considerable powers as a valuer,
seeing as he values so many of his own assets',[10] though
the *Statist*, attributing the decline in business to
competition, added: 'The fact that Mr Wheeler of the
Board of Trade has resigned his official position to
become deputy-chairman of the Company is an
indication that the financial control will be good.'[11]

Samuel Wheeler had acted as Official Receiver for a
number of well-known groups of companies, and it was
anticipated that his presence would bring a wealth of
financial acumen to the Board, especially as Whiteley
had never professed to have any great knowledge of
finance beyond the mechanisms of trade. The other
directors, apart from Whiteley, were William junior,

Frank, businessman Courtauld Thomson and James
Keith who was appointed managing director.

Almost at once, the new company experienced a
major commotion which had to be carefully contained.
Mr Wheeler had become uneasy about the founder's
informal valuations, and the curious omission of the
trading results of the farms from the prospectus. He
started to accumulate information to put before the
Board, and bombarded Whiteley with letters detailing
the results of his enquiries and asking for clarification.
Letters from Whiteley to his broker early in 1900 contain
repeated tetchy complaints that he had been receiving
long reports from Wheeler and was having to assemble
papers for a reply. On 13 February he wrote, '[Wheeler]
is still doing all he can to annoy me and to reduce the
value of the business as much as possible . . .',[12] and on
22 February, 'If Mr Wheeler is not removed he will
completely ruin the place.'[13]

Whiteley's usual response in such situations was to
try and delay matters, but he was fighting a more
determined class of opponent than the old Paddington
Vestry. Cluttons was brought in to examine the
inventories of trade fixtures sold to the company, and
discovered some serious anomalies, which included
fixtures charged to the company twice over. A report
was prepared which was submitted to the Board on
19 April, signed by Wheeler, James Keith and Courtauld
Thomson. It concluded that the profits of the business
had been misrepresented in the prospectus, and that
important facts relating to the business which should
have been disclosed to potential investors had been
suppressed. Whiteley was asked to refund £75,125 3s 1d
to the company with interest of 5 per cent. In the
absence of fair and reasonable proposals from Mr

Whiteley, the facts would be placed before an independent solicitor.

Predictably, these proposals were not forthcoming and so the matter was placed before Harold Brown of Linklater and Co., and by 24 July he was able to send Charles Russell, the company secretary, a memo of his recommended terms. This included the suggestion that Whiteley should lease the farms back from the company. Whiteley had, in the meantime, been making strenuous efforts to remove Wheeler as deputy chairman, or, failing that, to alter his rights under the original agreement, but it was one of those rare occasions when Whiteley found that he was powerless before the law. There must also have been something highly suspect about Frank's dealings with the farms, since Brown specifically stipulated that 'Mr F.E. Whiteley will not any longer interfere with the management of Hanworth and Hillingdon'. [14]

Matters were finally settled, though far from amicably. A letter from Charles Russell of 10 December states, 'Mr Whiteley has carried out all the recommendations of the auditors, and has received from the company a release and discharge from all claims.'[15] Whiteley, in vengeful mode, now did everything he could to remove Wheeler from the Board. Charles Russell had suggested the company make a payment to Wheeler, but this Whiteley would not countenance. On 15 January 1901 he wrote to Russell:

. . . there is one point in your letter to which I cannot agree and that is paying Blackmail. I am not a hasty man – I hope I weigh matters well before I come to a conclusion – but when I have come to the conclusion I stick to it – unless it can be most clearly proved to me that I am wrong and I fear the man is not yet born who can convince me that I am wrong . . . What we have to do is to get Wheeler out as we shall never do any good whilst he is here . . . He will not resign so we must vote him out and it will take a month to do that so do not let us waste any more time over it – I propose that you at once tomorrow take steps to remove him. If you will let me have the papers I will get them signed at once by 4 shareholders and myself calling the meeting – Please do not let us waste another day as I presume Mr Greenwell and Mr Young are agreeable to this course being adopted. . . . Yes I know how Mr Young has been treated over his Audit Fees and that is all Mr Wheeler's fault . . . [16]

Indeed, Turquand and Young felt they had been treated very shabbily over the question of their fees, which had unexpectedly decreased, and correspondence from that firm to Whiteley on 6 July 1903 shows some bitterness and reveals that the lease of the farms was an exercise in creative accountancy, whereby Whiteley paid the company £12,000 a year in order to protect the business capital and avoid alarming the debenture holders. He was effectively funding the payment of his own dividends.

With all this going on, Whiteley did not neglect the minutiae of his own investment portfolio as evidenced by the following blunt notes:

August 26 1901
Gentlemen
I have still laying at the Bank idle – earning nothing £11,000. Could not this be put to some use and earn some profit?

8 July 1902

Gentlemen

Excuse me reminding you that my balance at the Bank is now £13,000, and I do not like that amount laying idle and losing interest, say £10-0-0 per week, or 30/- per day and if anything can be done to remedy it I shall be very glad.[17]

The results for the year ended 28 February 1901 were not inspiring. Trading profits had fallen, the directors attributing the position to a general depression of trade caused by the war and the death of the Queen. This didn't fool the *Chronicle*:

unless common report and the opinion of commercial organs deserve no credit, there are other adverse circumstances which must be taken into consideration. . . . Rightly or wrongly the clients seem to think that they are not well catered for under the new as under the old regime. Many of the employees of the firm, after long years of service, have been dismissed, and in some cases have taken away customers with them, whilst among those still retained a sense of uncertainty and uneasiness prevails . . . there have been rumours of dissentions in the Board . . . It is no secret that the founder of the house retired to his tents like Achilles on the occasion of the last annual dinner, and thus gave currency to the idea that the differences between himself and his colleagues were more serious than the facts warranted.[18]

Whiteley, who had claimed ill-health as the reason for his absence from the 1900 dinner, may have taken that as a hint, and he was once again in the chair in November 1901 with Wheeler still there as vice-chair.

In 1901 Whiteley lost two of his oldest allies. In February, Charles Mills Roche died aged 73. His obituary in the *City Press* was full of praise, and the little ripple in the calm of his professional life had been forgotten.[19] Also in that year, James Keith retired after thirty-five years of loyal service.

The creation of a limited company had exposed Whiteleys' trading results to the critical gaze of the press, and in May 1902 the *Financial Times* made some disquieting revelations. The profits of the first three years were substantially lower than anticipated by the prospectus, and while the directors' report gave no clue as to the performance of the farm properties, it was easy to deduce that they were running at a loss, and had been for some years. The *FT* concluded that Whiteleys' trade was in decline, a fact which had been concealed from investors.[20]

At Christmas 1902, Whiteleys was again in conflict with the tradesmen of Westbourne Grove. Old methods were still in evidence and old rivalries as fresh as ever. Christmas day fell on a Sunday that year, and Whiteley had reduced the usual staff holiday from two days to one, on what the *Chronicle* called 'the well-worn but totally inadequate plea that he cannot close his banking department'.[21] The *Chronicle* suggested that the public should retaliate by boycotting the shop on Tuesday. A meeting was convened at the Paddington Baths by the Early Closing Association, where William Owen confirmed that of all the businesses in the area, only four or five had not agreed to close on Tuesday. 'The minority,' he said, 'were simply following the wake of the "Big Man". He would not mention names.' The

remark brought laughter and cries of 'Shame!' 'The
cause of the difficulty', he went on, 'was that they had a
big trader among them, and some of his neighbours were
afraid of him.'[22]

By January 1903 Wheeler had departed. John Lawrie,
a senior manager with many years' service, joined the
Board, and over the years his calm assured manner and
thorough knowledge of the business earned him the
considerable respect of his colleagues. Company events
such as tea dances and sports meetings continued but
while William Whiteley did occasionally attend, more
often than not the family was represented by William
junior and Frank. On 6 February 1903 Whiteley took the
chair at the annual 'Concordia' concert attended by over
2,000 people 'with all his accustomed "bonhomie",
introducing each of the artists with a few humorous
words'. The star turn was Harry Lauder.[23]

The following year it was Frank who took the chair,
and those present drank toasts to him and the lady at his
side – for he was now engaged to be married. The bride-
to-be was Ethel Annie Rostron, and the wedding took
place on 16 April at St Mary Abbots Church,
Kensington. Frank was 31, Ethel 23.

The couple, who departed for a Parisian honeymoon,
must have been cheered by the improving profits of
Whiteleys Limited. The *Chronicle* compared the results
of Whiteleys with its closest rival, William Owen,
which had also incorporated, and was shown to be one-
tenth the size of the Westbourne Grove leviathan. Both
had had a successful year, dispelling recent gloomy
rumours as to the depressed state of trade in the Grove;
nevertheless the *Chronicle* warned, 'It must not,
however, be assumed that the prosperity of these two
undertakings necessarily implies a like happy state of

things among the class of smaller traders. On the contrary, when tritons thrive, minnows are often having a bad time of it.'[24]

Before long, William Whiteley was looking forward to the birth of his first grandchild, and he must have been hoping for a boy. Frank's daughter, Ethel Nora Whiteley, was born on 20 January 1905. There was better news at the next AGM which showed that profits continued to be on the increase.

With the Board now settled according to his wishes, Whiteley must have enjoyed a relatively trouble-free time. His two sons were still his staunchest supporters, even though they seemed unwilling to work at the pace and intensity he might have wished. Both enjoyed the new recreation of motoring and liked to push their cars a little faster than was considered safe. In September 1902 William junior was stopped by a policeman for driving at 19 miles per hour. In court he tried to maintain that the condition of his car made this impossible, but was fined £5, not so much because of the speed, but because he had offered the policeman half a sovereign to forget all about it, something the chairman of the magistrates described as 'a most ungentlemanly act'.[25] Frank was an equally keen motorist and by 1917 had clocked up twelve appearances in court for speeding offences.

Potential employees were still expected to queue for a personal interview with the Universal Provider, but were no longer handed a list of fines. P.C. Hoffman, of the Shop Assistants' Union, later recalled his meeting with William Whiteley.

I can see him now, short and stocky, slightly bow-legged, with a rather large head, bald in front, with

white hair bushy at the top and back, and with long
white whiskers at the sides, other wise clean-shaven;
eyes large but bloodshot rather badly, at the lower lids;
dressed in frock coat, polo collar and white tie. His
formula for engaging was the same for all – 'Good
morning, young man' (spoken as if through his nose), 'I
have vacancies in my linen, furnishing, oriental, dress
and country order departments – supposing I was to
engage you. We close each evening at 6.30 p.m. in the
winter and 7 p.m. in the summer, with 2 p.m. on
Saturdays. We ask for no references, we give no
references; there is one moment's notice on either side.
You will have good food, a beautiful bed to lie upon,
there are no fines or deductions of any kind whatsoever.
What is the lowest possible salary you will take?'[26]

Instead of fines, a 'late list' was posted every day in a
glass case, giving the name of the offender, his
department and his excuse, with Whiteley's comments
scrawled thereon in red ink. Hoffman gave the following
examples:

Jones (Cabinets)	Unwell	No, he is not – lazy fellow
Smith (Silks)	Illness at home	Clear him out
Robinson (Drapery)	Relation ill	Fine excuse
Williams (Hosiery)	Lost the train	Yes, and will lose head, too if not careful[27]

When Hoffman left Whiteleys in 1906 he told his
employer that one of the objects of the Shop Assistants'
Union was to abolish the living-in system. 'Young man',
said Mr Whiteley, 'do you realise the grave moral

responsibility that rests upon your shoulders in regard to that matter?' Hoffman 'let him have a straight reply as to what went on in his own establishment, and I could tell him plenty'.[28]

Even in his 70s, Whiteley regarded morality as something for other people. An assistant who worked at Whiteleys from 1904 later recalled that he regularly took his buyers on trips to Paris, and the assistants used to duck behind their counters to avoid being asked to accompany him.[29]

The last year of William Whiteley's life must have been one of great contentment. As he approached his 75th birthday, he was still the centre of attention at social gatherings, and the press was eager to interview him on any matter of commercial interest. In March 1906 *Pearson's Weekly* ran an article penned by Whiteley on 'Why People Fail in Business' in which he stated: 'Let the budding aspirant to a successful career always bear in mind the maxim "be honest". The man who will go far is not the ultra-smart man who will steal a "commercial march" on a rival by underhand means, but the honest straightforward "plodder" who is not afraid to learn from others, but who would at the same time scorn to score a point by doing an action which would reflect to his discredit.'[30]

In September the *Daily Mail* interviewed him on the subject of married shop assistants. Whiteley believed that married men were more dependable. 'If one of my young men, earning, say, a salary of £80 a year came and asked that he might live out as he was going to marry, if there was nothing against him, permission would be given. But if he asked my advice, I should strongly recommend him to wait until he had improved his position.'[31]

Whiteleys, though a little faded, was still the heart of Bayswater. In April 1906 the *Chronicle* observed 'the report and balance sheet of William Whiteley Limited are looked for each year with keen interest by all who are concerned in the commercial prosperity of this quarter of London. These records may fairly be regarded as affording something akin to a barometrical indication of the rise and fall of business activity in the Bayswater district. . . .'[32] That year showed another increase in profits, the overall picture being one of steady and healthy growth.

There was, however, one project still dear to William Whiteley's heart. In July he wrote personally to the Paddington Borough Council Baths Committee saying that he was prepared to enter into negotiations for the purchase of the Queen's Road Baths. The Committee's report to the Council provoked a lively discussion. Some members thought it would be worth while to find out what kind of offer might be made, others were firm that the Baths should not be sold. Ultimately the matter was not pursued. Once again, Whiteley had to bide his time, confident that one day the property would be his and he could realise his dream of a single unbroken frontage the length of Queen's Road. Age had made him stiff in the knees, and he was moving more slowly than before, but he could still walk to work each morning, with a friendly word to passers-by, and the old street sweeper. As the year drew to its close he was looking forward to the birth of Ethel's second child – perhaps at last the longed-for grandson.

Sir Thomas Lipton, the grocery magnate, was a good friend who gave a picture of the Universal Provider's private life at this time. From Monday to Friday, Whiteley's only thought was of business, but on

Saturday he spent the day at the farm, of which he remained very fond. On Sundays he was at home with friends, and there were regular dinner parties with up to twenty at the lavishly provided table. His evening amusement was listening to music, and while he read neither newspapers nor books, he had someone read to him each evening. This was no sinecure, since he wanted not only to hear the news, but to have it explained to him until he understood it. Unsurprisingly, Lipton had never seen Whiteley berating his staff, and wrote of 'the extraordinary quietness of his manners . . .' and wondered how a man with such a business could keep up '. . . such an imperturbable temper'.[33]

Manners were about to be William Whiteley's downfall. Shortly before his fatal confrontation of 24 January 1907, he wrote, 'visitors from all parts of the world are to this day constantly enquiring whether it is possible to see me, and a request of this kind is invariably granted, at whatever inconvenience to myself.'[34]

TWELVE

The Man of Mystery

Shortly after 1 p.m. on 24 January 1907 William Whiteley junior, who had been working in Queen's Road, was about to go out for lunch when David Goodman, the chief cashier, approached him in a state of some distress. 'Have you heard of the accident?' exclaimed Goodman, who was too overcome to give the news in anything other than gulps.

'What accident?'

'To your father,' said Goodman.

'Where is my father?' demanded William, but the cashier had broken down and was unable to speak any more.[1]

William hurried to 43 Westbourne Grove. He must have known before he arrived that his father was dead. He found assistants standing behind their counters weeping, while grim-faced shopwalkers were ushering customers out into the street, the mass exodus causing a not unnatural consternation in the Grove where passers-by thought Whiteleys was on fire again. A crowd of directors and managers had assembled, and a screen had been moved into place enclosing an area outside the Universal Provider's tiny office. They tried to dissuade William from approaching, but he forced his way through, and pulled the screen aside. Two bodies lay on the floor at right angles, their feet almost touching. William Whiteley had been shot twice, once in the face and once in the head. Brain matter was oozing from the head wound and his long whiskers were streaked with blood. It was immediately obvious that he was beyond help. The other man was lying face down in his own blood. William scarcely looked at him, and arranged for Frank to be summoned by telephone. Meanwhile, Glyn James, who had been sent for a policeman only minutes before, had returned with Police Constable F. Bussey 175 F. There was a gun on the floor beside the assassin's right hand which Bussey took charge of, noting that three bullets had been discharged and three remained.

A telephone call had already been made to Dr John Gay French of Porchester Gardens. On arrival, French examined William Whiteley and confirmed that he was dead. His murderer was bleeding from wounds to his temple and face, and as French turned the body over, he exclaimed, 'This man is alive!'

'I am alive,' said the young man. 'Don't worry about me.' As French bandaged the wounds, his patient added, 'I am quite conscious.' Those present looked carefully at the assassin's face, but no one knew who he was. He was removed to St Mary's Hospital, Paddington.

There, the reason for the gunman's survival became apparent. His attempt to put a bullet in his brain had failed. He must have turned away as he pulled the trigger, and the shot had entered his head at an angle, tearing through his right eye, passing through the bridge of his nose, and exiting through the forehead. As casualty surgeon Herbert Batten dressed the wounds, he asked the patient for his name. He made a written note of the response. 'My name is Cecil Whiteley,' was the calm reply. 'I am the son of Mr Whiteley. I have shot Mr Whiteley. I have shot myself and made a mistake. Give me something to make me sleep away, there's a good boy. I am quite conscious.'

The police arrived at the hospital, but were told that the patient's condition was critical. He was too ill to be questioned, and there was nothing on him to confirm his identity which, in view of the extraordinary nature of his statement, was still considered to be a mystery. The police took possession of the man's clothing and found some leaves torn from a notebook, on one of which he had written:

To whom it may concern
William Whiteley is my father, and has brought upon himself and me a double fatality by reason of his own refusal of a request perfectly reasonable.
R.I.P.

The only money found on him was one shilling. No more clues were forthcoming and the newspapers – the *Chronicle* outlining each of its columns in black, a tribute usually reserved for royalty – could only speculate as to who the assassin was, hinting darkly that the circumstances of the 1881 divorce proceedings rendered it not unlikely that there could be an illegitimate son. The mystery man remained in hospital, and a constable was sent to guard him.

Whiteleys had been closed immediately after the murder, a black-bordered notice posted in the window, and staff who returned after their lunch break were sent home. Outside, crowds gathered on the pavement, exchanging reminiscences of William Whiteley, undeterred by the cold weather and small biting particles of snow. At 3 o'clock, an ambulance arrived, and a stretcher was carried into the shop. The onlookers waited for it to emerge with the body, but they waited in vain. One of Whiteleys' hearses had been taken round to

Douglas Place, and it was here that William Whiteley
left his empire for the last time – appropriately enough,
by the goods entrance.

The following morning, Whiteleys was open for
business as usual, including the department where the
shooting had taken place, which was naturally crowded
with visitors. An announcement appeared in the daily
papers:

> Mr Whiteley created this great business, but in his
> later years he was a sufficiently shrewd man to realise
> that it was a weak point to make it a one-man concern.
>
> With his consent, in 1899 a company was formed,
> and the business organised on lines which have made
> it quite independent of Mr Whiteley's personal
> management and direction. Though, of course, his
> loss will be deeply regretted on personal grounds, it
> would not in any way affect the working of the
> business.[2]

On 25 January Dr French carried out the post-mortem
on the body of William Whiteley. He found degeneration
of the mitral valve of the heart, which had become
enlarged under the strain, an old pleurisy in the left
lung and cysts in the kidneys, but no other disease. The
skin of Whiteley's left cheek and the back of his neck
were blackened by powder marks showing that the shots
had been fired from 9 to 15in away. The first shot had
entered the left cheek, and exited from the back of the
neck. It would not have been fatal. He must have
flinched away, and turned slightly, for the second bullet
entered behind his left ear, ploughed through the brain
and embedded itself in the bone above his right ear.
Death would have been almost instantaneous.

The police searches of Whiteleys' premises had missed one vital clue – the assassin's silk hat. It was found by an employee who discovered a cloakroom ticket in the lining, which he at once passed to the police. This led to Lancaster Gate tube station where an envelope in the name of H.B. Richards was found, containing documents which included pawn tickets, correspondence and a passport. The name of the assassin was Horace George Rayner, and it was soon established that he was the son of George Rayner and Emily Turner.

This revelation precipitated an intensive search for information into the origins and life of Horace Rayner. Everyone who had a story to tell was interviewed by the press, events twenty-five years in the past were dredged from memory, and newspapers rushed to get the revelations into print. Understandably, there was considerable variation between the newspaper accounts, even when the same people had been interviewed, and the result was a confused mass of detail, some of which was undoubtedly garbled, inaccurate or untrue. Statements made by those on the periphery of events often failed to distinguish between the two attractive Turner sisters, each with a small dark-eyed boy in tow. George Rayner, who might have offered some enlightenment, was suddenly absent from business and unavailable for comment. In due course, Horace would have his own story to tell, and of all the prime witnesses, he was the least reliable.

Horace George Rayner grew up with the triple stigma of illegitimacy, an alcoholic mother, and a father – George Rayner – who had no real interest in him. He had the advantage of good looks and cultivated manners, but behind the mask there festered a deep sense of inadequacy that led him to bolster his fragile image with boastfulness and lies. He also seems to have been afflicted with a strong disinclination to work for a living and the belief that it was his right to demand money from relatives.[3]

When George and Emily parted in 1888, Horace was sent away to school. He was educated in Brighton, Barnet, and a college in Eastbourne. On 30 January 1893 at the parish church of St George, Hanover Square, London, Emily Turner married Ernest Dudding, a farmer's son, who gave his profession as 'gentleman rider'. Ernest, who was 23, declared his age as 26. Emily also claimed to be 26. She was actually 35. The couple settled in Southampton where Dudding became a brewer's agent, not perhaps the most fortunate profession, given his wife's family weakness. Emily's fondness for the bottle was to lead to a gradual breakdown of both her health and the marriage.

On leaving college Horace went to live with George, and assisted him at the office, but this was not to last. George Rayner preferred his children at a distance. Eva was in a convent school, where she remained – in 1901 she was teaching there – and by 1907 youngest son Gordon had been packed off to Valparaiso. Horace's destination was Russia, where he was sent at the age of 17, probably to work as a clerk in a branch of an English company. One of the items found in the cloakroom at Lancaster Gate tube station was a letter of introduction from Lord Loftus to the British Consul at St Petersburg. The connection between George Rayner and Loftus, who had once been British Ambassador to St Petersburg, is unknown.

Accounts differ about how long Horace was in Russia on that occasion – anything from seven months to three years. He was certainly back in England by October 1899 when he applied for the post of correspondence

clerk with Tubes Ltd of Birmingham under the name of
Horace G. Payne. He claimed that he had been educated
at Rugby School and had been with a firm called
Godfrey Rayner and Co. of Jermyn Street for five years.
These credentials were not checked, and he was given
the job. Two months later, he approached his manager
and asked if he could make a statement to him in
private. Behind closed doors he confided that his name
was not Payne but Rayner, and that he was in hiding
from his family who were well-connected, and would
not want him to be confined to a clerk's desk. He
requested that the statement should be kept a secret.
Perhaps this did not produce the desired impression, for
shortly afterwards he made a second statement, that he
was the son of William Whiteley. The reactions of his
manager are not recorded.

Horace's curious behaviour may be explained by some
pivotal events in his life which occurred in the closing
years of the nineteenth century. Family friends were
later to comment that around the age of 20 or 21,
Horace's cheerful outlook changed, and he became
moody and depressed. Emily's health had been
deteriorating, and she eventually suffered chronic
kidney failure. Louie, who had been in Switzerland,
rushed home to nurse her. Emily slipped into a coma
and passed away in her sister's arms on 13 January
1898. She was 39. A few months later, Ernest remarried.
Quite apart from any filial grief, Horace must have
realised that Ernest Dudding, if he ever had been a
potential source of finance, was no longer concerned
with him. Nevertheless, as the eldest son of a man who
was 'something in the city' he must have considered his
prospects to be bright. He even started calling himself
George. [For the sake of clarity he will continue to be

205

referred to as Horace.] By now, however, his father had a new mistress, and another daughter, Mabel. In 1899, much to Horace's displeasure, George Rayner, aged 50, married Agnes Mary Allen, who was not quite 24. Suddenly, Horace found he could no longer obtain money from George and the prospect of being supplanted by legitimate issue loomed unpleasantly. There were rows, and George, especially after a few drinks, maintained that Horace was no son of his, and told him to go and see William Whiteley as he (Horace) had more claim on him. If Horace had not known before about his family's connection with Whiteley, he certainly knew it then.

At about the same time, there was a brief meeting between Horace Rayner and Herbert Cecil Whiteley Turner, Louie's boy (usually called Cecil), who was destined to enter the navy. Horace asked Louie who this boy was, and she told him. He never forgot it. It weighed on his mind. He must have compared his own fortunes with those which he imagined a son of William Whiteley might enjoy. It is not too wild a supposition to suggest that Horace envied Cecil, and might even have wanted to be him.

In April 1901 Horace abruptly left his job at Tubes Ltd saying he had obtained a position as private secretary to a gentleman of title. He had actually gone to work as a junior clerk with the Frederick Hotels Company.

Horace used to spend his summers with Gordon and Eva, who boarded during the school holidays at The Manor House in Bewdley, a quiet Worcestershire town. In Bewdley there resided two maiden ladies, sisters named Sarah and Annie Knowles. In 1901 Sarah was 60, her sister two years younger. They were the daughters of a successful timber merchant, and able to live comfortably on their own means. Horace made the acquaintance of these ladies at a social gathering, and was introduced to their niece, 21-year-old Alice May Knowles, a pretty, dark-haired blue-eyed girl with a fondness for large elaborate hats. Alice, the daughter of an engineer who had fallen on hard times, had initially been brought up by her grandparents, and then by her aunts, and it was no secret that she would eventually inherit their fortune.

Horace told the Knowles family that he was well connected in London, being the son of a stockbroker, and was engaged as private secretary to a financier, Mr Burdett-Coutts MP. Everything about his manner seemed confident, open and frank. Alice fell in love with Horace, and her aunts were enchanted, convinced that this was a young man who would go far. The only words of caution were from Alice's father Albert, who pointed out that they knew nothing at all about Horace except what he himself had told them. His instincts were correct, for if they had checked, they would have found that Mr Burdett-Coutts had never heard of Horace Rayner.

After a few months' courtship, Horace and Alice were married in Kensington on 23 November 1901. Horace gave his name as George Horace Rayner, and his profession as secretary. He declared his father's name to be George Edward [*sic*] Rayner, stockbroker. Sarah and Annie were the witnesses.

At first the marriage prospered. The aunts furnished a handsome home for the couple. They lived first in Harrow and then in Kensington. One of Alice's sisters visited them there in 1903, and later described their home life to the *Daily Chronicle*. They seemed to be in flourishing circumstances. Horace was working long hours – at any rate he did not return home till late in the evening – and she had the impression that he had a good many friends in the city. 'In his home he was all gaiety and geniality. He sang well, and played the piano, and his manners altogether were fascinating. He was very good-looking, polished and well groomed. His refined features and clean-shaven face gave him a boyish appearance. But his eyes were queer. . . . There always seemed some mystery lurking behind them. There was no suggestion of want of mental balance.' The Rayners' first child, a daughter, Etheldreda Alice, was born in 1903.[4]

Horace must have thought he had made a good impression at the Frederick Hotels, as he later gave his employer's name as a reference. Unfortunately the first person to take up this reference received a letter in reply which was not very cordial. It stated that while Horace Rayner had initially done his work well, he had later thrown up the job in a huff. 'He was always an independent foolish sort of young man. His supposed father was always reminding him of this, and he was always finding fault with his father.'[5]

For a time Horace drifted between failed attempts at self-employment, the family finances sliding into penury. The smart flat had to be given up. From 12 April to 13 May 1904, Horace and Alice were staying at a hotel in Millman Street run by a couple called Williams. Horace told them that he was taking an office in Bedford Row to start a business of employment agency, business transfer agency and company promotion. The Rayners quarrelled frequently, and on several occasions, Mrs Williams was obliged to intervene to prevent Horace from striking Alice. After they had left, Horace returned a few times to collect letters, and on the last occasion he said the business in Bedford Row was no good. He said he had borrowed £500 – the expression he used was 'knocked down the old girl', referring to one of Alice's aunts, and meant to go to Russia and have a good time with it.

The Rayners took lodgings in Camden Town. The landlady later recalled Horace having a picture of his mother, a beautiful woman with lovely eyes like his own. He placed the picture on the bedroom wall, and although showing a devotion to the portrait, was unwilling to talk about its subject. He did tell the landlady about his young stepmother, with whom he was not on good terms.

Horace had been advertising in the newspapers for businesses for sale and also for those who wished to invest, hoping to bring the two together and earn commission. It was through these advertisements that he met a man (whose name was never revealed) who wanted some City experience. They formed a partnership and went into business in a single room over a bank in Threadneedle Street as mortgage brokers. His partner, who had initially warmed to Horace's attractive personality, was quickly disappointed. 'He was volatile in disposition, and, very unfortunately, idle.' Unlike many who had spent time with Horace, he believed 'there was never a hint of mystery. Horace Rayner was always very serious and preoccupied, but that was all.'[6]

Horace introduced his new partner to George Rayner, who, with his brother Bernard, was in business in King William Street. George, like his son, had a 'very taking personality'. Horace said that George had negotiated large loans for local authorities and done very well out of them, but Horace's partner saw through the boast. George was an able man who had probably made quite a bit of money in his day, but it was obvious that he had

not done so well recently. The three men would
occasionally play billiards together, and Horace would
always address George as 'Father' while George
addressed Horace by his Christian name.

By December 1904, Horace's partner had had enough.
He wanted to wind up the business and take out what
money was left, but at first Horace would not agree,
taking the attitude, 'No, I shall sit tight; you can go to
the devil.'[7] Eventually he agreed to a buy-out but failed
to pay his partner the promised money. Unable to pay
the rent of the premises, the partners were given notice
to quit, and the partnership was dissolved. Horace tried
to continue in business at another address, but by the
middle of 1905 he had given this up. Money was now a
serious problem. Alice had given birth to a son, Eric
(referred to as Peter in the newspapers), and little
Etheldreda was sent to be looked after by the aunts in
Bewdley. The Rayners subsisted for a while on £1 a
week sent to them by Alice's aunts, but eventually they
were unable to pay the rent and were asked to leave.

In August 1905 Horace spent a few days at the Albion
Hotel, which was managed by the same Mr and Mrs
Williams who had once run the Millman Street Hotel.
He checked in as Horace Payne but Williams
recognised him and he was obliged to admit he was
Horace Rayner. When Mrs Williams asked after Alice
she was shocked by his declaring that she '. . . could go
to a warmer climate'. Horace admitted that he had only
married for 'the old girls' money', and said that he had
obtained money out of the aunts through Alice by
threatening to leave her.[8] That avenue of income was in
the process of drying up. The failure of a brewery in
which the aunts had invested had seriously reduced
the value of their capital. Horace had planned to walk

away from the unprofitable marriage as he had walked away from everything else, and was angry with Alice because, while he intended to swear that he had never married her, she insisted on sticking to the marriage certificate.

Horace, meanwhile, was off to a colder climate, and told his family he had obtained a situation with a Russian count. A Russian counting-house was nearer the mark – he became a cashier with the Union Cold Storage Company in Kozlov (now Michurinsk). Alice, her sister Gertie and Eric took rooms at 23 Highgate Road. The rent was 5s 6d a week.

Horace was in Russia until December, where his pleasant manners ensured that he was well-liked and trusted. He then absconded with £400 wages money. An extradition order was taken out for him, and a reward of £50 offered for his apprehension. By moving around – he was spotted in Birmingham and elsewhere – he was never in danger of arrest. He eventually rejoined his family at the Highgate Road flat, but was frequently away, sometimes for a week at a time, claiming that he was on business. Alice never knew where he was. He stayed in cheap hotels, where he represented himself as a single man.

He was at the Gerhard Hotel, 23 Red Lion Street, Holborn, for one night in mid-June, arriving without luggage, and signing the register with the name Horace Payne, giving an address in Russia, and paying 2s 6d for bed and breakfast. He then transferred to the Albion. The stolen money must have run out, for he was supporting himself by pawning things. That summer he visited his aunt Louie, who was then living in a flat in Great Woodstock Street, and took the opportunity to borrow money to redeem some clothes he had pawned.

In September 1906, Alice's landlord Tom Browning and his lodgers all removed to 14 Grove Park, South Tottenham, where the rent was 7s a week. Horace told Browning that he had no employment, and claimed he was doing everything he could to find some. He was becoming increasingly moody and withdrawn, and complained of insomnia. Alice found his repeated absences so worrying that she suggested a separation, but he refused to consider it. At the end of September 1906, with Alice three months pregnant, Horace disappeared again, and this time he left most of his clothes and possessions behind. He did not lose touch, however, sending Alice letters and telegrams three or four times a week, saying that he was sorry he could not come home as pressure of business kept him in the City, and Tottenham was such an awkward place to travel to.

Horace's 'business' was mainly at the Horseshoe Hotel where he was a regular visitor paying particular attention to pretty Dora Westbrook, the 18-year-old barmaid. She must have been impressed by his good looks and manners, his stories of Rugby School, his work as secretary to men of position, the businesses he had run, and the money he had made. Romance blossomed and they became engaged.

In November, Horace applied for a job at Sanatogen Ltd. When interviewed he claimed to have been educated at Rugby, and that his father was a medical man. He was not given the job. He next started placing advertisements in the newspapers, perhaps with the idea of starting an employment agency. A typical insertion read:

LADIES required to colour postcards at home, also Christmas cards, materials free; experience not necessary; remuneration.[9]

A box number was given for replies, and later many coloured cards were found among his possessions. Other advertisements were for grocers' assistants, secretaries, and typists. All produced responses which he never seems to have followed up.

On either 18 or 19 December 1906, Alice Rayner, Eric and Gertie left London to spend a fortnight at Bewdley, and Horace went to the railway station to see them off, telling them he was staying in London on business. Only later did he write to Alice informing her that he was going to give up the Tottenham flat.

Horace visited the rooms once or twice after that, to collect letters. The last time Browning saw his ex-lodger was on 23 December. Horace was very depressed, saying that the furniture was on the hire system and he could not keep up the instalments. He said he had not a brass farthing and had pawned practically everything. This was true. The nineteen pawn tickets later found at Lancaster Gate station told a sorry tale of both Horace and Alice pawning jewellery and clothing, with Horace appearing under a variety of names, such as Geo Payne, James Rayner and John Knowles. Six days later the Hackney Furnishing Company came and took away the furniture.

At the end of December, Horace left the Albion Hotel, leaving behind an unpaid bill and a trunk containing linen which was marked with several different names. For a while, Horace stayed in contact with his family. At Christmas and New Year he sent effusive love letters to Alice, but after that she heard no more from him. As the days passed she became increasingly anxious.

Horace hired a cubicle at a lodging house called Rowton House in Hammersmith, a place where upwards of 800 men stayed every night. The last item he pawned was a pair of trousers on 2 January for which he received two shillings. On 4 January 1907 he returned to the Gerhard Hotel, giving the name Rayner, although the proprietor, Jacob Gerhard, recognised him from the previous visit. His only luggage was a parcel, and he appeared to have few clothes other than what he was wearing. Horace told Jacob Gerhard that he was the son of a London businessman worth over £2 million who originally came from Yorkshire, a fact he had discovered two years previously. He also said he had learned the secret of his birth from his mother on her deathbed, which was impossible as Horace had not been with Emily when she died.

Horace tried to impress the other guests with boastful tales of adventures which they suspected he had gleaned from the newspapers, his expensive education at Rugby School, work as private secretary to wealthy gentlemen, and businesses where he had both made and run through enormous sums of money. He claimed to have twice lost highly paid jobs by being out of town when the vital telegrams arrived. To those who would listen, he complained about his father's marriage and that he could never obtain any money from him, though he hoped to receive some from two aunts.

It was at this time that Horace began to talk about his expectations of acquiring the sum of £1,000. He did not mention where this was to come from, only that he was busy making an arrangement with someone to receive the money. With these funds he intended to marry Dora, go to Canada and start up a business. He asked Gerhard's advice as to the best kind of investment.

As January progressed, Horace's mental state was obviously declining. He often complained of insomnia, and in the week before the murder he was noticeably

restless and depressed. On 19 January he told Gerhard
he had had nothing to eat all day. On the evening of
23 January, Horace asked Gerhard if he could be called
at 8 the next morning as he had an appointment and
wanted his breakfast early. After breakfast the following
day he left the hotel at 9.30 a.m. and did not return.
Three and a half hours later, he shot William Whiteley.

In the aftermath of the murder, the newspapers
carried many tributes to the Universal Provider, the *Mail*
commenting, with some truth, 'To many who have never
known him the tragic story of his death will come with
a sense of personal loss.'[10] Mr Courtauld Thomson – the
same gentleman who had signed the report which
revealed Whiteley's undervaluation of the business –
was both a colleague and a 'warm personal friend. . . .
I can say with confidence that if ever the real facts as to
this terrible tragedy are discovered, it will be found that
there is nothing in connection with them which can
reflect in any way on his honour as a man. . . . He was a
man who never said an unkind word of anyone.' The
same sense of honour, according to Thomson, extended
to Whiteley's business dealings. Mr Thomson's close
personal knowledge of William Whiteley did not extend
to knowing that he had two daughters, as he was only
aware of one.[11]

Stories emerged of Whiteley's many acts of kindness:
there was Mr Williams the old crossing sweeper who
had been a regular pensioner for five years, and an old
nurse to whom he had granted a payment of ten
shillings a week. Whiteley's tearful housekeeper, Miss
Kathleen Lockyer, said he had once refused a title
because of his 'modesty and love of retirement'. She
added that he looked nearer 60 than 75 because 'he
lived a good clean straight life'.[12]

In hospital, Horace Rayner was not lacking company. Some of the Whiteley employees had been brought in to look at him, but none could recall having seen him before. A constable had been placed there to guard him and obligingly read from the daily papers, which were not a great comfort, as Horace learned that Alice had heard what had happened. Horace had been brought up as a Catholic, and Father O'Neill, chaplain to St Mary's, was a regular visitor. When he and Horace conversed, a screen was drawn around them.

In Bewdley, Alice Rayner, now seven months pregnant, had read about the murder, but even after Horace was identified, refused to believe it was anything to do with her husband until a telegram arrived. She retired to her bed, murmuring weakly that she must go to 'George', while the people of the little town, with pitying glances at the stricken house, talked of nothing else.

On 25 January, Jacob Gerhard read about the murder in the newspapers and searched Rayner's room where he found a box of cartridges. He reported his find to the police, and then went to the hospital to identify the patient. He found Rayner lying flat without a pillow (not sitting up as artists depicted him in the newspapers), his head swathed in bandages down to the level of his mouth. Initially, Rayner refused to recognise Gerhard, but later grudgingly indicated that he did.

'I suppose you know he is dead?' said Gerhard.
'Yes, I know my father is dead,' said Rayner. 'I am glad I did it. I hope I shan't pull through.'[13]

Gerhard visited again two days later and found his former lodger in a surly mood. He asked Horace if any of his friends had been to see him to which the reply was, 'No, and I don't want to see any.' He refused to give any information beyond the fact that he still hoped he would die.[14]

Harriet Whiteley, who had been staying in Bath, told reporters that she had never heard of the Turners or the Rayners. It is not hard to detect in her statements some lingering affection for her husband, and a wistful feeling that the marriage could somehow have been saved, if only for the children's sake. 'I was always ready to be a good wife to him. . . . How I worked for the man . . . slaved for him . . . it was not I who brought about the separation. I was willing to do what I could to make things as happy as possible. My daughters were still young. But he practically drove me into a corner by sending me a solicitor's letter. Then things came to my knowledge that left me only one course. . . . Ours should have been the happiest of marriages. He was a fine business man and could be generous and kind when he liked.' This was not the time to reveal some of the unpleasanter sides of William Whiteley's character, and tastefully, she refrained.[15]

At 10 a.m. on the day after the shooting, Horace Rayner was operated on at St Mary's Hospital. The remains of his injured eye were removed, as were the bullet fragments embedded in his forehead. Horace, a more efficient assassin than he was a suicide, was expected to make a full and rapid recovery, although his good looks would be gone for ever. A sensational trial was now, for the thrill-hungry public, a real and enticing prospect.

THIRTEEN

Burying the Past

The inquest[1] into the death of William Whiteley opened on Monday 28 January 1907 at the Coroner's Court, Paddington Green, which adjoined the mortuary where the body had lain since the preceding Thursday. Dr George Danford Thomas, Coroner for the Central London District, presided. Charles St John Roche, the son of Charles Mills Roche, appeared for the Whiteley family and Henri Pierron for Horace. Such was the importance of the event that the Mayor and Town Clerk of Paddington were there. As the enquiry opened, the court was packed to overflowing, and those who could not gain entry gathered outside, eager to hear the result. Harriet arrived, but was conducted to a private room where she remained during the hearing.

William Whiteley junior was the first witness to be called, and as he stepped into the witness box, 'keen and intellectual looking', according to the *Globe*, the court was blanketed in a sympathetic hush. He started to give his evidence clearly and firmly but, describing how he had found his father's body, broke down, and was able to go on only with difficulty, his voice shaking with emotion. He confirmed that he had never seen Horace Rayner before that day. One by one the witnesses to the tragedy told their stories. Inspector Fuller said that he believed the motive for Rayner calling on Whiteley was blackmail. 'He had carefully concealed his identity in case he might be arrested.' Fuller had not traced the ownership of the revolver, which he thought had probably been stolen, though not necessarily by Rayner.

Dr French produced photographs of the relative positions of the two bodies. These were not of the bodies themselves – he had asked two friends to lie in the correct positions. He revealed that William Whiteley's brain had weighed 52oz, which was abnormally heavy.

The Coroner had no doubt that it was a case of murder and directed the jury to return a verdict accordingly. The jury was able to do so without leaving the box to confer, and Horace Rayner was committed for trial at the Central Criminal Court. The body of William Whiteley, in a polished oak coffin with brass fittings, was conveyed to 31 Porchester Terrace and placed in the drawing room.

The funeral took place on Wednesday 30 January.[2] It was bitterly cold, yet thousands of people lined the streets, and at noon, as a mark of respect, all the leading business houses of the main thoroughfares put up their shutters, drew their blinds, and closed. The coffin was eased down the steps of the house, and placed in a glass-panelled horse-drawn hearse. It was laden with floral tributes, the main one being a large harp with a symbolically broken string, from Harriet.

The chief mourners, who were all family members apart from Miss Lockyer, followed in five carriages, and another twenty carriages were required to take the remaining mourners, directors and managers of the company, aldermen, councillors, Mr Roche junior, and other prominent gentlemen including Sir Thomas Lipton. The crowd lining the route to Christ Church, Lancaster Gate, was so dense that there was hardly room for the cortège to pass, yet so quiet and orderly that the police had no difficulty in seeing the carriages through.

At the church, which had places for 1,700 people, the demand for admission was such that those employees who had served for twenty years had to be given preference, and were issued with tickets. One hundred and fifty carriages were said to have set down outside the church and discharged their occupants, but most of these could only watch from outside. The total list of floral tributes printed in the *Chronicle* covers over a column, since they represented not only family and friends, but each of the departments in the great company. The fish department, for example, supplied one in the form of an anchor, and the stables a horseshoe. Harriet and her four children (this was a rare public outing for Clara) occupied the front seats for a long and moving service with organ music and full choir. As the coffin was carried from the western door, William and Frank followed, while Harriet and her daughters remained kneeling in prayer as the dead march boomed forth from the organ. The coffin was taken to Kensal Green cemetery, a journey of 3 miles along streets lined with onlookers and closed shops. Only the chief mourners and ticket holders were allowed in for the final ceremony. A marquee had been erected over the open grave, beside which was the resting place of little Walter who had died in 1867, and here the remains were committed to the earth, the mourners afterwards passing by in single file, for a final farewell.

The other demise was the reputation of William Whiteley. As the biographer of barrister Richard Muir commented:[3] 'But the facts quoted and others concerning William Whiteley's early liaison having been published in the Press, a wave of sympathy for the

assassin ran throughout the whole country. The more
the public realized what a canting humbug Whiteley
had been, the more the sympathy increased.'

These revelations added fuel to the blackmail
scenario, and some colourful and highly unlikely stories
briefly gained credence. A gentleman who claimed to
have known Rayner for three years told the *Daily Mail*
that Rayner had told him he was connected with
Whiteleys and regularly obtained money from that
source. In one short period the sum of £8,000 was
supposed to have passed through his hands.[4] The *Mirror*
alone of all the papers rejected the lone assassin theory
and decided that Horace was part of a conspiracy,
claiming that the police were on the verge of arresting
the remainder of the gang.

George Rayner felt it necessary to issue a statement to
the press through his solicitors, which is interesting as
much for what it leaves out as what it says.

Many statements have been appearing in the Press
during the past few days connecting our client, Mr
George Rayner, with the man now lying in St Mary's
Hospital, accused of the murder of the late Mr
William Whiteley.

Our client feels very acutely that his name has been
used and published in this way. We are therefore
instructed to give you a definite statement of the facts
concerning which so much has been written, and we
trust that, after having these facts clearly set out, no
further liberties will be taken with our client's name.
The facts are briefly as follows:-

There were two sisters, one by name Emily Turner,
and the other, Louie Turner, Louie Turner being an
assistant at William Whiteley's. The other sister was

visited by Mr George Rayner. Some time after Mr George Rayner made the acquaintance of Miss Emily Turner, he was informed that Miss Emily Turner had given birth to a child, and that the child was his. Mr Rayner thereon assumed the duties and obligations thus thrust upon him and proceeded with the upbringing and education of this son.

About two years after this, Miss Emily Turner was again about to give birth to a child, she thereupon confessed to Mr George Rayner that the son he was bringing up as his own son was in fact neither his son nor her own, and in fact, that she did not give birth to it. This confession being made, it was mutually agreed between Mr Rayner and Miss Turner that the son should be relegated to its proper parents. Miss Emily Turner informed Mr Rayner that the child she was about to give birth to was his child, and although Mr Rayner had grave reasons to doubt this, owing to the position in which he found himself, he felt it incumbent upon him to accept responsibility, and promised Miss Turner that the child should be properly educated. Shortly after this, Miss Turner left Mr Rayner and was married. Mr Rayner has kept his promise to Miss Turner and has acted as foster-father to this latter son, who is the man now lying in St Mary's Hospital. The infant was registered by Miss Emily Turner wrongfully in Mr Rayner's name, the only name to which he is entitled being that of this mother.[5]

On the morning of 19 February, Detective Inspector Fuller, accompanied by a sergeant, went to St Mary's Hospital to arrest Horace Rayner for the murder of William Whiteley. Horace declined to make a statement, and was taken to Paddington Green police station where he was formally charged.

Later that day Horace appeared at the police court. He looked thin and ill. His old clothes had been brought out of pawn for him, and he was clad in a crumpled grey suit and tried to shield his face with a tweed cap. The scar of the bullet entry wound was clearly visible, the bridge of his nose was flattened, and a glass eye had been placed in the right socket, the flesh of which was swollen and blackened. The story of his life, his lies and fantasies, his theft in Russia, violence towards Alice and plans to abandon her and the children had all appeared in the eagerly devoured newspapers, yet his appearance invoked a wave of public pity which swept away all memory of his past.

> . . . broken on the wheel of circumstances [wrote the *Evening Standard*]; laid low by injuries self-inflicted; patched and prepared for a second life struggle by the surgeons; his bearing was that of one rendered by torture unable to display emotion or to take a coherent interest in his surroundings . . . an unkempt beard has grown about his chin, heavy lines mark down the corners of his mouth; the artificial eye which the hospital doctors have given him emphasises the listlessness of his expression; his profile from the right suggests nothing but a retrospect of suffering and a blank, unbroken prospect.[6]

Committed for trial, Horace was removed to the police infirmary where his health and appearance gradually improved.

The trial of Horace George Rayner, described as a 'clerk', opened at the Central Criminal Court on Friday

22 March 1907. The judge was Viscount Alverstone, later referred to as 'probably the strongest and most dominating personality that has ever sat upon the English Bench'.[7] Born in 1845, he had been appointed Attorney General in 1885 and became Lord Chief Justice in 1900.

The prosecuting counsel was Richard Muir. Born in 1857, he had been called to the Bar in 1884. His shrewd and logical grasp of the facts of a case brought him rapidly to prominence, and he was involved in many of the famous cases tried in the first two decades of the twentieth century. Hard-working and relentless, he tempered these qualities with a warm, generous nature, and was known to be sympathetic in cases where he felt there were extenuating circumstances. Appearing for Horace was George Elliott KC, and his junior was a young Henry (later Sir Henry) Curtis-Bennett.

Horace, wearing the same suit he had worn during the police court hearings, stepped quietly into the dock. His wounds had healed, and the only signs of his terrible injuries of two months before were the flattening of the bridge of his nose, and his glass eye. The *Mail* described him as 'a gallant-looking fellow . . . a bold determined boyish figure . . . a splendidly built man, with a well-poised head and wavy black hair'.[8] In a barely audible voice Horace pleaded 'Not Guilty', then lapsed into an impassive silence, neither consulting with counsel nor using any of the writing materials provided.

The opening statement of the prosecution revealed aspects of William Whiteley's personal life he had wanted to keep securely hidden, yet Muir was careful not to go too far. 'It is necessary,' he said, 'that a little, and as little as possible only, should be stated and proved relating to the early history of the prisoner and

of an episode in the life of William Whiteley.'[9] Muir
took great care to emphasise the dates on which events
had happened. The prisoner, he said, had been born in
April 1879, and his aunt had entered the service of
William Whiteley in 1882. 'That is the earliest date at
which any member of the Turner family in any way
came into contact with William Whiteley.'[10] Louie, he
said, had gone to live under the protection of William
Whiteley in January 1883, and in that year Whiteley and
Louie had first visited George Rayner and Emily. So far
as was known that was the first time the prisoner's
mother ever saw Mr Whiteley. Horace would then have
been 4 years old. When he was 5 he had been taken to
Whiteleys at Westbourne Grove and Louie had told
Whiteley that the boy was her sister's son. Muir went on
to reveal the existence of Louie and Whiteley's son,
who, for the purposes of the case, he referred to as Cecil
Whiteley, and described this boy's meeting with Horace.
Muir firmly rejected any question of justification for the
murder, which was entirely unprovoked, and neither
did he believe that it had taken place in a sudden fit of
rage. There was, on the contrary, ample evidence of
deliberation. As for motive, the prisoner's history
showed that he was in dire financial straits. He might
have reasoned that Whiteley was a man of public
position, to whom a few hundred pounds was of no
consequence, but the revival of an old scandal was of
great consequence. The motive was blackmail:
'blackmail and succeed, or fail and commit suicide'.[11]

Muir concluded by submitting to the jury that there
could only be one conclusion from the facts – that the
crime was one of deliberate and wilful murder.

The first witness was Sir George Lewis. Lewis was
probably the most famous lawyer in England. Born in

1833, by 1907 he was close to retirement, having in his stellar career acted in numerous celebrated cases, including the Baccarat affair, and the Dilke divorce case. It was said he knew the true facts behind every society scandal, but one reason for his enormous success was that his illustrious clients knew they could rely upon him for absolute secrecy. In this respect he did not fail the memory of the late William Whiteley. Lewis told the court that he did not know Horace and had never given him authority to use his name to obtain an interview with Whiteley. He had not acted in the Whiteley divorce proceedings nor in any action between Whiteley and George Rayner. Asked if he had acted for Mr Whiteley in any matter relating to Louisa and Emily Turner, he protested, 'My Lord, there is really no occasion to go into what those communications were.'[12] His Lordship permitted him to do no more than confirm that he had acted in that matter, and stopped the questioning when Elliott sought to probe further. Lewis departed the witness box, his reputation untarnished. When he retired in 1909, he destroyed all his papers.

'A slim lady of medium height, dressed in black, with a black veil and wearing pince-nez' now stepped into the witness box.[13] This, at last, was Louie Turner, who had recently retired to live at Berry Villa, Silverton, Devon. Every eye must have stared keenly at the woman who held so many secrets. She spoke in a subdued voice, and seemed painfully aware of the powerful searchlight that was being thrown on to that long-hidden area of her life. Louie said she had met George Rayner about a year before Horace was born. She knew that George had repudiated the older child, but Emily had told her that George was the father. At the time she entered the service of William Whiteley, Emily had been living with

George as his wife for about three years. She did not believe that George and Whiteley had known each other at the time. Louie confirmed that the house in Greville Road had been taken in the name of Rayner even though George and Emily had never lived there, only stayed there as visitors. A receipt was put in evidence, for furniture bought for the house, stating 'Received from George Rayner, on payment by Wm. Whiteley, the sum of £300.' Elliott was careful to elicit from her the Turner family's long acquaintanceship with the bottle. Emily, Louie admitted, had eventually given way to drink, the same failing of both her mother and her grandmother.

As Elliott rose to make his opening speech for the defence, it was obvious that there was only one line he could take. Even though the prisoner stood calmly in the dock, and had been considered perfectly competent to stand trial, Elliott would have to try and convince the court that his client was insane, if only at the time of the murder. Sensibly, he did not try to prove that Rayner was Whiteley's son. For the case he was about to make it was necessary, and indeed preferable, only to show that Horace believed it. He sought to show that:

. . . his vicissitudes, acting on a mind never of a powerful equilibrium in a parentage associated with constant habits of indulgence, weakened the mental and moral fibre in the man. At the time of going to Mr Whiteley, the prisoner was, in fact, insane . . . [the jury] had heard of his antecedents and would understand that he was a degenerate. A man with parentage like that of the prisoner, might be able to stand a certain amount of trouble, but when the psychological moment came, when more trouble came upon him than he could bear, then a man like that, until then quite rational, might become as mad as any raging lunatic in an asylum.[14]

In particular, Elliott protested against the suggestion that it was a premeditated murder.

Alice May Rayner, eight and a half months pregnant, pretty and pale, stepped into the witness box. Horace bowed his head as she told of the problems of her married life, and how her husband's failure to find work affected his temper and made it hard for him to sleep at nights. Sometimes, she admitted, Horace was not very kind to her. 'He used to call me all sorts of names and say he wished he had not married me,' she confessed.[15] Annie and Sarah Knowles also gave evidence saying that when they had seen Horace last November, his eyes had been bloodshot and he had not had food for two days.

By the time Horace was called, the crowds in the gallery must have looked on him with sympathy, if only for the ruination of his once handsome face. His voice, said the *Standard*, was 'clear though not self-assertive, and with a conciseness and absence of colour that convinced many people who heard him, that though misguided and criminal, he was not lying'.[16]

After his return from the second visit to Russia, said Horace, he had been unable to find employment and had gone without food a good deal. He recalled that when his mother had been quarrelling with George she had said that if ever he needed a friend he should find one in Mr Whiteley. He gave no date for this conversation, which, if it had taken place, must have been before 1888. He also recalled George's hints that Horace might not be his son. The two stories seemed to add up. He had, he said, considered blowing his brains out when he had been at Rowton House, except he did not then have the funds to fetch his revolver out of pawn. He believed that he was justified in approaching Whiteley, gambling his own life against the Universal Provider's goodwill. Horace's account of his talk with William Whiteley is the only version of the events that took place behind the closed door of the little office. There is no way of knowing how much of his statement is true, or what he may have omitted. In common with many another criminal, Horace claimed to recall nothing of those incidents he was least comfortable describing. The interview began with Horace admitting that he had not after all, come from Sir George Lewis. Giving his name he said, 'I believe I am right in stating, Mr Whiteley, that your son is speaking to his father?'

'Is that so?' said Whiteley. 'And when did you see me last?'

Horace explained the circumstance of their last meeting and Whiteley said, 'And what can I do for you?'

I mentioned my desperate straits with regard to money and my wife's condition. I made no propositions to him with regard to helping me. Mr Whiteley asked me what business I had been brought up to, and after talking some time, without getting much nearer the object of my visit, I put it to him: 'Can you assist me in any way? I shall be pleased if only I could obtain employment.' I mentioned no question of money to him, except in so far as it might be taken by inference. He said I must not mix myself up with the past, or words to that effect. He also said it was all very fine, but there were two sides to every question, and I had only presented one side. I made no comment, and he said, 'Why don't you go abroad?' I said I had no capital, but he said that many young fellows went abroad without capital and did well. He said, 'I should advise you to go to one of the emigration agencies, such as the Salvation Army.' I was very much nettled to think that he showed so little sentiment in speaking to a blood relation, and there was a revulsion of feeling in my mind. I said, 'Do you absolutely refuse to assist me, even by employment?' He said, 'I must not.' Thereupon I said, 'Then I must tell you that I made up my mind before I came here that I will blow my brains out, if unsuccessful in my application to you.' He said, 'Don't be so silly.' I was excited and produced the revolver, and put it to my head. He said, 'Put that thing down,' and I put it behind my back. I was staggered for a moment as to what was best to do. My head was in a whirl, and I thought, 'Well if he is not amenable to sentiment and to what ought to be his sense of duty, perhaps he may be amenable to a sense of fear.' I therefore made up my mind that I would play that as the last card without any intention at all of carrying it into effect. So I put the revolver in my pocket and sat down, tore a leaf out of my note-book, and started to write.

After I had written the best part of it, Mr Whiteley got up and went towards the door. I asked him if he would stop. He took no notice. I got up to see what had become of him and saw him standing outside. It occurred to me that he had thought he would wait outside to hear me shoot myself. I think my mind was not improved by the knowledge of that fact. I went towards him, and extended my hand in a friendly way, and asked him to come in again and not leave the matter like that. He said, 'No. I have sent for a policeman.' That is all I remember of the circumstances. The actual shooting and what was in my mind at the time I know nothing about.[17]

Rayner's story fails to explain why Whiteley was rendered pale with fury, his fists clenched in anger. Few things could have produced such a reaction, a demand for money being the most obvious. Based on immediate past events, it is a reasonable conclusion that Horace asked Whiteley to give him £1,000, to enable him to go to Canada. He must have made this request based on his claim to be Whiteley's son, though whether there was also an attempt at blackmail must remain in doubt. The waving of a revolver was more than sufficient reason for the police to be called to remove the unwanted visitor.

When Horace had told his story the court waited with anticipation for Mr Muir's cross-examination. It never came. To everyone's astonishment, the prisoner was not questioned further and left the witness box. It was most unlike Muir's usual thorough work, and there was some speculation that either he was sympathetic to the accused, or had received special instructions to do nothing which would intensify the scandal. Horace's career as a serial liar, work-shy sponger, thief, wife-abuser and intended bigamist was therefore never aired in court.

Muir's next actions tend to counter the 'sympathy' argument. Two medical witnesses were brought, and both testified that Horace had suffered from mental instability and diminished self-control. They thought that such a person would commit acts and recover without knowing what had happened. Elliott had opened the door, offering the jury a chance to show mercy, but Muir immediately shut it. He asked both

doctors if the prisoner was insane now. Both answered
'No'. Muir submitted that no case of insanity had been
made out to go to the jury, and the judge agreed.

At 4.20 in the afternoon, the Lord Chief Justice began
his summing up. He told the jury they must dismiss any
question of sanity or insanity. It was impossible that the
shooting could be accidental. If they decided that the
prisoner drew a pistol on Mr Whiteley intending to kill
him then they must find a verdict of guilty of wilful
murder. This, after deliberating for just nine minutes,
they did. Horace took the news without flinching, and
listened impassively as he was sentenced to hang. As he
stepped from the dock, the bank holiday attraction at
Madame Tussauds was already in preparation – William
Whiteley and Horace George Rayner.

There was an immediate tidal wave of sympathy for
the condemned man. The great warm-hearted Victorian
public had taken Horace Rayner to its collective bosom,
and campaigned tirelessly for his reprieve. His
solicitor's office was so besieged by people wanting to
sign a petition that he had to open special addresses for
them to go to and appoint a team of clerks to handle the
deluge of mail. The newspapers were inundated with
letters of which the following are typical:

> The heart of man revolts against the thought of
> nursing this poor prisoner back to life in order that he
> may be legally put to death.

> No-one can read the pitiful story without realising
> that Rayner was impelled along the path of
> destruction by forces and conditions – mainly the
> fault of society, largely those of other persons – almost
> beyond his control.[18]

One correspondent even suggested that 'Rayner's crime almost amounts to justifiable homicide'.[19]

There were a few steelier souls who regarded the campaign as 'misguided and ill-judged sentimentality', and as one correspondent pointed out, 'the late Mr Whiteley may have been a roué, but none of his victims suffered want, whereas Rayner was courting a young lady, and at the same time his wife was in want'.[20]

In a few days, Pierron's clerks distributed petition forms sufficient to hold over a million signatures. On 31 March he was just about to post a large batch of completed forms when the telephone rang, and an unknown caller asked if it was true that Horace had been reprieved. Pierron immediately phoned the Home Office, and was told that a messenger was on his way and he could save his stamps. He at once sent a telegram

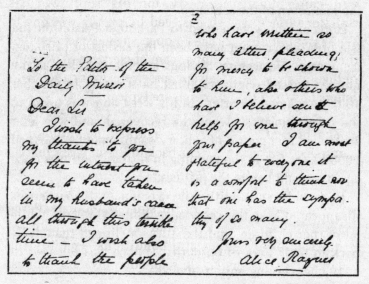

The 'thank-you' letter written by Alice Rayner to the *Daily Mirror*.

to Alice. She must have gone into labour shortly after receiving the news, for her daughter Christine was born at 4.30 a.m. on 1 April.

Not everyone approved. The *Chronicle* commented: 'The only intelligible ground upon which the Home Secretary can have advised his Sovereign to exercise the prerogative of mercy was anxiety for the safety of the miserable wife about to become a mother, an anxiety which her depraved husband does not appear to have shared in any degree.'[21] Horace, moved out of the condemned cell, was pleased for Alice's sake, but commented: 'I would have preferred to get the whole business over and done with, instead of having to endure years of misery behind iron bars.'[22] Alverstone, in his memoirs, made his feelings on the matter quite plain. 'The crime was a deliberate one and obviously planned beforehand, but for some reason which I was never able to fathom, the then Home Secretary advised the remission of the sentence.'[23]

Horace, who was moved to Parkhurst Prison on the Isle of Wight, cannot have been the easiest of prisoners to manage. He was an obvious suicide risk, but as the months passed, vigilance must have eased. In October 1907 he opened an artery in his wrist and was taken to the prison hospital, where he recovered, and was later sentenced to a period of solitary confinement.[24] In April 1908 he set fire to the bedding in his cell, and was once again brought before the justices.[25]

Horace Rayner with his dreams and obsessions disappeared from the knowledge of the Whiteleys, while Alice, her children, and the Turners slipped thankfully back to their lives of obscurity. Horace was released in 1919 after serving only twelve years.[26]

The Legacy of William Whiteley

Whiteley's will was a matter of enormous public interest. The man who had not been noted for great generosity during his lifetime had left the bulk of his fortune to charity. There were a number of small bequests to hospitals, and he had left £5,000 to a fund for promotion of sporting activities, and £5,000 to supply annual Christmas gifts to the deserving poor of Paddington. To each of his sons he left £50,000 (approximately £3 million today), and to his daughters an annuity of £1,000 on the death of their mother. Harriet, who had already been provided for, received nothing. There were the usual small bequests to servants, nieces, nephews, and £1,000 each to his brother-in-law Henry Mason, and Charles Roche junior. The annuity of £150 to Louie was to continue.

The largest bequest, amounting to something like £1 million (a staggering £60 million today) was for a project to which he had obviously devoted a great deal of thought. For William Whiteley, the store which carried his name was not a sufficient monument to his memory. He wanted something bigger. He had therefore determined that the money should be used to create a village of homes for the aged poor, and had left detailed instructions as to how this was to be done.

The will appointed eight trustees, including his sons, and specified that they should purchase freehold land in one of the western suburbs of London or the adjacent country, and if possible within 10 miles of Charing Cross. The site 'shall be in as bright cheerful and healthy spot as possible' and the buildings 'of good and substantial character and of a plain and useful design'. Those qualified to be inmates 'shall be persons of good character and of sound mind and not affected by any infectious or contagious disease, and not having been convicted of any criminal offence, and being male of not less than sixty-five years and being female of not less than sixty years of age'. Preference would be given to persons or wives of persons who had been engaged in commercial or agricultural pursuits.[1]

It was obvious from the start that there was going to be trouble. At the first meeting of the trustees on 5 June 1907, William and Frank proposed that the land at Hanworth might be suitable, but discovered that the other trustees thought it would be better to build homes on more than one site. This was a suggestion William and Frank strenuously opposed, as something they believed was contrary to their father's wishes. It was obvious, however, that the work was not to happen for some time, as most of the estate consisted of shares, and the state of the stock market indicated that it would be best to wait before realising the capital.

In June 1909 the executors were at last able to offer the bulk of the company shares to the public. That July the trustees commissioned two independent reports on whether it would be better to have the Whiteley homes on one site or several. When the reports were delivered both were in favour of several sites, but William and Frank dug their heels in and said that was not what their father had intended. The continued impasse could only be settled in a court of law. The case came before Mr Justice Eve on 23 February 1910, and his judgment

referred to 'the wish and intentions of the testator –
obvious throughout his will – that his benefactions of a
public character should be permanently and
prominently associated with his name . . .'. He added: 'I
think it is impossible to read the will without coming to
the conclusion that the testator was a man of strong
individuality, the nature of whose charitable
dispositions was, in part, determined by his wish
therewith to identify his personality, and thereby to
perpetuate his memory.' Pointing out that the will
always referred to a 'site' not a 'site or sites', he held
that the trustees were not entitled to select more than
one. William and Frank had won.[2]

A site at Shirley Park Estate, Croydon, was approved
by the majority of trustees but rejected by William and
Frank, so it was back to court again, and Mr Justice Eve,
who agreed with the brothers that Croydon was not a
western suburb. By March 1911, however, there was
unanimous agreement on the 225 acres at Burhill
outside Weybridge, and work started on clearing the
heavily wooded area.

Six architects were invited to submit their designs for
the village, and the winner was R. Frank Atkinson who
proposed a distinctive central octagonal layout. While
changes were later made to the scheme it is this feature
which survived the later planning stages. Seven
architects were then asked to design the cottages, and
Sir George Frampton was commissioned to design a
memorial to William Whiteley. Surprisingly, he did not
propose to erect a statue of the founder, instead
suggesting a figure symbolising trade, with a bust of the
founder on the pedestal. Even more surprisingly, the
trustees approved it. The foundation stone was finally
laid on 21 July 1914. Two weeks later, war was declared.

The builders suggested that in view of lack of men and materials, the work should be suspended for the duration of the war, but the trustees decided to press on.

While all this was happening, the company was moving into an era of increased prosperity. The directors now had a confidence in the future which enabled them to contemplate a fundamental change in the business. The leases on five of the Westbourne Grove properties were soon to expire. The company could have bought the freehold, but instead, it was decided to move its centre of operations to Queen's Road. This was part of a major scheme which involved not only the construction of a new building but remodelling the existing properties to provide a unified unbroken row of Whiteleys stores. The whole project would cost £250,000 (about £15 million today), and central to its success was the purchase of the Paddington Baths. Negotiations between the company and the Council had started and stopped several times over a number of years amid disputed valuations, objections by councillors, opposition from local ratepayers, and an enquiry at the Town Hall, and by March 1910 had ground to a frustrating halt.[3]

That month brought for some people a terrifying memory of the great Whiteley fires of the 1880s, when smoke was seen to be pouring out of a basement in Westbourne Grove. Eleven firemen, with no kind of protection again the fumes, lowered themselves inside. After a while, they failed to respond to shouts from their comrades, and men with smoke helmets went down. All eleven had been overcome and were unconscious. Fortunately they were brought out and later recovered in hospital. The fire itself was soon put out, with only £800 worth of damage done.[4]

A few days later the sale of the Baths was finally agreed, and it closed its doors for the last time on 31 August 1910. A demolition team soon reduced it to rubble, and on 28 October the Mayor of Paddington laid the foundation stone of Whiteleys' new premises. At the celebratory luncheon John Lawrie, replying to the Mayor's toast to 'the firm' said they hoped the new building would become the greatest commercial enterprise in the country. It would extend from Porchester Gardens to Douglas Place, with a frontage of 600ft and a depth of 300ft on a site of 4 acres. There would be five floors, a large centre dome 150ft high and twenty-four passenger lifts. He promised 'many novelties', some of which they would keep up their sleeves – they wanted the opening of the store to cause a sensation.[5] An enticingly worded brochure was distributed to the guests. 'Imagine the most dignified and beautiful store you can conceive, the centre of a thousand interests, an institution running as smoothly as silk slips from a reel, and you will begin to have a glimmering of what the New Whiteleys will mean . . . Whiteleys will be more than a store – it will be a first class club – a social centre.'[6]

The new store, which opened on 21 November 1911, was everything that had been promised, a veritable palace of shopping, with much to delight and astonish. The frontage was of smooth-faced white granite with Corinthian columns, and on entering the store the visitor stepped into a rotunda surmounted by a dome which was a reproduction of that of the church of Santa Maria della Salute in Venice. The galleries around the rotunda were occupied by sale counters, and on the top floor there was a tea room and café with access to an Italian roof garden to be used as a restaurant. There were telephone stations, a wireless telegraphy station on the roof, a lounge for ladies, a reading room, and a smoking room for gentlemen. The store's 115 departments required 5,000 staff. A whole floor was set aside for children who would be able to amuse themselves on an imitation seashore in the charge of nurses while their mothers were shopping.[7]

The whole scheme was still incomplete when it attracted the attention of the *Architectural Review* in 1912. There were now two rotundas which extended the whole height of the building with connecting floors at different levels. The *Review* revealed that the graceful twin marble columns of the rotundas were not weight bearing, but had a core of steel and concrete. The whole weight of the building was taken by a steel frame, weighing nearly 3,000 tons. 'The two main considerations in the design of the interior were – large space for display, and effective fire-protection . . . as regards the fire-protection of the building this is so elaborate as to merit somewhat extended notice.' There was to be no skating around the regulations in the new Whiteleys. Fire-resistant glazing was used throughout and there were steel shutters that could be wound up and down. The floors were of hollow clay blocks reinforced with steel rods. There was also a sprinkler system, a fire detection and alarm system, a hydrant system and fire escape staircases.[8]

In the three years following the opening of the great store, the company results more than bore out the surging confidence of its directors. In 1914, with the outbreak of war delaying the building of the Whiteley Homes, and the increased prices of coal and petrol making trading conditions less favourable, Frank Whiteley had another problem on his mind.

Two years previously while on holiday in Eastbourne, Frank and Ethel had met Captain Lancelot Fane Gladwin and his young wife, who was very ill. They had become friends, but shortly afterwards, Mrs Gladwin died. The Whiteleys had offered sympathetic support. Lancelot had visited Frank and Ethel, and later gone travelling with them. In 1913 Lancelot, with the full knowledge of Frank, had stayed in a hotel in Minehead where Ethel and the children had also been staying, while Frank was detained in London on business. Early in 1914 Ethel complained of feeling unwell and said she needed to go to Brighton for a change. She departed on 21 January, and the next day Frank received a letter from Lancelot, confessing his adultery with Ethel. Matters had been precipitated by the fact that Ethel was pregnant. On 28 July Frank was informed that Ethel had given birth to a son. The marriage was dissolved a few days later.[9]

Another grave concern was the health of Frank's son, Frank junior, born in March 1907, Whiteley's only grandson of the legitimate line. The child was afflicted with tuberculosis, and in the summer of 1916 it became apparent that the condition had spread to the brain. He died of tuberculous meningitis on 20 August, aged 9.

* * *

Despite the difficult trading conditions during the war, Whiteleys came through with satisfactory results. Many of the young men had joined the forces, and in their absence increasing numbers of women were taking senior posts. In April 1920 Whiteleys gave a dinner at the Connaught Rooms in honour of the employees who had served in the war, also the Red Cross and VAD workers. Two hundred women employees had worked in their spare time for the hospital services. Fourteen hundred men had joined the forces, and eighty-five had died. Eleven had won decorations, chief of those being Sergeant C. Spackman of the 1st Border regiment, who had gained the VC and the *Médaille Militaire*. In June 1923 a memorial shrine on the fourth floor of the rotunda was dedicated to the fallen.

In October 1917, the first villagers were able to take up residence in the Whiteley Homes. Numbers and amenities increased over the years, and by 1920 there were over 224 residents enjoying a village social club, a lending library, a communal kitchen and a church. In May 1921 the King and Queen made a visit. By then the village, with 300 inhabitants, boasted a hall for films, plays and concerts, a post office, allotments, a recreation ground and a hospital.

William and Frank were there to guide the royal couple, and Frank's daughter Nora presented the Queen with a bouquet. Their Majesties toured the village, planted some trees, were entertained by the village choral society, declared the new clubhouse open and had tea. Whiteleys did the catering.

The early twenties were years of record profits for the company – in 1921 over £300,000. Times were changing. Fewer employees were living in and the farm at Hanworth, which William and Frank had been so eager to offer to the trustees in 1907, was finally disposed of. At the AGM in March 1923 William junior, chairman of the company, spoke optimistically of the future, but these were to be the company's last good times, and William's last AGM. Shortly afterwards (the exact date is unknown), he suffered a riding accident, shattering a leg and a shoulder so badly that a year later he was still confined to bed. At the 1925 AGM John Lawrie announced that William had taken the decision to retire from business. Lawrie was unanimously elected chairman.

William left London, for 'Bencomb' in Mickleham, Surrey, where he lived quietly. His new home was only 8 miles from the Whiteley Village. He corresponded regularly with the other trustees and from 1927 he was able to attend the annual general meetings at the village. He was also a generous subscriber to local charities, and impressed everyone with his kind nature. There seemed to be no bitterness about the accident which had robbed him of his busy life at the heart of the thriving Whiteley empire.

In 1923 the company was paying handsome dividends of 20 per cent to its ordinary shareholders. In the next three years it maintained this rate, adding a 5 per cent bonus. Steadily falling profits were explained away as due to the extensive building work involved in the remodelling of the Queen's Road frontage. The optimism of the company meetings had a hollow centre, invisible beneath the cloak of rich dividends. The success of Whiteleys had depended on its position at the heart of an upper-middle-class suburb, but the glory days of Bayswater were over. It was no longer a unified community of prosperous families, but had a diverse and increasingly cosmopolitan population with wholly different requirements, which traders could not afford to ignore. The loss of cachet meant that customers from outside the area who might once have made their way to Westbourne Grove were now shopping in Oxford Street.

One of Whiteleys' many rivals was Selfridges, opened in 1909 by American entrepreneur Harry Gordon Selfridge. In 1926, a negotiator called Jimmy White, keen to enjoy a handsome commission, hinted to

Selfridge that he might be able to purchase Whiteleys, but preliminary talks came to nothing. At the March 1927 AGM, Lawrie stated, 'We have now a most beautiful and well-laid-out store, second to none, with ample space for comfortable and pleasant shopping, fully equipped with the latest and most up-to-date requirements.' There had been setbacks which he attributed to the General Strike and a coal strike, but he expressed confidence for the future. He confirmed that there had been an offer for the business but that negotiations had fallen through.[10]

White's persistence won through, however, and just over a week later the terms of amalgamation of Whiteleys and Selfridges were published in the newspapers. The offer was extraordinarily, even foolishly, generous, and suggests that ego rather than common sense was at work. Selfridges was to purchase a controlling interest in Whiteleys and would guarantee that the ordinary shareholders would receive a dividend of 25 per cent every year for ten years. In the event of Whiteleys not making enough profit to pay such a dividend, Selfridges agreed to make up the difference. John Lawrie, recognising an unmissable deal, was happy to recommend it to the shareholders, but to his dismay, they did not see things his way. An extraordinary general meeting was held on 12 April where it was apparent that the shareholders were strenuously opposed to the transfer of control, and were highly critical of the directors who had agreed to retire from office. Lawrie, dropping the optimistic tone he had used at the AGMs, was obliged to remind everyone that the profits of Whiteleys had been in decline for the last few years, whereas Selfridges' profits had increased, but his views seemed to carry no weight, especially when it was revealed that all the directors would receive handsome compensation for their loss of guaranteed income. With the continued spirited opposition of the shareholders, Lawrie must have thought the deal would fall through, but instead, Selfridges offered improved terms. The company was now prepared to guarantee the 25 per cent dividend for fifteen years. The shareholders jumped at the offer, and the merger was agreed. It was an arrangement that Gordon Selfridge came to regret bitterly.

The takeover marked the final severing of all connections between the company and the family of its founder. Frank Whiteley did not enjoy his retirement for long. He died in Bayswater on 19 November 1929, from chronic bronchitis and heart failure. He was 57.

William Whiteley junior had become a familiar figure in Mickleham, spending a great deal of time, especially in the summer months, standing on crutches at the entrance to Bencomb Drive, with his personal attendant, watching the stream of traffic moving along the road.[11] Privately, he may have consoled himself with alcohol, for he died of heart failure and cirrhosis of the liver on 11 March 1937 at the age of 65.

Harriet was too frail to attend the funerals of either of her sons. She had retired to a nursing home in Worthing where she died in 1940 aged 95. Her daughters never married. Clara died in 1946 and Ada in 1951.

The new directors of William Whiteley Limited were obliged to make some radical changes. The properties used as sleeping quarters for the living-in staff were disposed of, as they were no longer needed. The farm at Hillingdon had not been used for some years and had become derelict. It was sold for building land. Profits remained disappointing. Customers still flocked to Whiteleys but individually they were spending less.

The large Bayswater residences where families had brought up broods of children and employed servants were being split into flats for the smaller units required by a more mobile population with different spending patterns. Unwanted town houses were demolished and blocks of flats took their place. At the centre of the changes, Whiteleys in all its Edwardian splendour was failing to keep pace.

In no year following the takeover did Whiteleys earn enough to pay the 25 per cent dividend, and each time Selfridges had to make up the difference. The guarantee, which was now recognised as a serious error of judgement, was an onerous burden, and, as the directors were eventually obliged to admit, 'too much success was probably responsible for the over-confidence which has resulted in such serious over-expansion'.[12] A gradual, encouraging improvement in the 1930s was suddenly reversed in 1938, when the threat of war decreased public confidence, and spending declined. The Whiteley profits plummeted once more, and by 1940, with the company making losses for the first time since the fires of the 1880s, Selfridges had had enough. A total of £663,350 had been paid out under the guarantee and the liquidity of Selfridges was under threat. A scheme was put in place cancelling the guarantee in return for stock in Selfridges. Gordon Selfridge was ousted from the board of directors, and gambled away his fortune, dying in poverty in 1947.

During the Second World War, trading was difficult for all businesses due to an exodus of the population from London, and lack of merchandise, but Whiteleys benefited by being called upon to supply over 5,000,000 items of equipment, such as tents and gas masks. Of 560 staff serving in the war, 16 were killed and many were

decorated, one with the George Medal. The shop was
not struck by bombing, but in March 1945 a rocket fell
nearby breaking the glass and frames of the large show
windows, and it was some time before it was possible to
obtain permission to replace them.

In the postwar years the company limped along with
modest results, hampered by the increasing expense of
maintaining the huge premises, while government-
controlled profit margins curtailed income. At the end
of 1952, 61-year-old Colonel George Stanley Brighten,
chairman of a number of London property companies,
acquired on behalf of himself and some colleagues, a
large interest in the ordinary share capital of Whiteleys
Limited, and joined the Board. He intended to carry out
a complete reorganisation of the business. One of his
ideas was to build a new international air terminal at
the rear of the store in Queensway, though the project
met with difficulties at the planning stages and was
soon abandoned. The reorganisation was expensive,
profits disappeared, and the payment of dividends was
suspended. Nevertheless in July 1954 Brighten said he
viewed the future with confidence.[13]

Whether or not Brighten's 'new broom' tactics would
have worked in the long run will never be known. Just
over two months later, Brighten was driving through
Newchapel in Surrey, when he lost control of his car,
which swerved across the road, plunged through a
hedge and ditch into a ploughed field, and came to a
sudden stop against a large tree. He was taken to
hospital but was found to be dead on arrival.

He was not therefore able to offer an explanation for
the fact that in the year ended March 1955 the company
suffered a loss of nearly a quarter of a million pounds.
In November 1955, with the losing trend continuing, the

chairman Sir Sydney Harold Gillett announced that 'the selling space was too large for the present turnover and running expenses were higher than would be the case if all the selling space available could be utilised'. The floor space, he admitted, was 'large enough to service a turnover of four times its present size'.[14] The company was obliged to let the substantial Kensington property, and sell off others. The upper floors of the Queensway store were converted to offices, the spectacular light wells obliterated by concrete. The space was let to Esso Petroleum.

In 1961, though there were signs of recovery, ordinary shareholders had not had a dividend since 1953, and the company was taken over by United Drapery Stores. The bid was £1,750,000. In real terms, the company was worth one-fifth of its original value.

By contrast, Whiteley Village remained a success. It was substantially modernised in the 1960s and still thrives today, remaining true to its founder's ideals. There is a village open day on the third Saturday in July, and on the Sunday nearest to William Whiteley's birthday a service is held to commemorate the founding of the village.

But no one could save Whiteleys stores. As the company slid into losses again, UDS held a market survey to see what could be done, and discovered that the customers were satisfied – there were just not enough of them. In 1981 it was announced that Whiteleys, which had only 300 staff, was uneconomic, and would be closing down. The final sale was on 3 October that year, when a rush of 200,000 people cleaned out all the remaining stock. The doors closed, and as the years passed, and the building remained unsold, neglect and vandalism took its toll.

That could have been the end – but it wasn't.

In 1986 the building was purchased by a consortium of property developers, who sold it to the Standard Life Assurance Company in the following year. A massive restoration commenced during which modern additions were demolished to restore the beauty of the original façade and interior of the Grade II listed building. Concrete was broken away to reveal the light wells, which once again could illuminate the sweep of the great staircase and tiers of balconied galleries. On 26 July 1989, Whiteleys reopened, offering a varied, attractive and comfortable environment for shopping and leisure. The development coincided with the social and economic revival of Bayswater following extensive rebuilding programmes, which had brought young professionals and wealthy families to the area.

Customers who enter Whiteleys today looking for bargains, or heading for the eight-screen cinema, gymnasium or restaurants, should pause a moment to look at the soaring marble columns, elegant staircase, classical glass domes, gilded lettering and fine plasterwork, which evoke the days of Edwardian grandeur. On this spot once stood the great warehouses dubbed 'Whiteley's Folly' by his competitors, twice burned to the ground by a bitter enemy. Around the corner in Westbourne Grove flourished the row of shops where he made his reputation, and here one can imagine the crush of ladies in their long sweeping gowns battling over lengths of silk, and hard-pressed assistants in neat black dresses, concealing with a smile their fear of the great man's temper and his more personal attentions, while supervising it all is a short, stocky Yorkshireman with a frock coat and a welcoming smile, ushering you in to the great glory of its age which was and is Whiteleys.

Whiteley Genealogy Table 1 – Ancestry and Siblings

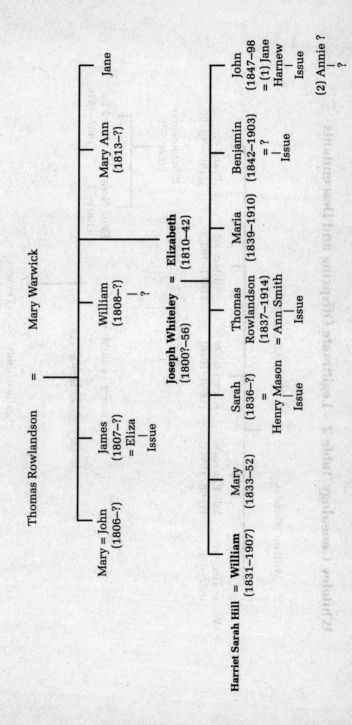

Whiteley Genealogy Table 2 – Legitimate Offspring and Descendants

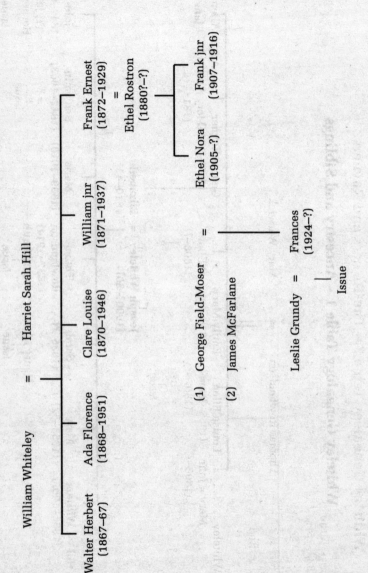

ONE: BANKRUPTCY AVENUE

1. Genealogical data from official records at the Family Record Centre, London; the International Genealogical Index and the parish records of Featherstone and Warmfield, West Riding Archives.
2. *MAP* and Anon., 'William Whiteley, Universal Provider', in *Fortunes Made in Business*, Amalgamated Press, London, 1901, pp. 94–101.
3. 'Tragic End of the Universal Provider', *Wakefield Express*, 26 January 1907, p. 3.
4. *MAP*, p. 504.
5. *Ibid.*
6. *Ibid.*
7. Lambert, p. 16. Lambert's 1938 biography has not been used as a factual source, except on the rare occasions, which are indicated, where it is clear that he had access to records which I have not been able to trace. It should be pointed out here that Lambert's account of William Whiteley's parentage is incorrect.
8. *MAP*, p. 505.
9. C. Hawley, *The Drapery Trade before the Public*, John Heywood, 1878, Manchester, pp. 15–16.
10. *MAP*, p. 505.
11. *Ibid.*
12. 'Topics', p. 11.
13. *MAP*, p. 505.
14. 'Topics', p. 11.
15. *Ibid.*
16. *MAP*, p. 505.

TWO: THE MAKING OF WESTBOURNE GROVE

1. 'Topics', p. 11. In the nineteenth century and well into the twentieth, the word employee was spelt employé. I have used the modern spelling throughout.
2. *Fortunes*, p. 96.
3. 'Topics', p. 11.
4. W.P. Frith, *My Autobiography and Reminiscences*, Richard Bentley and Son, London, 1889, p. 289.
5. *MAP*, p. 505.
6. 'Topics', p. 11.

7. The *Bayswater Chronicle* was continued as the *PKB Chronicle* in 1873.
8. 'William Whiteley (Limited)', *PKB Chronicle*, 4 June 1898, p. 5.
9. 'The Widow Interviewed', *Daily Chronicle*, 28 January 1907, p. 5.
10. 'Kildare Rowing Club', *Paddington Times*, 15 July 1871, p. 3.
11. 'The Late Mr James Flood', *PKB Chronicle*, 6 November 1886, p. 5.
12. 'Public Baths and Washhouses', *Paddington Times*, 21 January 1871, p. 3.
13. 'Paddington Vestry', *Paddington Times*, 8 April 1871, p. 3.
14. 'Troubles of a Wedding Trousseau', *Bayswater Chronicle*, 4 March 1871, p. 7.
15. *Bayswater Chronicle*, 23 March 1872, p. 4.
16. 'Co-operation Extraordinary', *Paddington Times*, 9 March 1872, p. 3.

THREE: WHITELEYS' WINDOWS

1. *Paddington Times*, 19 April 1873, p. 3.
2. 'Westbourne Grove Approaches', *Paddington Times*, 17 January 1874, p. 2.
3. 'Widening Westbourne Grove', *Paddington Times*, 23 May 1874, p. 2.
4. 'Lunch with the Linen Drapers', *Graphic*, 3 August 1872, p. 98.
5. 'Kildare Dramatic Society', *Paddington Times*, 22 February 1873, p. 3.
6. 'Whiteley's' Christmas Bazaar', *Paddington Times*, 19 December 1874, p. 2.
7. *Fortunes*, p. 98.
8. 'Kildare Dramatic Society', *Paddington Times*, 9 January 1875, p. 2.
9. 'Whiteley's New Premises, Queen's Rd Bayswater, and the Commissioners of Baths and Washhouses', *Paddington Times*, 13 February 1875, p. 3.
10. 'Paddington Vestry', *PKB Chronicle*, 10 April 1875.
11. 'Paddington Vestry', *Paddington Times*, 6 March 1875, p. 3.
12. 'Paddington Vestry', *PKB Chronicle*, 20 March 1875, p. 5.
13. 'Paddington Vestry', *Paddington Times*, 10 April 1875, p. 3; 'Paddington Vestry', *PKB Chronicle*, 10 April 1875, p. 5.
14. *PKB Chronicle*, 10 April 1875, p. 4.

15. 'Whiteley's Windows', *Paddington Times*, 1 May 1875, p. 2.
16. *Paddington Times*, 8 May 1875, p. 2.
17. 'Paddington Vestry', *PKB Chronicle*, 24 April 1875, p. 5.
18. *Paddington Times*, 15 May 1875, p. 2.
19. 'Mr Whiteley's Grand Furniture Emporium, Queen's Rd Bayswater', *Paddington Times*, 25 September 1875, p. 3.
20. 'Whiteley's' Grand Christmas Bazaar', *Paddington Times*, 18 December 1875, p.2.

FOUR: A SADDER AND A WISER MAN

1. *PKB Chronicle*, 29 July 1876, p. 4.
2. *PKB Chronicle*, 29 July 1876, p. 5.
3. *Ibid.*
4. 'Mr Whiteley and the Westminster Aquarium', *PKB Chronicle*, 16 September 1876, p. 5; *ibid.*, 'Local Gossip'.
5. 'The Westminster Aquarium', *Paddington Times*, 21 October 1876, p. 3.
6. *New York Daily Graphic*, 12 May 1876.
7. 'A Commercial Eutopia', *Essex Weekly News*, 3 November 1876, p. 8.
8. 'Whiteley's Grand Provision Emporium', *Paddington Times*, 4 November 1876, p. 2.
9. '"Rattening" against Cheap Food', *Land and Water*, 18 November 1876, p. 357.
10. 'Guy Fawkes Day in Westbourne Grove', *PKB Chronicle*, 11 November 1876, p. 5.
11. *Ibid.*
12. 'Wholesale Butchery in Bayswater', *PKB Chronicle*, 11 November 1876, p. 5.
13. *PKB Chronicle*, 25 November 1876, p. 5.
14. *PKB Chronicle*, 6 January 1877, p. 5.
15. 'The Alexander Street Opening', *Paddington Times*, 18 May 1878, p. 2.
16. 'Local Gossip', *PKB Chronicle*, 2 December 1876, p. 5; *ibid.*, 'Local Gossip', 9 December 1876, p. 5.
17. 'Local Gossip', *PKB Chronicle*, 13 January 1877, p. 5.
18. 'Local Gossip', *PKB Chronicle*, 3 February 1877, p. 5.
19. *Paddington Times*, 15 February 1877, p. 3.
20. *Paddington Times*, 14 July 1877, p. 2.
21. 'Ratepayers' Association', *Paddington Times*, 24 June 1876, p. 2.
22. *PKB Chronicle*, 27 May 1876, p. 5.

23. 'Kleptomania by a Married Woman', *Paddington Times*, 3 March 1877, p. 3.
24. 'Kleptomania', *PKB Chronicle*, 17 November 1877, p. 5.
25. 'Tassell *v* Whiteley', *PKB Chronicle*, 9 June 1887, p. 5.
26. 'Local Gossip', *PKB Chronicle*, 4 August 1887, p. 5.
27. 'Westbourne Gazette and Belgrave Herald', *Paddington Times*, 15 September 1877, p. 3.
28. 'Whiteley's Christmas Bazaar', *Paddington Times*, 22 December 1877, p. 3.

FIVE: FROM A PIN TO AN ELEPHANT

1. W. Whiteley, 'Why people fail in business', *Pearson's Weekly*, 22 March 1906, no. 818, p. 669; *Magazine of Commerce*.
2. *Magazine of Commerce*, p. 127.
3. W. Whiteley, 'How to succeed as a Shopkeeper', *London Magazine* Vol. 9, pp. 189–92; *Magazine of Commerce*.
4. *Truth*, 24 May 1877, p. 644.
5. 'Local Gossip', *PKB Chronicle*, 26 May 1877, p. 5.
6. 'How to Succeed', p. 191.
7. 'The Murder of William Whiteley. A Personal Tribute', *Globe*, 25 January 1907, p. 7.
8. 'Montgomery *v.* Whiteley and Bear', *PKB Chronicle*, December 7 1878, p. 5; 'Montgomery *v.* Bear and Whiteley', *PKB Chronicle*, 7 April 1879, p. 2.
9. 'Westbourne Grove', *Paddington Times*, 23 February 1878, p. 2.
10. 'The Electric Light in Westbourne Grove', *PKB Chronicle*, 7 December 1878, p. 5.
11. *PKB Chronicle*, 1 February 1879, p. 4.
12. 'Mr Whiteley and the Douglas Place Improvement', *PKB Chronicle*, 15 March 1879, p. 5.
13. 'Mr Whiteley and the Douglas Place Improvement', *PKB Chronicle*, 19 April 1879, p. 4.
14. 'Collapse of the Douglas Place Improvement Scheme', *PKB Chronicle*, 10 May 1879, p. 4.
15. 'The allegations against a Bayswater solicitor', *PKB Chronicle*, 1 March 1879, p. 5; 'Meeting of Creditors', *City Press*, 15 February 1879, p. 5.
16. 'Young London. I. Westbourne Grove and There-abouts', *Daily Telegraph*, 2 June 1879, p. 5.
17. 'Local Gossip', *PKB Chronicle*, 7 June 1879, p. 5.

18. W.P. Frith, *My Autobiography and Reminiscences*, R. Bentley and Son, London, 1888, 7th edn, pp. 287–9.
19. *PKB Chronicle*, 29 November 1879, p. 3.
20. 'Local Gossip', *PKB Chronicle*, 6 December 1879, p. 5.
21. 'Common Pleas division. In the Matter of Charles Mills Roche, a Solicitor', *The Times*, 19 April 1880, p. 4.

SIX: CONFLICT AND COMPROMISE

1. 'Paddington Vestry', *PKB Chronicle*, 23 October 1880, p. 2.
2. 'Action for Libel against the Bayswater Chronicle', *PKB Chronicle*, 23 October 1880, p. 5; *ibid.*, 'Personal', 30 October 1880, p. 5.
3. *PKB Chronicle,* 5 March 1881, pp. 4–5.
4. 'Mr Whiteley's New Premises', *PKB Chronicle*, 26 March 1881. p. 5; *ibid.*, 'Local Gossip'.
5. 'The Inquiry at the Paddington Baths', *PKB Chronicle*, 10 September 1881, p. 4.
6. 'The Paddington Baths and Mr Whiteley', *PKB Chronicle*, 10 September 1881, p. 5.
7. 'Paddington Vestry', *PKB Chronicle*, 29 October 1881, pp. 2 and 5; *ibid.*, 'Paddington Vestry – the Baths and Mr Whiteley', p. 5.
8. Alverstone. A delightful piece of marginalia is to be found in the edition of Lord Alverstone's memoirs held by the British Library, where someone has scribbled on page 273, 'To the writers [*sic*] knowledge Whiteley was a thorough-paced unctuous old hypocrite and in the habit of taking different women practically every week to the Castle Hotel, Hastings.'
9. 'The Widow Interviewed', *Daily Chronicle*, 28 January 1907, p. 5.
10. 'Whiteley *v.* Whiteley, Probate and Divorce Court', *PKB Chronicle*, 19 November 1881, p. 5.
11. *Whiteley* v. *Whiteley*, National Archives, J77/264/2.
12. 'Whiteley *v.* Whiteley, Probate and Divorce Court' *PKB Chronicle*, 19 November 1881, p. 5.
13. 'Whiteley *v.* Whiteley', *Daily Chronicle*, 16 November 1881, p. 6.
14. 'Whiteley *v.* Whiteley, Probate and Divorce Court', *PKB Chronicle*, 19 November 1881, p. 5.
15. 'The Divorce Court', *PKB Chronicle*, 1 July 1882, p. 5; 'Whiteley *v* Whiteley', 8 July 1882, p. 5.

16. 'Whiteley *v.* Whiteley', *PKB Chronicle*, 5 August 1882, p. 5.
17. 'Mr William Whiteley's Murder', *Kidderminster Times*, 2 February 1907, p. 3.

SEVEN: WILLIAM AND LOUIE AND GEORGE AND EMILY

1. 'Killed on the Railway', *The Times*, 11 February 1875, p. 5.
2. 'Mrs Turner tells "The Star" the Story of her Daughters' Romantic Lives', *Star*, 30 January 1907, p. 2.
3. *Ibid.*
4. 'Reminiscences of Cetewayo', *Pall Mall Gazette*, 11 February 1884, pp. 1–2.
5. 'Cetewayo in Westbourne Grove', *PKB Chronicle*, 26 August 1882, p. 5.
6. 'Paddington Vestry', *PKB Chronicle*, 8 July 1882, p. 3.
7. 'Sketches in Paddington Vestry', *PKB Chronicle*, 8 July 1882, p. 5.
8. 'Paddington Vestry *v.* Whiteley', *PKB Chronicle*, 15 July 1882, p. 5.
9. 'Paddington Vestry', *PKB Chronicle*, 5 August 1882, p. 5.
10. 'Great Fire at Whiteley's', *PKB Chronicle*, 18 November 1882, p. 5.
11. 'Extraordinary Scene in Westbourne Grove', *PKB Chronicle*, 16 December 1882, p. 5.
12. 'Notes', *PKB Chronicle*, 16 December 1882, p. 5; *ibid.*, 'Extraordinary Scene in Westbourne Grove'.

EIGHT: OUT OF THE ASHES

1. 'Paddington Vestry', *PKB Chronicle*, 10 March, p. 2; *ibid.*, 'Mr Whiteley the Vestry and the Baths', p. 5.
2. 'The Vestry and Mr Whiteley', *PKB Chronicle*, 5 April 1884, p. 5.
3. 'Paddington Vestry Elections Ward 1', *PKB Chronicle*, 26 May 1883, p. 5.
4. 'Alleged Frauds on Mr Whiteley', *PKB Chronicle*, 8 October 1881, p. 2.
5. 'Rooney *v.* Whiteley', *PKB Chronicle*, 15 July 1882, p. 5; 'Rooney *v.* Whiteley', *PKB Chronicle*, 30 June 1883, p. 5.
6. 'Saturday in Westbourne Grove', *PKB Chronicle*, 16 February 1884, p. 4.
7. 'Great Fire in the Metropolis', *PKB Chronicle*, 3 May 1884, p. 6.

8. *Ibid.*, p. 5.
9. *Ibid.*
10. *Ibid.*
11. *Ibid.*
12. *Ibid.*
13. *Ibid.*
14. 'Great Fire at Whiteley's', *Pall Mall Gazette*, 26 April 1884, p. 8.
15. *Ibid.*
16. 'Great Fire in the Metropolis', *PKB Chronicle*, 3 May 1884, p. 5.
17. *Ibid.*
18. 'Great Fire at Whiteley's', *Pall Mall Gazette*, 26 April 1884, p. 8.
19. Lambert, pp. 176–7.
20. 'Paddington Vestry', *PKB Chronicle*, 10 May 1884, p. 2.
21. 'Topics', p. 12.
22. 'Maori King at Whiteley's', *PKB Chronicle*, 28 June 1884, p. 5.
23. *PKB Chronicle*, 22 November 1884, p. 5.
24. 'Fire at Whiteley's', *Pall Mall Gazette*, 17 June 1885, p. 8; 'Great Fire at Whiteley's', *PKB Chronicle*, 20 June, p. 5.
25. *PKB Chronicle*, 27 June 1885, p. 5; *ibid.*, 'The Fire at Whiteley's'.
26. 'Prosecution of a Lady by Mr Whiteley', *PKB Chronicle*, 25 September 1885, p. 5; *ibid.*, 'Mr Whiteley's Recent Prosecution'; 'Mr Whiteley's Recent Prosecution', 10 October 1885, p. 5; 'Mr Whiteley and the Prosecution of a Lady', *PKB Chronicle*, 17 April 1886, p. 5.
27. *PKB Chronicle*, 3 April, p. 5; *ibid.*, 'Mr Whiteley and the Photographers', 29 May 1886, p. 5.

NINE: THE BURNING FIERY FURNACE

1. 'Westbourne Grove in the Season', *PKB Chronicle*, 4 June 1887, p. 5.
2. 'Royal Visit to Westbourne Grove', *PKB Chronicle*, 26 December 1885. p. 5.
3. *PKB Chronicle*, 20 November 1886, p. 5; 'Marylebone Police Court', *The Times*, Tuesday 16 November 1886, p. 3.
4. 'Jubilee Week in Paddington', *PKB Chronicle*, 18 June 1887, p. 5; *ibid.*, 'Mr Whiteley's Display', 25 June 1887, p. 5.
5. 'The Great Fire at Whiteley's', *PKB Chronicle*, 13 August 1887, p. 8.

6. W.L. Longstaff, 'Whiteley's Fire: What it looked like Out of the Crowd', *Paddington Times*, 13 August 1887, p. 5.
7. 'The Great Fire at Whiteley's', *PKB Chronicle*, 13 August 1887, p. 5.
8. *Ibid.*
9. *Ibid.*
10. 'The Great Fire at Whiteley's', *PKB Chronicle*, 13 August 1887, p. 8.
11. 'The Fire at Whiteley's', *Globe*, 8 August 1887, p. 5.
12. 'The Great Fire at Whiteley's' and 'Sympathy with Mr Whiteley', *PKB Chronicle*, 20 August 1887, p. 5.
13. *Paddington Times*, 13 August 1887, p. 4.
14. 'The American Press on the Fire at Whiteley's', *PKB Chronicle*, 27 August 1887, p. 5.
15. 'Why is Whiteley's so often Burned Down?', *Pall Mall Gazette*, 10 August 1887, p. 3.
16. 'Rules of W. Whiteley's Establishment', *TRUCK: William Whiteleys. Fines deducted from wages*, Public Record Office, HO 45/9802/B5581.
17. 'The Late Fire', *PKB Chronicle*, 22 October 1887, p. 5.

TEN: OLD FARMER WILLIAM

1. 'Mr William Whiteley's Murder', *Kidderminster Times*, 2 February 1907, p. 3.
2. 'Notes', *PKB Chronicle*, 25 February 1888, p. 5.
3. 'Why Whiteley's Was Burnt Out', *PKB Chronicle*, 14 July 1888 p.5
4. 'Notes', *PKB Chronicle*, 21 April 1888, p. 5.
5. 'Mr Whiteley and the Budget', *PKB Chronicle*, 31 March 1888, p. 5.
6. 'Is Mr Whiteley Going to Holloway?', *PKB Chronicle*, 5 January 1889, p. 5.
7. 'Alleged Blackmailing of Mr Whiteley', *PKB Chronicle*, 1 June 1895, p. 5; *ibid.*, 'Fraud on Mr Whiteley', 21 September 1895, p. 5.
8. 'The Art of Shoplifting at Whiteley's', *PKB Chronicle*, 17 February 1894, p. 5.
9. 'The Princess of Wales at Westbourne Hall', *PKB Chronicle*, 3 May 1890, p. 5.
10. 'The Orchid Show at Whiteley's', *PKB Chronicle*, 16 May 1891, p. 5.
11. 'Mr Whiteley's Fruit and Flower Farm', *PKB Chronicle*,

18 July 1891, p. 5.

12. *Ibid.*
13. *Ibid.*
14. 'Guests at a Guinea a Head', *PKB Chronicle*, 3 January 1891, p. 5.
15. 'The Scare in Westbourne Grove', *PKB Chronicle*, 9 July 1892, p. ?.
16. *Orchards and Gardens*, p. 241.
17. 'Mr Whiteley Arraigned by the Selborne Society', *PKB Chronicle*, 9 June 1894, p. 5.
18. Lambert, p. 227.
19. *Orchards and Gardens,* p. 32.
20. *Orchards and Gardens,* p. 86.
21. 'Mr Whiteley Fined, but is Personally Exculpated', *PKB Chronicle*, 14 April 1894, p. 5.
22. 'Police', *The Times*, 12 December 1894, p. 3; *ibid.*, 'Police', 2 January 1895, p. 3; *ibid.*, 'Law Reports', 9 January 1895, p. 13; 'Notes', *PKB Chronicle*, 19 January 1895, p. 5; 'Presentation to Mr Whiteley', *PKB Chronicle*, 12 October 1895, p. 5.
23. 'Whiteley as Omnibus Proprietor', *PKB Chronicle*, 23 March 1895, p. 5; *ibid.*, 'The Whiteley Omnibus Service', 6 April, p. 5.
24. 'Whiteley's House Dinner', *PKB Chronicle*, 9 November 1895, p. 5.
25. 'Whiteley's House Dinner', *PKB Chronicle*, 13 November 1896, p. 5.
26. 'Moscow Road Improvements', *PKB Chronicle*, 5 February 1898, p. 5.
27. 'Life in the Shop. Part 1', *Daily Chronicle*, 4 February 1898, p. 5.
28. 'Life in the Shop', *Daily Chronicle*, 7 April 1898, p. 7.
29. 'William Whiteley (Limited)', *PKB Chronicle*, 4 June 1898, p. 5.

ELEVEN: HOW TO SUCCEED IN BUSINESS

1. 'Whiteley's Dinner', *PKB Chronicle*, 19 November 1898, p. 5.
2. HSBC archives, 889/2 bundle 6, handwritten notebook, undated, p. 9.
3. 'An Up-to-date Universal Provider', *Irish Financial Times*, 15 May 1899, p. 2.

4. HSBC 889/2/6 notebook, p. 2.
5. HSBC 889/2/7.
6. HSBC 889/02/1.
7. 'William Whiteley Limited', *Financial Times*, 7 June 1899, p. 4.
8. 'William Whiteley, Limited', *Economist*, 10 June 1899, p. 840.
9. 'William Whiteley Limited', *Investors Review*, 10 June 1899, p. 822.
10. 'Capel Court Echoes', *Money*, 10 June 1899, p. 359.
11. 'Whiteley's Debentures', *The Statist*, 10 June 1899, p. 921.
12. HSBC 889/2/7.
13. HSBC 889/2/9.
14. *Ibid.*
15. *Ibid.*
16. *Ibid.*
17. *Ibid.*
18. 'Notes', *PKB Chronicle*, 1 June 1901, p. 5.
19. 'Obituary', *City Press*, 20 February 1901, p. 5.
20. 'The Whiteley Report', *Financial Times*, 26 May 1902, p. 2.
21. 'The Christmas Holidays in Bayswater', *PKB Chronicle*, 24 December 1902, p. 5.
22. 'The Christmas Holiday Difficulty in Bayswater', *PKB Chronicle*, 24 December 1902, p. 5.
23. 'Whiteley's "Concordia" Concert', *PKB Chronicle*, 14 February 1903, p. 5.
24. 'Notes', *PKB Chronicle*, 9 April 1904, p. 4.
25. 'Speed of Motor Cars', *The Times*, 12 September 1902, p. 3.
26. P.C. Hoffman, *They Also Serve: the Story of the Shop Worker*, Porcupine Press, London, 1949, pp. 21–2.
27. *Ibid.*, pp. 39–40.
28. *Ibid.*, p. 40.
29. Conversation on 28 February 1983 with Mrs Montgomery, Whiteley Village Trust archives.
30. W. Whiteley, 'Why People Fail in Business', *Pearson's*, 22 March 1906, no. 818, p. 669.
31. 'Bachelors in Business', *Daily Mail*, 30 August 1906, p. 3.
32. 'Notes', *PKB Chronicle*, 7 April 1906, p. 4.
33. 'The Private Life of Mr Whiteley', *Daily Mail*, 26 January 1907, p. 6.
34. 'Success in Business', *Daily Chronicle*, 25 January 1907, p. 6.

TWELVE: THE MAN OF MYSTERY

1. Details of the murder and investigation are from witness depositions in the Public Archives, reference CRIM/104/9.
2. 'Business As Usual', *Star*, 25 January 1907, p. 3.
3. The story of Horace George Rayner's life has been pieced together from evidence given at the police court and trial, and interviews with his family, friends and colleagues reported in the aftermath of the murder by the leading newspapers of the day.
4. 'Rayner's Married Life', *Daily Chronicle*, 28 January 1907, p. 6.
5. 'Who is Rayner's Father?', *Globe*, 28 January 1907, p. 7.
6. *Ibid.*
7. *Ibid.*
8. 'Confessions', *Star*, 25 January 1907, p.3.
9. 'The History of Mr Whiteley's Murderer', *Daily Mail*, 26 January 1907, p. 7.
10. 'The Universal Provider', *Daily Mail*, 25 January 1907, p. 7.
11. 'The Murder of William Whiteley', *Globe*, 25 January 1907, p. 7.
12. 'How Mr Whiteley Refused a Title', *Daily Mirror*, 26 January 1907, p 3.
13. 'Mr Whiteley's Murder', *Standard*, 26 January 1907, p. 7.
14. 'Assailant Hopes To Die', *Globe*, 28 January 1907, p. 9.
15. 'The Widow Interviewed', *Daily Chronicle*, 28 January 1907, p. 5.

THIRTEEN: BURYING THE PAST

1. *Globe*, 28 January 1907, p. 7; 'Whiteley Murder', 'The Murder of Mr Whiteley', *PKB Chronicle*, 2 February 1907, p. 5; 'Whiteley Tragedy', *Evening Standard*, 29 January 1907, p. 11; 'Inquest on the Late Mr Whiteley', *Daily Mirror*, 29 January 1907, p. 3; witness depositions in the Public Archives, reference CRIM/104/9.
2. 'Funeral of Mr W. Whiteley', *PKB Chronicle*, 2 February 1907, p. 5.
3. Felstead, p. 228.
4. 'I Can go to Whiteley', *Daily Mail*, 28 January 1907, p. 7.
5. 'Whiteley Tragedy', *Evening Standard*, 29 January 1907, p. 11.

6. 'Whiteley Mystery', *Evening Standard*, 19 February 1907, p. 6.
7. Felstead, p. 228.
8. 'The Murder of Mr Whiteley', *Daily Mail*, 23 March 1907, p. 5.
9. 'The Whiteley Murder', *Globe*, 22 March 1907, p. 5.
10. *Ibid.*
11. *Ibid.*
12. *Ibid.*
13. 'The Whiteley Murder', *Globe*, 22 March 1907, p. 5
14. *Ibid.*, p. 7.
15. 'The Prisoner's Wife', *Evening Standard*, 22 March 1907, p. 12.
16. 'Whiteley Murder Trial', *Standard*, 23 March 1907, p. 7.
17. 'Rayner's Trial', *Globe*, 22 March 1907, p. 7.
18. 'The Murder of Mr Whiteley', *Daily Mail*, 25 March 1907, p. 4.
19. 'The Sentence on Rayner', *Daily Mail*, 30 March 1907, p. 2.
20. 'The Murder of Mr Whiteley', *Daily Mail*, 30 March 1907, p. 5.
21. 'Notes', *PKB Chronicle*, 6 April 1907, p. 5.
22. 'Rayner Reprieved', *Daily Mail*, 1 April 1907, p. 5.
23. Alverstone, pp. 273–4.
24. 'Attempted Suicide of Mr Whiteley's Murderer', *The Times*, 23 October 1907, p. 8.
25. 'The Convict Rayner', *The Times*, 17 April 1908, p. 17.
26. Felstead, p. 233.

FOURTEEN: THE LEGACY OF WILLIAM WHITELEY

1. Will of William Whiteley, Probate Record Office.
2. 'In Re Whiteley – Bishop of London *v.* Whiteley', *The Times*, 24 February 1910, p. 3.
3. 'Sale of Municipal Baths', *The Times*, 19 January, p. 7; *ibid.*, 'Sale of Paddington Baths', 3 February 1909, p. 10; 'The Proposed Sale of Paddington Baths', 4 March 1909, p. 14.
4. 'Fire at Messrs Whiteleys', *The Times*, 15 March 1910, p. 16.
5. 'Messrs Whiteleys New Premises', *The Times*, 29 October 1910, p. 15.
6. 'Laying the Foundation Stone of the New Whiteleys', *PKB Chronicle*, 29 October 1910, p. 5.
7. 'The New Whiteleys', *The Times*, 12 October 1911, p. 12.

8. John Belcher, R.A., and J.J. Joass, FRIBA, 'Current architecture. Whiteleys New Premises', *The Architectural Review*, March 1912, pp. 164–78.
9. 'A Company Director's Suit', *The Times*, 1 August 1914, p. 4.
10. 'William Whiteley', *The Times*, 25 March 1927, p. 23.
11. 'Death of Mr William Whiteley', *Dorking and Leatherhead Advertiser*, 12 March, p. 9.
12. 'Selfridges and Co. Limited', *The Times*, 22 January 1941, p. 9.
13. 'William Whiteley', *The Times*, 29 July 1954, p. 13.
14. 'William Whiteley Losses', *The Times*, 26 November 1955, p. 11.

Bibliography

ARCHIVES

HSBC Archives
Greenwell papers relating to William Whiteley Ltd, accession no
  889/02/1-10

National Archives
Defendant: Rayner, Horace George, Charge: Murder, CRIM/104/9
TRUCK: William Whiteleys. Fines deducted from wages, HO
  45/9802/B5581
Whiteley v. Whiteley, J77/264/2

West Yorkshire Archives
Parish Records of Warmfield and Featherstone

Westminster Archives
Whiteley papers, accession number 726

Whiteley Homes Trust
The Whiteley Homes Trustees Minutes Book

Record of conversation with Mrs Montgomery, 28 February 1983

Records of births, marriages, deaths, probate and census returns
  held at the Family Record Centre, London
Wills held at the Probate Registry, London

BOOKS

Adburgham, A. *Shops and Shopping*, George Allen and Unwin,
  London, 1964
Amalgamated Press, 'William Whiteley, Universal Provider',
  Fortunes Made in Business, Life Struggles of Famous People,
  Amalgamated Press, London, 1901, pp. 94–101

Anon, *Reminiscences of an Old Draper*, reprinted from the *Drapers' Record*, London, 1876

Anstey, F. *The Man from Blankleys'* (A Comedy of the Early Nineties), Hodder and Stoughton, London, 1927

Barnard, A. *Orchards and Gardens Ancient and Modern, with a description of the orchards gardens model farms and factories owned by Mr William Whiteley of Westbourne Grove, London*, Sir Joseph Causton and Sons, London, 1895

Darwin, B. *John Gully and His Times*, Cassell, London, 1935

Felstead, S.T., Lady Muir, eds, *Sir Richard Muir – a Memoir of a Public Prosecutor*, John Lane, London, 1927

Ferry, J.W. *A History of the Department Store*, Macmillan, New York, 1960

Frith, W. P. *My Autobiography and Reminiscences*, R. Bentley and Son, London, 1888, 7th edn

Goodchild, John, *Wakefield*, Tempus, Stroud, 1998

Hawley, C. *The Drapery Trade before the Public*, John Heywood, Manchester, 1878

Hoffman, P. C. *They Also Serve. The Story of the Shop Worker*, Porcupine Press, London, 1949

Honeycombe, G. *Selfridges. Seventy-five Years. The Story of the Store 1909–1984*, Park Lane Press, London, 1984

Juxon, J. *Lewis and Lewis*, Collins, London, 1983

Lambert, R.S. *The Universal Provider*, George G. Harrap, London, 1938

Lancaster, B. *The Department Store. A Social History*, Leicester University Press, Leicester, 1995

Munro, J.M. *The Royal Aquarium; Failure of a Victorian Compromise*, American University of Beirut, Beirut, 1971

Rappaport, E. 'The Halls of Temptation', *Journal of British Studies*, Vol. 35, 1996, pp. 58–83

Reeder, D.A. 'A Theatre of Suburbs: Some Patterns of Development in West London, 1801–1911', in *The Study of Urban History*, H.J. Dyos (ed.), Edward Arnold, London, 1968

Walker, J.W. *Wakefield its History and People* (2 vols), Wakefield, privately printed, 1939

Webster, R.E. Viscount Alverstone, *Recollections of Bar and Bench*, Edward Arnold, London, 1914

White, W. *Directory and Gazetteer of Leeds, Bradford, Halifax, Huddersfield and Wakefield*, W. White, Sheffield, 1853

Whitehead, J. *The Growth of St Marylebone and Paddington*, Jack Whitehead, London, 2001

Index

Index

Index